Making Housing Happen

Faith-based Affordable Housing Models

Making Housing Happen

Faith-based Affordable Housing Models

Jill Suzanne Shook, EDITOR

CHALICE
PRESS

ST. LOUIS, MISSOURI

Bible quotations, unless otherwise noted, are from the *New Revised Standard Version Bible,* copyright 1989, Division of Christian Education of the National Council of the Churches of Christ in the United States of America. Used by permission. All rights reserved.

Scripture quotations marked (NIV) are taken from the HOLY BIBLE, NEW INTERNATIONAL VERSION®. NIV®. Copyright © 1973, 1978, 1984 by International Bible Society. Used by permission of Zondervan Publishing House. All rights reserved.

Scripture quotations marked (NLT) are taken from the *Holy Bible, New Living Translation,* copyright © 1996. Used by permission of Tyndale House Publishers, Inc., Wheaton, Illinois 60189, U.S.A. All rights reserved.

Scripture marked NASB is taken from the NEW AMERICAN STANDARD BIBLE ®, © Copyright The Lockman Foundation 1960, 1962, 1963, 1968, 1971, 1972, 1973, 1975, 1977, 1995. Used by permission.

Those quotations marked RSV are from the *Revised Standard Version of the Bible,* copyright 1952, [2nd edition, 1971] by the Division of Christian Education of the National Council of the Churches of Christ in the United States of America. Used by permission. All rights reserved.

Cover photos: Getty Images and Hui-Chu Wang
Cover and interior design: Elizabeth Wright

Visit Chalice Press on the World Wide Web at
www.chalicepress.com

10 9 8 7 6 5 4 3 2 1   06   07 08 09 10 11

Library of Congress Cataloging-in-Publication Data

Shook, Jill Suzanne.
  Making housing happen : faith-based affordable housing models / Jill Suzanne Shook.
      p. cm.
  Includes bibliographical references.
  ISBN-13: 978-0-827223-32-5 (pbk.)
  ISBN-10: 0-827223-32-3 (pbk.)
  1. Housing–United States–Finance–Case studies. 2. Self-help housing–United States–Case studies. 3. Housing rehabilitation–United States–Case studies. 4. Low-income housing–United States–Case studies. 5. Home ownership–United States–Case studies. 6. Housing–Religious aspects–Christianity–Case studies. 7. Church work with families–Case studies. 8. Christian leadership–United States–Case studies. I. Title: Affordable housing models. II. Title: Faith-based affordable housing models. III. Title.
  HD7293.Z9S52 2006
  261.8'32–dc22   2005037540

Printed in the United States of America

Contents

Foreword

DR. JOHN PERKINS

In 1942 when I was 12 years old, I received fifteen cents for a day of backbreaking labor in Mississippi. Though a poor, uneducated, black youngster, I was smart. I quickly figured out that ownership of the wagon, the mule, and the land would lift people from poverty. Since that day, I determined to struggle with solutions that would break the crippling poverty cycle. I have committed my life to the kind of community development across the U.S. and beyond that challenges the church to bring about a more equitable redistribution of land and community resources. And this is what *Making Housing Happen: Faith-based Affordable Housing Models* is about.

I have had the honor and privilege of knowing and mentoring many of the authors in this book—including Jill Shook, who lived and worked with us at the Harambee Center in Pasadena, California. Jill has taken this book beyond my own focus on community development to include models of community organizing—a process that provides a voice for the faith community to address public policy. This book is about both public and personal transformation. By including cohousing, cooperative housing, and community land trusts, Jill speaks to the core of so much of the loneliness, isolation, individualism, and materialism that is destroying our society.

Making Housing Happen goes to the root of the housing crisis, a crisis that today has contributed to an all-time high in homelessness, but is also affecting middle- and low-income populations. Yes, I figured out early on that land ownership and the skills to manage it would go a long way in shaking off the bonds of poverty, but God had to first get at my heart and show me how to walk in his grace and love. The process of personal and public transformation is unique to each person and each community. Each story in this book gives us a glimpse of God's expression in the world. Just as the Bible tells stories of God's work in individuals, communities, and nations, this book tells God's story of how affordable housing has been created by churches across our landscape. Principles of best practice are embedded into these stories...as well as principles of faith. This book tells how God has orchestrated housing ministries beyond what small and large churches dared to dream could be done. They stepped out, trusting in God's provision, believing that God cares deeply that everyone has a decent, safe, and affordable place to call home.

This book powerfully unfolds some of the best theological thinking that is foundational for an effective housing ministry—how land is a central theme of the Bible and is at the core of the gospel. It also shows the grip of racial issues that still play an integral part in housing inequity today, keeping people in poverty–isolated and without hope.

   Making Housing Happen provides hope. It shows how denominations from coast to coast have dreamed outside the box and come up with creative housing solutions that are cutting across economic and racial boundaries, and stand as demonstrations of God's love.

Acknowledgments

As a team player, I couldn't have accomplished this book without the eyes, ears, hearts, and sharp minds of many gracious people who joined the team. My dearest friend Terry Carter deserves the team player of the year award. Since that first gathering in May 2002, when Bert Newton, Diane Harris, Ed Mahoney, Jude Tiersma-Watson, Mark Schmidt, and Paul Smith came together to discuss how to make the dream of this book a reality, Terry has given her heart and soul to making this book a success. During the last year of writing, we met each Saturday from about ten in the morning to ten at night–either at her place in Koreatown in Los Angeles or my place in Pasadena. We grappled with how to truly hear each other, seeking to climb into each other's brains on how we viewed our outline, word choices, and key concepts. It was excruciating…but rather than tearing us apart, we grew closer. DarEll Weist joined that initial team, providing a broader voice to the mix. Carmen Berry gave direction on the book proposal. Dwight Ozard helped to secure our publisher.

Beatrice Carranza, Kimitra Flowers, Diane Harris, and Mark Schmidt spent hours transcribing interviews. Then, just as the final editing push came, a dog up the street bit off the tip of my index finger! Coming to my rescue, Diane Lewis, Lisa Knofel, Mary and Grace Lilienthal, Karen Peacock, Rebecca Straayer, Brian Ward, Marlene Yoder, and Susan Young became my hands as they typed editorial comments into chapter drafts. Tom Baden bought me a computer with voice recognition software. Steve and Linda Kane graciously loaned me their laptop–enabling me to recreate a tiny office from kitchen tables in Maine and Church of the Saviour's guest house in Washington, D.C., to coffee shops in the west. The laptop allowed Terry and I to work in tandem at her place or mine.

Fuller Professor Mark Lau Branson brought Richard Beaton, Quentin Kinnison, Dr. Richard Slimbach, and Pastor Inman Moore together for a "read" on the first draft of the theology chapter. Fuller Old Testament professor John Goldingay and Matt Rindge, who taught at Azusa Pacific, also reviewed this chapter.

Bill Branner, Terry Flood, Peter Drier, Ray Bakke, and Joe Shuldiner provided essential pieces of research. Michele Zack helped us pare down the "Rude Awakening" chapter to a reasonable size.

Many others spent hours editing and/or attending "reads": Mary Allen, Doris Anderson, Lynn Anderson, Maggie Brandow, Tom Flanagan, Timothy Fowler, Daryn Kobata, Alex Linna, Ayanna Bridges, Albert

Durstenfeld, Eric Getty, Esther Cannon, Dorthea Tillford, Kurt Florman, Musiki Glover, Eddie Boylan, Jerome Hannaman, Pastor Henry Johnson, G. Alan Kingston, Regina Korossy, David Lewis, Diane Lewis, Claire Lewis, Pastor Camelia Joseph Lloyd, Robbie McPherson, Raquel Marquez, Pastor Linda Marshall, June Miley, Don Miner, Pastor Inman Moore, Mary King, Cindy Neubreck, Tim O'Connell, Dayna Olsen, Paul and Nelly Patag, Joan Peace, Derek Perkins, Tanja Sacco, Mark Schmidt, Donna Shook, Donna Sider, Reggie Simon, Blair Thompson, and Katie Tocce. Sharon Calkins, my walking partner; Tephillah Chi, my roommate; Susan Young, my massage therapist; and Deb Schafer from church, each went the extra mile in editing multiple chapters. Steve Pelletier went the second and third miles by doing a final read on all the chapters, making indices and double-checking the footnotes. Beatrice Carranza and Terry Carter were especially helpful in obtaining copies of quotes from their original source.

Still others helped indirectly through their prayers, monthly contributions to my support, or bringing remedies to numerous expensive and untimely setbacks, such as the termite damage to my home. My mother's Bible study group got involved in praying for very specific requests during trying episodes. I missed numerous social and family events—at times feeling like a hermit—a rather tough role for an off-the-charts extrovert! Indeed, this book was a labor of love for those who missed my presence over those five years, for those who helped ease my anxieties, and those who jumped at the chance to be on the team and play their part to bring about a biblical vision for healthy, housed communities.

Contributing Authors

ROGER BAIRSTOW is chair of Snake River Housing, an affordable farmworker housing organization in Washington state, and director of Mano á Mano, a nonprofit organization dedicated to asset building for low-income and disadvantaged populations. He was assistant professor with Oregon State University Extension Service, where he initiated micro-enterprise programming and directed a local leadership program for low-income and minority populations. Roger has worked in Oregon, Michigan, and Pennsylvania, implementing community economic development programs, and has conducted international development work in Senegal, Kenya, Guatemala, and Costa Rica.

J. R. BERGDOLL JR., was project manager of the Temescal Cohousing Project during development and construction, and remains an active owner. Bergdoll is currently housing development director for Habitat for Humanity-East Bay, managing site acquisition and project development in the Oakland area. He earned a B.S. in Architecture from the University of Virginia and a Master of City Planning from the University of California at Berkeley. He worked for the San Francisco Planning Department in urban design, neighborhood planning, and project review and has been a leader of church missions for Rockridge United Methodist Church in Oakland, California.

MARIAN BRAY has authored more than twenty books and more than 150 stories with various publishers, including David C. Cook, Chariot Books, Scholastic, Zondervan, Harold Shaw Publishers, Tyndale House, Doubleday, and Augsburg Press and in various Christian and secular magazines. Marian was a college instructor with the Children's Institute of Literature, Learning Tree University in California, and Biola University, and has instructed workshops at various writing conferences. Marian lives with her husband and daughter Piper, along with horses, dogs, cats, guinea pigs, and chickens on the high desert in New Mexico.

TERRY CARTER works for Century Housing, one of the largest affordable housing agencies in Southern California. She attended Biola University and graduated from California State University at Fullerton. She has worked for two international relief and development agencies, World Vision and Food for the Hungry. She actively participates in community-organizing efforts through her church's membership in One L.A., the Industrial Areas Foundation (IAF) affiliate in Los Angeles. She is part of the One L.A. Housing Strategy Team.

SHANE CLAIBORNE is founding partner of The Simple Way, a radical faith community that lives among the homeless in Kensington, North Philadelphia (http://www.thesimpleway.org/). Shane graduated from Eastern University, and studied at Princeton Seminary. He spent a ten-week stint with Mother Teresa and a year at Willow Creek Community Church near Chicago. Shane serves on the board of directors for the Christian Community Development Association. He writes and travels extensively, speaking about peacemaking, social justice, and Jesus.

LISA TREVINO CUMMINS is president and founder of Urban Strategies in Arlington, Virginia (www.urbanstrategies.us), which connects, resources, and tools nonprofit organizations to affect change among communities in need. Recently she launched a three-year, $10 million national project, Reclamando Nuestro Futuro/Reclaiming Our Future, that resources Latino grassroots organizations to impact the lives of at-risk and adjudicated youth. She served in the White House Office for Faith-Based and Community Initiatives as associate director, leading several Cabinet-level agencies in program design and strategic alliances within the faith community. She also served as senior vice president of Community Development in one of the country's largest financial institutions.

MILLARD FULLER is founder and former president of Habitat for Humanity International, one of the top twenty house builders in the United States. In 2005 he started the Fuller Center for Housing, with offices in Americus, Georgia. Habitat has helped more than 125,000 families in more than 3,000 U.S. cities and 82 other countries. More than 625,000 people now have safe, decent, affordable shelter because of Habitat's global work. Author of nine books about his life and work with Habitat for Humanity, Fuller received the Medal of Freedom from President Clinton in 1996 and was named the 1995 Builder of the Year by *Professional Builder* magazine. Fuller continues to receive honorary doctorates and achievement awards for his leadership toward meeting the goal of eliminating poverty housing worldwide.

JOHN HEINEMEIER was pastor of the Resurrection Lutheran Church, Roxbury, Massachusetts, and has a Masters in Sacred Theology from Concordia Seminary in St. Louis. He served four growing and vital congregations in New York for more than thirty-one years. He helped create powerful church-based citizens' groups: East Brooklyn Congregations and South Bronx Churches. These two organizations have now built some 4,000 owner-occupied Nehemiah Homes for the working class and have established three high-achieving alternative public high schools. In 1994, Pastor Heinemeier assisted in establishing The Greater Boston Interfaith Organization, called by the Boston Globe (March 19, 2000), "the strongest grassroots political force this area has seen since the 1970's."

MARY KING is an investment consultant in Beverly Hills, California. She holds the first B.A. degree awarded in Economics and Religion (with honors) from Harvard University, where she specialized in ethics in finance and socially responsible investing. She is the author of academic research published in The Journal of Investing and several articles in popular magazines, including *Christianity Today*. Mary serves on the boards of the Foundation for Christian Stewardship and Floresta and is a contributing editor to Prism, a publication of Evangelicals for Social Action. She also has worked for KLD Inc. & Co., a premier research firm tracking corporate *ethics*.

DARYN KOBATA is an editor and writer with great interest in poverty issues. Most recently editor of California Institute of Technology's award-winning faculty and staff newspaper, Daryn has also had articles published in *Charisma* and *World Christian* magazines and the World Pulse missions newsletter. She also has been a writer with Food for the Hungry in Africa, Asia, and the U.S., and with World Relief in Darfur, Sudan (2005). She earned her B.A. in English at the University of California-Davis and is completing her M.A. in theology at Fuller Theological Seminary in Pasadena, California.

ANDY KRUMSIEG is cofounder and the current director of the Jubilee Christian Development Corporation in St. Louis and the Jubilee Community Church, along with Pastor Leroy Gill Jr. He graduated from Wheaton College, majoring in biblical studies. Andy served at Lawndale Community Church in Chicago and was the director of St. Louis World Impact. He is married to Debbie, who grew up in the Congo as the daughter of missionaries. They have four children, Ben, Christy, Aaron, and Caleb. Caleb, born in St. Louis, is the sixth generation of Andy's family living in the same neighborhood.

DR. ROBERT C. LINTHICUM is president of Partners in Urban Transformation in California (www.piut.org), which equips the church for engagement in public life. Dr. Linthicum is Distinguished Professor Emeritus at Eastern University in Philadelphia, Pennsylvania, and adjunct faculty at the Claremont School of Theology in California. He directed the Office of Urban Advance for World Vision International. Ordained with the Presbyterian Church (USA) he pastored in Milwaukee, Detroit, Rockford (Ill.) and Chicago. More than 17,000 pastors, mission leaders, and students from more than seventy cities in twenty-one countries have participated in 120 urban ministry consultations and workshops led by Dr. Linthicum since 1986. He authored seven books, most recently, *Transforming Power: Biblical Strategies for Making A Difference In Your Community.*

BOB LUPTON is founder and president of FCS Urban Ministries, a community development organization in Atlanta (www.fcsministries.org). For the past thirty-five years he has lived and served in the inner-city, where he has created a wide range of human services, developed mixed-income subdivisions, organized a multiracial congregation, started businesses, and created housing for hundreds of families. He has a Ph.D. in psychology from The University of Georgia and is the author of four books on urban ministry

ED MAHONEY works to create a healthy home environment for abused and emotionally disturbed children at the residential Hillsides Home for Children in Southern California. He earned degrees in Religious Studies and English at Westmont College, Santa Barbara. In 1994 he completed his Master's from Regents College in Canada.

DON MINER has twenty years experience in property management and trust real estate at two major banks—Bank of America and Wells Fargo. With a degree in economics from California State University Los Angeles, he sees his profession as a ministry helping clients to recognize and meet their housing needs. His passion has always centered on human rights issues, and social and economic conditions throughout the world. He is currently focusing on the discussion pertaining to the Kurds in the Middle East.

EDWARD F. MONCRIEF is the executive director of Neighborhood Housing Services Silicon Valley (www.nhssv.org). He was a Franciscan friar, living in the Old Missions of California. After leaving seminary, he earned a Master's of Social Work, and has studied law, real estate, and finance. He is a published writer and poet. He spent thirty-five-years directing nonprofit housing development and housing finance organizations. He was the director of *El Porvenir*, self-help housing launched by the American Friends Service Committee with farmworkers of the San Joaquin Valley. As founding executive director of Community Housing Improvement Systems and

Planning Association, Inc. (CHISPA), he worked for the development of more than seven hundred homes for farmworker families of the Salinas Valley.

MARY NELSON is past president of Bethel New Life, a faith-based community development corporation on Chicago's low-income west side. Bethel has developed more than 1,100 units of affordable housing and has brought more than $100 million of new investments into the credit-starved community. She serves on the boards of Call to Renewal, Christian Community Development Corporation, and Good City, and is past board president of Woodstock Institute and National Congress of Community Economic Development. She has her Ph.D. from Union Graduate School, and is now doing consulting and teaching.

BERT NEWTON serves as an associate pastor at Pasadena Mennonite Church in Pasadena, California, is a staff associate for Mennonite Central Committee (as a peace and justice educator), and is on the steering committee for Affordable Housing Action (AHA). He has taught Bible courses for Heston College and the Center for Anabaptist Leadership. He earned his M.Div. at Fuller Seminary.

LOWELL NOBLE was called into missions in Appalachia. He received his M.A. in religion from Seattle Pacific College and a B.A. in anthropology and M.A. in anthropology from Wheaton College. He received a Specialist in Arts Degree in 1975, then taught sociology and anthropology at Spring Arbor College. He and his wife, Dixie, volunteer six months of the year at Antioch Community in Jackson, Mississippi, working closely with Dr. John Perkins as the training (education) director for the Spencer Perkins Center.

SUSAN P. ORTMEYER is a writer living in Pasadena, California, with her husband, John Neff, a scientist. Susan has an active interest in issues affecting the poor. She graduated from University of California-Berkeley in 1987 with a B.A. in history; and from UCL.A Law School in 1993. Susan worked for ten years as a labor and employment lawyer, and for four years specializing in employment discrimination investigations. She was the legal director with Public Interest Investigations, Inc., then began a career as a writer, potter, and homemaker.

JILL SHOOK works with churches and community leaders bringing housing justice to Pasadena and beyond. She recently founded PAHA–Pasadena Affordable Housing Alliance. Jill earned a M.A. in biblical studies from Denver Seminary and is working on her doctorate in "Transformational Leadership for the Global City" at Bakke Graduate School. She serves on the boards of the Pasadena Neighborhood Housing Services and the Golden Rule Affordable Housing Trust Fund. Jill was a campus minister, serving campuses in California and Oregon. She worked with Food for the Hungry International designing and implementing a program for work-teams from Berkeley to Harvard to serve in developing nations. She also designed workshops for pastors and teachers looking at Jesus as the Master Teacher, which she taught in Boliva and Mexico. Jill founded Students and Tutors Achieving Real Success (STARS), a ministry of Lake Avenue Church, where hundreds of volunteers work with at-risk students. Her Web site is www.makinghousinghappen.com.

THOMAS AND CHRISTINE SINE are the cofounders of Mustard Seed Associates, which encourages Christians to create imaginative new models of life and faith including new forms of housing, community, and lifestyle. Tom is a consultant in futures research and planning for both Christian and secular organizations. He has authored many books, earning the Christian Booksellers Association's Gold Medallion Award and *Christianity Today*'s book of the year list in 1996. Christine is an Australian physician who developed and directed the healthcare ministry for YWAM's Mercy Ships, and has also written several books. They coauthored *Living on Purpose: Finding God's Best for Your Life*. They are adjunct professors for Fuller Theological Seminary in Seattle.

PAUL A. SMITH serves with InnerChange, a Christian order among the poor. InnerChange ministries flow from relationships formed when teams move into poor neighborhoods. The emergence of local leaders in Los Angeles resulted in Comunidad Cambria, a tenant-controlled nonprofit corporation. Comunidad Cambria received the National Association of Professional Organizers Community Service Award in 1995 and Southern California Association of Non-Profit Housing Project of the Year in 1998. Smith has an A.B. from Harvard University and a M.S. from the California Institute of Technology.

REV. CANON RONALD SPANN was rector of Church of the Messiah for twenty-five years in Detroit. The parish spread faith-based development through its Housing Corporation. Spann led the effort to form the Islandview Village Development Corporation. He is director of Christ Church Grosse Pointe Spirituality Center and on the faculty of CREDO, a clergy wellness initiative. He is a charter member of the Christian Community Development Association and serves on its advisory board.

RAY STRANSKE earned degrees from Biola University and Denver Seminary. He cofounded Hope Communities, Inc., which has built or renovated more than 650 units of affordable housing in the urban Denver area. Ray is an active member of the Five Points Business Association, and board member of Housing For All, Colorado Housing Consortium, US Bank Community Advisory Board, and the Enterprise Foundation network (since its inception in 1982). Ray is also active with many state and local housing development associations, such as Colorado Housing Affordable Partnership, and Colorado Housing Now.

MARILYN STRANSKE is president and national organizer of Christians Supporting Community Organizing (CSCO), an effort to involve Evangelical and Pentecostal congregations in faith-based community organizing. She has addressed more than 400 national and regional leaders. Marilyn earned a B.S. from Northwestern University and a M.Ed. from Georgia State University. She cofounded Hope Communities with her huband, Ray. She is a board member and an associate with Partners in Urban Transformation. The Stranskes met in an urban church in 1974 in the neighborhood where they still live. The joys of their lives are children, Jon and Clarissa, travel, and their church, St. John's Episcopal Church.

DR. LEE STUART directed SBC Nehemiah—the development entity of South Bronx Churches. She was lead organizer of South Bronx Churches Sponsoring Committee, Inc., a broad-based organization affiliated with the Industrial Areas Foundation, which is a primary force changing social conditions in the South Bronx since 1987. Lee received her Ph.D. in Ecology from San Diego State University and the University of California Davis and completed postdoctoral work at Virginia Tech in biology. She founded SHARE–Self Help and Resource Exchange, an ecumenical food assistance and community development program that serves 11,000 families per month throughout the United States, Mexico, and Guatemala.

RICHARD TOWNSELL is the executive director of the Lawndale Christian Community Development Corporation (LCDC), and has overseen 30 million dollars of housing development. He and LCDC have received more than a dozen awards for the housing development including the Local Initiatives Support Corporation (2001) as the Community Builder of the Year; the Leadership for a Changing World Award from the Ford Foundation (2003); and a National Award for Social Justice Leadership (2004). He was named the Distinguished Fellow at the twentieth anniversary of Leadership Greater Chicago. He holds degrees from Northwestern University, Spertus College in Chicago (M.A. in urban housing development) and a Certificate in Business Administration from the University of Illinois-Chicago's Business School. He is an adjunct faculty member of Northwestern University, Wheaton College, and the University of Illinois at Chicago.

REV. DR. DARELL T. WEIST has been a campus minister; theological professor in Sierra Leone, West Africa; church administrator; local pastor; and foundation president. He is now the president and CEO of a faith-based affordable housing corporation. The corporation's housing has received a prestigious Southern California award from Union Bank. Weist has a B. S. from Westmar College, Le Mars, Iowa; a M. Div from Garret Evangelical Theological Seminary in Evanston, Illinois; and a Rel. D. from Claremont School of Theology in Claremont, California.

Falling Bodies

JILL SHOOK

Too often our outreach projects are catching bodies as they come over the waterfall, but we don't go up to see what is causing the situation and then seek to prevent it.

Ray Bakke[1]

Growing numbers in this country are struggling with a need as basic as shelter. They are "falling over the waterfall," as the above quote from Ray Bakke suggests. It is my prayer that this book will help you catch a glimpse of how congregations are preventing bodies from going over waterfalls—bodies caught in poverty and all its trappings, bodies caught in long commutes to and from work that keep loved ones apart and cause undue stress on families. These bodies must be caught before the damage caused by broken homes, homelessness, ghettoization, and poor living conditions take devastating lifelong tolls on children—our future. The affordable housing crisis is so pervasive, complex, and daunting that most of us feel defeated before considering what the body of Christ can actually do to help alleviate this problem. This book provides hope! It helps us see new structures that break the cycle of poverty and find ways to battle our subtle acceptance of the damage caused when communities are stratified—when people of resource are disconnected from people of need. The inspirational stories in this book show a renewed richness, diversity, and vitality in our communities. *Making Housing Happen* illustrates in concrete ways how congregations and faith-based groups across the nation have successfully developed affordable housing in their communities.

My Journey

In 2000, I was angry that friends were forced to leave Pasadena because of soaring rents, while my property skyrocketed in value. My father had helped me with a generous down payment. My friends were not so fortunate.

This dilemma propelled me to become involved with Affordable Housing Action, a local advocacy group. There I learned about the severity and complexity of our local crisis in Pasadena and of advocates in cities across the country with similar scenarios.

I see the same core principles I learned in the 1970s and 1980s from my seven-year career as a campus minister and my theological training at Denver seminary at play now in the various chapters in this book. These core principles insist that righteousness has both a personal and a public expression and that Christ is in the heart of that expression. My passion concerning affordable housing is rooted in my relentless belief that affordable housing is a deeply biblical issue.

I have spent most of my adult life with one foot firmly planted in communities of need and the other foot in various theological training institutions seeking to understand what the Bible teaches regarding public holiness—then designing appropriate ministries around my discoveries. In the early 1980s as a campus minister at Willamette University I helped found a shelter for migrant workers in Woodburn, Oregon. One family lived under a tree in the dead of winter. The image of a child found there with her socks frozen with urine still haunts me. My goal was to expose students to injustices that migrant workers suffered—especially regarding housing.

In the latter 1980s, I worked with Food for the Hungry International, designing a ministry through which U.S. university teams served together with nationals in the Dominican Republic, Kenya, and Mexico. Working side by side with fun-loving *campesinsos* dispelled stereotypes. The Americans could easily see that the poverty they witnessed had nothing to do with laziness, but rather resulted from a broken government system. I longed to see similar boundary-breaking relationships build bridges of hope between churches and low-income communities in the U.S.

Moving to Pasadena in 1990, I learned how the children of immigrants struggled with school, so I began STARS (Students and Tutors Achieving Real Success). This "wedded" hundreds of at-risk children with volunteers from Lake Avenue Church in long-term, intimate, and mutually beneficial relationships through an after-school program. "Connecting people" emerged for me as an ever-persistent gift, bringing people of resource together with people of need. Youth have been transformed, and volunteers are experiencing the exhilaration of meeting Jesus in new ways as they give of themselves.

Many outsiders now perceive Lake Avenue Church, with five thousand plus members, as caring for the vulnerable. Dr. Percy Clark, superintendent of Pasadena public schools, publicly praised this church as a model for our city due to their involvement in an "adopt-a-school" program. When asking new members why they join Lake Avenue, many now say it's because the church is involved with needs of the community.

Most people give a look of disbelief when I tell them the God-sized accounts of congregations building affordable housing that I have witnessed. People's disbelief begged for more information. How did they do it? What would motivate a church to do that? Where did they get the money? How did they get an alliance of churches to agree and cooperate around this single issue? Eyewitness accounts needed to be told. Jesus told us:

> You are the light of the world—like a city on a mountain, glowing in the night for all to see. Don't hide your light under a basket! Instead, put it on a stand and let it shine for all. In the same way, let your good deeds shine out for all to see, so that everyone will praise your heavenly Father. (Mt 5:14–16, NLT)

The housing represented in this book represents some of Christendom's best-kept secrets—secrets that need to be broadcast from the rooftops, "glowing for all to see."

This book presents a continuum of housing ministries. Some of the stories tell of housing ministries on the edge of the stream snatching bodies (chapter 16) involved with direct assistance such as temporary shelter, paying part of the rent or utilities, or helping someone find and move to a better apartment. These are essential ministries—opportunities to demonstrate the love of Christ. We must also catch bodies before they are dashed on rocks. Some churches do this by connecting people to financial literacy classes and jobs. Others partner with first-time homebuyers and down payment assistance programs (chapter 16). Still other ministries are involved with preventing bodies from falling in the first place. I love Henri Nouwen's thoughts on this:

> [S]ervice needs to be more than that, it should also have long-term goals in view. It should respond to crisis, but also build for the future. It should respond to need, but also seek to develop structures that may eliminate such need.[2]

Sometimes the bodies coming over the waterfall are our friends. They may feel like refugees, relegated to the outer edges of sprawled megalopolises where they can afford housing, isolated far from their place of work, worship, friends, and family. Other times, we are so close to our friends and their housing struggles that we are blind to the dynamics that have caused them to go over the waterfall—the history of legislative decisions and many other dynamics that have caused segregated low-income communities where poverty cycles keep churning, with few places to climb to shore. For example, I finally discovered why the northwest part of Pasadena ended up as a blighted area. I met Katherine Watson while riding my bike. She recounted how they, an African American family, came to live on my street. In 1962, having money for a generous down payment, they shopped for a home in the nicer parts of the city, but no one would sell to them. Realtors stated plainly, "We don't sell to black families." Racial covenants can still be seen crossed out on some Pasadena home deeds. At that time, the people of color, the majority of whom were lower income, could live only in one part of town. Also, at that time obtaining loans to improve older homes was almost impossible, so property values dropped. Then the 210 Freeway sliced through the middle of a vibrant African American business district that never fully recovered. These are only some of many reasons bodies go over the waterfall in my own neighborhood.

In South America, I had the opportunity to view the magnificent Iguasu Falls from a helicopter. I could see the banks of those majestic falls, which border Brazil, Argentina, and Paraguay. Some examples in this book view the housing crisis from a helicopter's vantage overhead, looking over all the rivers and streams that lead to the falls, redeeming the broken systems of society; they deal with root causes and are the seeds of social movements. Jim Wallis describes these historical movements as "changing the direction of the wind":

> Moral leaders like Martin Luther King Jr., Mahatma Gandhi understood this. To accomplish their bold agendas, they knew their movements would have to change the way people think. The very spiritual climate of the nation would be altered. Change the wind, and the necessary political reforms will follow.[3]

The body of Christ must participate in all of the above, from pulling bodies from the stream to changing the wind. Effective housing ministries along this continuum revitalize both the church and the whole community. The world is crying out for a church that tangibly demonstrates a love that breaks across all racial and economic barriers. Affordable housing puts a tangible and visible structure on love. *We need God-given, God-driven, and hope-filled strategies that bring us into relationship with the people in need of housing in today's world.* And we need a clear biblical theology that allows us to reflect on structural sins that perpetuate housing injustice. As Ray Bakke's book title says, we need *A Theology as Big as a City.*[4] We need ministries that

- provide temporary shelter
- help lonely seniors barely able to maintain their older homes on their fixed incomes (and possibly rent rooms to those who have none)
- preserve our aging housing stock—some of the only affordable dwellings left in our cities
- help congregation members shed NIMBY (Not In My Back Yard) attitudes toward affordable housing development
- create dwellings that are affordable and ministries that help people qualify to live in those dwellings
- create and strengthen new laws and policies in our cities, states, and nation that relate to just housing policy

- build partnerships and alliances across denominational lines, and with banks and other institutions
- organize and mobilize our churches to dream beyond what they ever thought possible to become agents of change

In *Making Housing Happen* you will read of churches rediscovering a corporate faith and purpose, and of the joy of obedience to Christ's foremost command: to love our neighbors as ourselves. They are discovering that it is impossible to separate loving God from loving their neighbors and loving themselves. Many wealthy people are finding fulfillment and joy by serving the poor. Many pastors and leaders are finding the joy of discovering a public witness for the first time as they build partnerships to accomplish their God-given dreams.

Joseph, Esther, Nehemiah, and Daniel partnered with their governments to bring about God's purposes. When Jim Ortiz, an Assembly of God pastor in Whittier, California, (chapter 9) began a company to rehab repossessed homes, he gained much favor with the Department of Housing and Urban Development (HUD). HUD flew him to Washington, D.C., several times to help simplify the red tape involved for churches' involvement. While looking for funding sources for her Lutheran church's housing ministry, Mary Nelson (chapter 5) came up with the idea of tax credits (while serving on government commissions). Today, this is the main source of funding for nonprofit affordable housing. Those people featured in this book understand something about a God who owns everything and is above all rulers and authorities, a God who operates in and through all things, who does more than we can imagine, multiplying our efforts for divine purposes (Col. 1; Eph. 3).

About the Authors

In November 2001, I asked Bob Lupton if his story of the prison-turned-GlenCastle had ever been published. When he said no, I asked if he would write about it for this book. (See chapter 5.) Bob's eager acceptance of my challenge clinched the deal in my heart. God was in this. With the name of Bob Lupton—widely known for amazing faith-based affordable housing projects—I developed a diverse list of viable, nationally respected models that reflect best practices combined with Christian faith.

This book recounts how God allowed ordinary people to do what none of them ever dreamed he or she would be able to do: create affordable housing. You will read of changed lives, transformed congregations, and housing ministries that have become the foundation for starting many other ministries and congregations. You will read about the transformation of neighborhoods and the creation of "community" born out of the soul of God's people seeking to "love thy neighbor." Even today, God is demonstrating glimpses of his kingdom on earth as in heaven.

The authors featured here were motivated by a wide variety of reasons—the emotional stress of migrant farm workers and the resulting devastation for their children (chapter 13), a vision for more livable cities with a mix of income levels (chapter 8), a passion for family values, joy in giving money and skills so others may have a decent place they can afford, and visions of the body of Christ united around a common goal for the common good (chapters 3, 9, 11).

The visionaries featured have authored their own chapters (a few share authorship with professional writers) and speak from their own experiences. Each author is a well-respected and gifted leader not only in the field of housing (now) but also as a pastor, missionary, priest, nun, or lay leader. They responded to God-orchestrated visions of how to love their neighbors in this tangible way. As they stepped out in faith to follow God's lead, the faith of their congregations grew as well. They found like-minded colaborers and workable, God-inspired strategies and solutions. Their lives speak loudly of the power of God and God's love for those in need.

Substance of the Book

The book is organized around three parts: "The Foundation," "Tangible Structures," and "Intangible Structures."

Part I, "The Foundation," consists of two chapters that lay the groundwork for a church's involvement in affordable housing. Chapter 1 discusses the severity of and reasons for our nation's housing crisis. Chapter 2 provides a biblical framework for a church's involvement in this ministry.

Part II gives readers a chance to peek into the "Tangible Structures" of actual housing units created by congregations across the country. Each chapter represents a different denomination and introduces a different model of how they have created affordable housing. I have narrowed the focus to sixteen congregations, ministerial associations, and mission groups involved in housing across the United States representing a broad diversity of ethnicities. In this part, each chapter begins with a description of the model. At the beginning of each chapter is an introduction to the model employed in that chapter. Most chapters are written by the practitioners who developed the housing. They tell their stories from their own intimate experiences.

Part III, "Intangible Structures," highlights visionaries who have not actually built affordable housing, but have set the stage for affordable housing to take place—sometimes by changing laws and sometimes simply by calling attention to the need. Local, regional, and nationwide, faith-based strategies are featured in this chapter.

The final chapter of the book highlights success factors common to the models featured in this book and shows how to get started.

Vast arrays of approaches are offered in this book. There are no cookie-cutter approaches to affordable housing. Therefore, a list of technical how-tos is inappropriate. Every community's needs and desires are unique, so every neighborhood must find its own affordable housing solutions. The approaches illustrated here should help you to consider what might be appropriate for your own community and neighborhood. For further information on how to make housing happen and additional stories, visit www.makinghousinghappen.com.

Jesus repeatedly said, "The kingdom of God is at hand." In the stories featured in this book, we see the Kingdom breaking into the present, giving us hope and bringing much glory to God. I pray the church will feel the urgency and take up its appointed position as servants to those caught in long commutes and those living in unthinkable conditions. Churches cannot meet all the needs, but they can set the pace, be a model in our cities, and change the direction of the wind in regard to the perception and commitment to affordable housing. It is my prayer that congregations across the nation will seek out the reasons why bodies are falling over the waterfall in their communities and be moved to action. We must first learn from those congregations who have blazed the trail for us, successfully addressing the affordable housing crisis.

PART I

The Foundation

Some friends in Idaho figured out a way to build a high quality home for 60 percent of the materials cost by ordering it "pre-engineered" from Canada. It arrived on a semi, precut and ready to place onto the foundation. The only problem was, the foundation was slightly off, thus creating a nightmare.

Chapter 1 wakes us up to the magnitude of the national housing crisis—its scope and complexity and why we have a housing crisis today. We must learn from the successes *and* from failed experiments and errant foundations so we might wisely build on a solid foundation.

Chapter 2 helps us lay an accurate foundation for a successful housing ministry. It starts with listening to God. The Bible reveals God's heart and desire for our lives, our faith communities, neighborhoods, cities, and towns. If we are slightly off target, a clear understanding of the scriptures serves to square up our miscalculations:

> "I will show you what it's like when someone comes to me, listens to my teaching, and then obeys me. It is like a person who builds a house on a strong foundation laid upon the underlying rock. When the floodwaters rise and break against the house, it stands firm because it is well built. But anyone who listens and doesn't obey is like a person who builds a house without a foundation. When the floods sweep down against that house, it will crumble into a heap of ruins." (Lk. 6:47–49, NLT)

The Bible lays out a blueprint for healthy, well-engineered communities—so that all have access to adequate shelter.

Our Nation's Housing Crisis

A Rude Awakening from the American Dream

TERRY CARTER AND JILL SHOOK

The American Dream: a charming little home (white picket fence optional) on a piece of land you can call your own. The street: tree-lined. Your job: nearby, with a salary adequate for a family of four.

The Reality: one-third of the nation is struggling with housing affordability—an entire third![1] When you add in the millions of families who are homeless and millions who live in crowded conditions and/or substandard housing, it becomes clear that we are a country with a severe housing problem.

The Evidence:

- Affordable housing shortage in every state[2]
- Rush hour travel time tripled since 1980[3]
- Affordable homes distant from jobs
- By some estimates, the homeless population tripled during the 1980s and now stands at an estimated 3.5 million annually; nearly 40 percent are children[4]
- Record homeownership rate, but rising delinquencies, defaults, foreclosures[5]
- As a rule of thumb, affordable housing equals 30 percent of income; in the early 1900s, housing cost 20 percent of a typical income, while by 1998, it had risen to 40 percent[6]
- Nearly one third of the workforce earned less than $10.00 an hour in 2003[7]
- A one-bedroom apartment at Fair Market Rent requires a wage of $13.23 an hour[8]—while the federal minimum wage is $5.15 an hour.
- 60+ percent of those earning minimum wage are heads of household or a spouse[9]

- 42 percent of homeless are employed but can't afford housing[10]
- 3.4 percent of the nation's total income goes to the poorest 20 percent of households[11]
- The "double whammy": climbing housing costs, falling earning power

This evidence calls the church to action. Journalist Barbara Ehrenreich's experience explains the crisis we face. She worked in various entry-level jobs, trying to get by on what she earned:

> The problem of rents is easy for an economist, even a sparsely educated low-wage worker, to grasp: it's the market, stupid. When the rich and the poor compete for housing on the open market, the poor don't stand a chance. The rich can always outbid them, buy up their tenements or trailer parks, and replace them with condos, McMansions, golf courses, or whatever they like. Since the rich have become more numerous, thanks largely to rising stock prices and executive salaries, the poor have necessarily been forced into housing that is more expensive, more dilapidated, or more distant from their places of work…Insofar as the poor have to work near the dwellings of the rich—as in the case of so many service and retail jobs—they are stuck with lengthy commutes or dauntingly expensive housing.[12]

She states earlier in her account that her coworkers' housing, in almost every case, was the "principal source of disruption in their lives, the first thing they fill you in on when they arrive for their shifts."[13]

How Did We Get Here?

This chapter looks at the scope and complexity of the national housing crisis and how it got this bad. We do this by examining housing policy decisions over the last one hundred years[14] and their repercussions.

A good deal has been accomplished, but severe problems persist. Government housing policies often did nothing to remedy entrenched economic and racial segregation, and often made them worse. Poorly designed housing policies sometimes led to brand new problems, such as abandoned urban areas and sprawl. These consequences, combined with media attention on some glaring failures, such as Chicago's notorious Cabrini Green, have stigmatized affordable housing.

We suffer a severe shortage of quality, affordable housing in well-planned, integrated neighborhoods. But the problem can be addressed. Parts of Europe and Canada have successfully met their housing needs for all income levels. The public and private experiments we chronicle here have never gone quite far enough to remedy enduring housing problems.

Late 1800s to Early 1900s:
Improving Disease-breeding Tenements; Tax Breaks

As early as the 1850s, wealthy American philanthropists discovered housing reform as an outlet for their generosity. They funded model tenements across the country with innovative designs that included open space in common areas, more privacy, indoor plumbing, natural light, and better air ventilation. These changes helped prevent slums from breeding crime and disease. Many renowned architects got on the bandwagon, including Frank Lloyd Wright, who designed a two-story model tenement in Chicago in 1895.

New York City's Tenement House Act of 1867 was the first comprehensive law regulating construction standards. The revised 1901 version expanded the regulations and became a model for other cities. Nobel Peace Prize winner Jane Addams started Settlement Houses, characterized by a democratic approach that recognized the dignity and initiative of poor residents. Among other things, Settlement House organizers called for stronger building codes.

Raising the bar for housing quality with legislative reforms that incorporated building codes for the first time increased the cost, demonstrating the need for a housing subsidy. This eventually set the stage for public housing.

Also during this period, the first federal income tax was introduced in 1913 and, with it, the mortgage interest deduction designed to help family farmers and small businesses pay off debt. After World War II, this deduction was expanded to help more families take advantage of the improved economy.

1920s: Zoning Laws Reinforce Segregation

Land was viewed as a relatively limitless commodity during our country's early years. As we became increasingly urban, city governments exercised more control over land. Local land use laws started appearing in 1916, again with New York City at the forefront. Such laws became standard in most states by the 1930s. The poor had little political voice when it came to land use decisions. Without federal land use laws, municipalities left to themselves generally listened to the wealthy. These land use policies provided the backdrop for future neglect of urban populations and institutionalized segregation. For example, today when municipalities zone for affordable multifamily housing production, "exclusionary" zoning practices often ensure that it is not built in affluent neighborhoods. This

Don't steal the land of defenseless orphans by moving the ancient boundary markers, for their Redeemer is strong. He himself will bring their charges against you. (Prov. 23:10, NLT)

reinforces a divided society, preventing meaningful relationships between neighboring rich and poor. When the poor are ghettoized, they are kept poor.[15]

1930s: Public Intervention Begins

In an effort to recover the collapsed economy during the Great Depression, President Herbert Hoover initiated the Federal Home Loan Bank Act in 1932. Despite the widespread poverty and the "Hooverville" shantytowns springing up, Hoover sought to avoid direct public assistance whenever possible and promoted self-reliance and free enterprise as the way out of the economic misery that had engulfed the country. Most Americans prior to the Depression shared this view. As the economy grew worse, however, the voice of those who argued for public assistance grew louder.

President Franklin D. Roosevelt's Public Works Administration attempted to kill two birds with one stone: build housing and, in so doing, create construction jobs. In addition the National Housing Act of 1934 created the Federal Housing Administration (FHA), which aimed more toward stabilizing the banking industry than assisting the poor. The FHA acted as a review board for banks and lending institutions and allowed them to offer guaranteed risk-free loans to middle-class households able to afford the 10 percent down. With this government-subsidized, risk-free money, families often found it cheaper to build a new home in the suburbs than to maintain their home in the city. Contributing to the movement out of the city, FHA discouraged loans for rehabbing existing structures or for building multifamily units. This lending policy resulted in all-white subdivisions, justified by citing the specter of "crowded neighborhoods" and "lower class occupancy."[16] FHA manuals instructed lenders to steer clear of areas with "inharmonious racial groups" and recommended that cities pass racially restrictive zoning ordinances and racial covenants (clauses on deeds stating that a house could never be sold to blacks or other minorities).[17]

With the nation suffering economically as a result of the Great Depression, housing assistance during that period became a national priority, with unions, policy makers, and the building industry joining together. The prevailing pull-yourself-up-by-your-bootstraps sentiment of the time called for self-sufficiency. The trouble was, there were no bootstraps for many folks. Even with full-time jobs, many simply could not afford an adequate roof over their heads.[18]

For most of the seventy years since this first large-scale public intervention, with some exceptions, the commitment to good policy and sufficient budget outlays has been inadequate. Today, despite a growing crisis, between 1976 and 2003 HUD's budget authority dropped by a whopping 60 percent.[19]

1937: Public Housing Is Born, Some Growing Up to Become "The Projects"

With the establishment of the U.S. Housing Act of 1937, the first public housing in the United States was built. The legislation was intended to create a federal housing authority, but cities protested and, through the court system, were granted the right to organize local housing authorities. These built housing for low-income families with federal money, bypassing the private building industry. Also, cities could decide where and when to build public housing. A suburb that did not want public housing simply refused to create a housing authority.

Special interest groups, such as real estate industry lobbyists, ensured that the Housing Act of 1937 produced public housing only for the poor, not a mixed-income population, as housing advocates originally envisioned. Despite this economic segregation, the first public housing projects had no stigma attached to them. During the Depression, many formerly working class folks were finding themselves in poverty. Elvis Presley, Glen Campbell, Kenny Rogers, and Jimmy Carter all lived in public housing.[20] The Housing Act of 1937 linked slum clearance to public housing, ensuring that the number of units torn down would be replaced with an equal number of public housing units. Unfortunately, a later law would overturn this requirement. The 1937 law did not help solve the intractable problem of segregation.[21]

After the Depression, WWII, and the Korean War, many public housing projects became a way to warehouse the poor. Adding to the numbers needing housing, the early 1940s saw the beginning of unparalleled migration of blacks to the North.[22] In Chicago, as blacks began to move into public housing, attempts to integrate caused conflicts of riot proportions. Public housing in Chicago became 99 percent segregated.[23] At first the rent structure of public housing enabled it to be self-supporting, including enough income for normal building maintenance. By 1970 the rent structure for public housing was based on income level, which meant that low-paid workers paid lower rents, at levels insufficient to cover proper maintenance. If the buildings had been economically mixed, the rent structure would have helped to support operating costs.

1949: The Most Lofty Federal Housing Policy Goal—Ever!

In 1949, Congress enacted another U.S. Housing Act, which called for "a decent home and suitable living environment for every American family," the most ambitious and comprehensive goal in the history of national housing policy. During World War II, defense industry jobs brought many to the cities; after the war, returning servicemen were seeking housing in

Those who shut their ears to the cries of the poor will be ignored in their own time of need. (Prov. 21:13, NLT)

record numbers. This created an unprecedented housing shortage. Building supplies went to the war effort rather than housing construction. Veterans and their families were forced to live in attics, basements, chicken coops, and boxcars.[24]

Housing was becoming one of the largest political issues of the middle class, joining them with the working class. Broad coalitions began to grow. Unlikely bedfellows such as business leaders, veterans groups, labor unions, and civic organizations joined with those who had been calling for public housing during the Depression. Newspapers and magazines printed numerous articles about the housing crisis. Public information films appeared in local theaters. Civic and religious groups organized community forums and invited public officials to speak on the subject of housing. This movement succeeded in making housing a dominant political issue despite a growing apprehension of activist government assistance programs that to some smacked of socialism. Despite this shift to the right, President Harry Truman won reelection largely with a pro-housing, anti-slum platform. Truman would boldly state, "There is nothing more un-American than a slum. How can we expect to sell democracy to Europe until we prove that within the democratic system we can provide decent homes for our people?"[25]

The fiftieth anniversary of this 1949 landmark act revealed a mixed public opinion on the Act's legacy. One editorial proclaimed that legislation "such as the Housing Act of 1949 can help every American look back with pride at the scope and planning of such a lofty goal."[26] Since the 1949 Act, the nation's plumbing moved indoors (one third of the country's homes lacked complete plumbing systems in 1949), and the average home size has doubled. Because of federally backed mortgages, almost two of every three Americans own their homes.

But the lofty language of the Act didn't match its provisions. Public housing fell far short of authorized production goals.[27] A research summary concluded: "Despite the best effort of many supporters, the possible impact of the housing act on race and income segregation not only remained unaddressed, but was actively ignored."[28]

The Act eliminated the 1937 provision that one unit of housing be built for every unit destroyed. Thus, it did not relieve the housing shortage. The 1949 Act allowed for an even larger use of public funds for slum clearance; neighborhoods were demolished, and businesses and families displaced to open up land for industries and highways. Guaranteed loans were restricted for new housing only, not to refurbish older homes. This effectively pushed America to the suburbs, where there was land for new

"The godly know the rights of the poor; the wicked don't care to know. (Prov. 29:7, NLT)

construction. Lenders practiced redlining, mapping out "undesirable" neighborhoods and, rendering those areas ineligible for credit and investment. Minorities were prevented from integrating into other neighborhoods, and because they couldn't get loans for home improvements, their property values plummeted.

1956: Hello Freeways, Hello Suburbia

The U.S. Housing Act of 1949 started dismantling city cores and creating suburbs. The 1956 Interstate Highway Act finished the job. Highways often sliced through minority neighborhoods, devastating once-thriving business districts that still have not recovered. This Act subsidized an easy exit out of the city for middle-class families. Most of our nation's city cores were left without a mix of income levels necessary to weave a strong social fabric. One report describes today's resulting problem in its title, "Sprawl Hits the Wall."[29] People are unwilling to drive any further, and many who can afford it are moving back into the city and competing with the poor for the same housing, driving up prices. What's often driving the exit to the suburbs today is affordability, not a preference for suburban life. But low density and far-flung suburbs cannot support public transportation systems, and these suburbs are often poorly planned, characterized by a separation of homes from job centers, cultural institutions, and vibrant city centers.

1960s: An Era of Renewed Commitment

In 1965, the Department of Housing and Urban Development (HUD) became a Cabinet level department. Housing was once again, as in 1949, seen as being among the top agenda items. With several experimental programs, HUD began a new approach: allowing local public housing authorities to rent privately owned housing to low-income tenants. This program was a precursor to the voucher-based Section 8 program, which is now the primary vehicle for providing housing assistance to the poor.

Also, housing segregation began to be addressed. Just a few months before the 1966 mid-term elections, President Lyndon B. Johnson submitted the Fair Housing Act to counter discriminatory housing practices such as redlining and racial covenants. The 1968 Fair Housing Act[30] prohibits discrimination in the sale or rental of housing on the basis of race, color,

> If you give special attention and a good seat to the rich person, but you say to the poor one, "You can stand over there, or else sit on the floor"—well, doesn't this discrimination show that you are guided by wrong motives?...Yes indeed, it is good when you truly obey our Lord's royal command found in the Scriptures: "Love your neighbor as yourself." But if you pay special attention to the rich, you are committing a sin, for you are guilty of breaking that law. (Jas. 2:3–4, 8–9, NLT)

religion, sex, or national origin. Twenty years later, the Act was expanded to include people with disabilities and families with children. Florida amended its Fair Housing Act so that it also essentially includes the protection of all low-income people.[31] Also in 1968, Congress reaffirmed the 1949 goal of meeting the nation's housing needs and again stated the problem as primarily a housing shortage. They set daunting ten-year subsidized housing production goals and, for the first few years, rigorously followed their timetable with unprecedented production results.

Springing from the civil rights movement, Community Development Corporations (CDCs) emerged in the 1960s. These were local nonprofits working to bring economic revival to their own low-income areas. The early CDCs of the 1960s received generous federal funding and were seen as a compliment to the Johnson Administration's "Great Society" efforts.[32]

1973: Goodbye Projects! The Introduction of Scattered Sites

In 1972, the notorious Pruitt-Igoe public housing development in St. Louis was demolished. These massive high-rises created the equivalent of a small town of concentrated poverty. (Pruitt-Igoe included thirty-three buildings designed to house some 15,000 people.) The poor design separated the project from the surrounding community and street grid, creating large, isolated open spaces that gangs eventually took over.[33] Moreover, the project, designed in the early 1950s, was meant to house whites in the Igoe apartments and blacks in the Pruitt apartments. Whites were unwilling to move in, and the entire Pruitt-Igoe project became completely black.[34]

In 1973, President Nixon declared a moratorium on public housing.[35] Whether a fair assessment or not, public housing had become the symbol of failed social policy. Large federal involvement as a developer of housing was coming to a close. Federal funds for public housing were last appropriated in 1994, but little has been built since the early 1980s. Fueling the disenchantment with public housing were the seminal Gautreaux court battles. The Chicago Housing Authority had built more than 10,300 units of public housing between 1954 and 1967—more than 99 percent of them in poor, segregated areas. Some brave folks fought this isolation and changed federal housing policy forever. Beginning with their first lawsuit in 1966, and culminating in a landmark 1976 Supreme Court case, *Hills v. Gautreaux,* thousands of poor black families claimed that it was discriminatory to offer no housing options for the poor except in areas of concentrated poverty.

As a result, more than 25,000 voluntary participants over the next twenty years were provided with special Section 8 vouchers allowing them to rent apartments in neighborhoods where no more than 30 percent of the residents were black. These participants were carefully studied, revealing powerful results. Poor, single-parent black families, when living in the midst of a middle-class neighborhood, were more likely to be employed. In addition, their children were four times less likely to drop out of school and more than twice as likely to attend college. About 75 percent of these children were employed, compared to only 41 percent in the poor, segregated control group.[36] The Gautreaux studies illustrated the benefits of scattered sites that ensure that the poor are not isolated. The flip side is that "they" might be moving in next door. "Not In My Back Yard," or NIMBY, is the phrase used to describe resistance to including "those people" in our neighborhoods.[37]

Despite NIMBYism, the majority of voters today are concerned about the skyrocketing cost of housing. More than 70 percent want government to make affordable housing a higher priority.[38] But when it comes to having "them"–those who qualify for affordable housing–live next door, the outcry of resistance rings loudly. Some of "them," by the way, are families making as much as 120 percent of area median income. Many reading this book are likely to be "those people."[39]

A big question on a NIMBY's mind is, "Will affordable housing lower my property value?" In thirty-one case studies across the country, nineteen showed that proximity to affordable housing did not impact property values of neighboring homes. Seven showed increased property values. Three were inconclusive. In only one out of thirty-one studies was there a confirmed negative impact on home values.[40]

NIMBYs fear increased crime. One of the nation's foremost public interest law and policy centers found no evidence that affordable housing brings crime to a neighborhood. "In fact, affordable housing, as a tool of economic development, can often help to lower crime rates...Most affordable housing residents are seeking safe and decent housing that will allow them to live self-sufficient lives in a good community."[41] The National Crime Prevention Council lists quality affordable housing as a primary crime deterrent strategy.[42]

1974–1977: Public/Private Partnership

The Gautreaux lawsuits shifted housing policy toward scattered sites–solutions aimed at preventing the isolation of the poor. In 1974, HUD's Section 8 program was created with two components. Project-based Section 8 (funding given to a project site) offered a subsidy to private developers in exchange for providing low-income housing (for twenty to forty years). Tenant-based Section 8 (funding granted to qualified individuals) allowed

For this is what the Sovereign Lord says: Enough, you princes of Israel! Stop all your violence and oppression and do what is just and right. Quit robbing and cheating my people out of their land! Stop expelling them from their homes! You must use only honest weights and scales, honest dry volume measures, and honest liquid volume measures. (Ezek. 45:9–10, NLT)

households with certificates (referred to as "vouchers" today) to use them anywhere in their city; it is dependent on an adequate supply of housing and participating landlords. Both programs were designed to ensure that the virtual ghettos created by huge public housing projects were not replicated and to scatter subsidized housing throughout a city. This private/public partnership helped close the gap caused by the moratorium on public housing development.

Also enacted in 1974 was the Community Development Block Grant (CDBG) program, providing funding to cities, counties, and states for, among other things, acquisition, rehabilitation, or demolition of real estate (not new construction). This program only required that 70 percent be used for low- or moderate-income recipients. Since its inception, 28 percent of CDBG funds have been used for housing.[43] The CDBG program has been the most significant source of federal funding for CDCs.[44]

The year 1976 was the high watermark for subsidized housing assistance, with HUD providing funding for an incremental increase of 435,000 more subsidized units. The next year the outgoing Ford administration requested an additional 506,000 units, the largest increase ever requested, but Congress did not approve the budget at the requested amount. The 1976 high point has never been duplicated, nor has any HUD budget request approached those levels, despite the growing need. If the federal government had been adding 500,000 units per year since 1977, these would be serving more than 14 million families today—the current number of families with critical housing needs.[45]

In 1977, Congress enacted the Community Reinvestment Act (CRA), requiring banks to provide credit products to the communities in which they are chartered.[46] The Act was designed to prevent redlining and encourage banks to meet the needs of their entire communities, especially low-income households. For the past twenty-five years, CRA has allowed underserved segments of the population access to small business loans, community development loans, and mortgages, much of it funneled into the community through CDCs.[47]

Housing assistance is the least funded of all federal low-income assistance programs. Even in 1976, the high watermark year, HUD's programs were never aimed at serving all who needed assistance. HUD serves approximately a quarter of the households that qualify for housing assistance.[48] Thousands are spending years on Section 8 waiting lists across the country.

To make matters worse, significantly more people need affordable housing than just that small group the government defines as "poor." Poverty level is calculated by taking bare-bones food costs and multiplying that amount by three, an archaic method developed in the 1960s that, with today's housing costs, vastly undercounts the numbers of households struggling to meet very basic needs. To identify those in the community in need, many social service agencies have created an additional designation for families and individuals above the official poverty level who are still experiencing great hardship. Some call this group "near poor" or "low income." These people find it difficult to meet expenses such as transportation, childcare, healthcare, and even food if housing costs eat up too much of the family budget.

1980s: A Withering Commitment[49]

Every president from Franklin D. Roosevelt to Jimmy Carter, regardless of party affiliation, increased federal housing assistance. The general consensus had been that the federal government must play a role in solving our country's housing needs, leading to relatively steady progress toward successfully housing the country. However, during the Reagan years, new annual funding for HUD was more than halved, from $31 billion in 1981 to only $14 billion in 1989. By 1982, President Reagan called for an end to the project-based, production component of Section 8, leaving the rent certificates as the only large-scale housing subsidy program.[50]

The Tax Reform Act of 1986 affected housing production in several ways. First, it repealed accelerated depreciation and related tax deductions, features in tax law that encouraged development. This prompted a sharp drop in the production of multifamily housing. The 1986 Act also limited the amount of money that states could issue in the form of tax-exempt bonds for multifamily housing production.[51] Finally, the 1986 Act favored the production of ownership housing over multifamily housing by increasing the mortgage interest deduction. To compensate for these disincentives to multifamily development, the Act created the Low Income Housing Tax Credit (LIHTC). Many of the successful housing developers in this book are faith-based CDCs using these tax credits.[52]

States also actively compensated for this federal drop in housing assistance. Yet with city and state budgets across the country experiencing economic troubles, by the end of the decade it was becoming "increasingly clear that only at the federal level did enough resources exist to seriously address the housing crisis."[53] At the close of the decade, fraudulent activity involving HUD contracts and kickbacks became known and investigations began, eventually leading to prosecution and guilty verdicts in 1996. Speaking to the House of Representatives in 1989, longtime Indiana Representative Lee H. Hamilton said, "The real scandal, though, is that the housing needs of millions of people were slighted…HUD's ostensible constituency, people who need low-income housing, are powerless and nearly invisible. The actual constituency, affluent developers and politicians, often use HUD grants for personal or political gain."[54]

Fed by the media's focus on public housing failures and HUD scandals, many came to believe that no solution existed beyond market forces. A "been there, done that" hopelessness—even cynicism—began to color any belief we still had in our ability to solve the housing problem. This is the legacy the 1980s left us.

1990s: HUD on the Chopping Block

Attacks on HUD were getting more strident and ominous. People were getting tired of so many housing experiments. In 1994 House Speaker Newt Gingrich was quoted in *The Washington Post* declaring that HUD's "weak political constituency makes it a prime candidate for cuts." "Politically, HUD is about as popular as smallpox," observed the paper in 1995.[55]

Among the attempts to streamline and answer some of its detractors, HUD introduced the Home Investment Partnerships Program (HOME), a housing block grant program. Policymakers favoring housing production and those who favored vouchers debated long and hard. Passage of the National Affordable Housing Act of 1990 initiated HOME. This put the debate to rest by leaving it up to state and local governments to decide. States and localities were now required to set aside at least 15 percent of HOME funds for Community Housing Development Organizations (CHDOs). HOME currently supports a wide variety of programs, including new construction, down payment assistance, and rental assistance to low- and extremely low-income tenants. HOME has financed nearly 800,000 affordable homes since its inception.[56] Today, HOME, LIHTC, and private activity bonds,[57] are the primary building blocks of our country's affordable housing production and preservation.

The 1990s also saw the establishment of the HOPE VI program, a part of the VA-HUD-IA Appropriations Act of 1993. HOPE VI is aimed at the revitalization of severely distressed public housing. While it meets a critical need of remedying bad housing, it continues the dubious tradition of the 1949 Act: it does not require one-for-one replacement of units demolished in dilapidated projects. As of September 2004, the program planned to replace only half of the demolished public housing units with affordable units.[58]

It would take building a quarter million units of affordable housing per year for the next twenty years to close the gap between the affordable housing stock and those in need of affordable housing. It's not that affordable housing isn't being built. It's just that the national stock of lower-cost housing is disappearing faster than it is being produced.[59]

Where Are We Today?

We haven't recovered from the downgrading of the importance of affordable housing over the last three decades. Despite today's crisis, housing receives almost no attention. "Why, then, is housing barely on the political radar screen?" asks leading housing expert and Occidental College professor Peter Dreier.[60] His answer, in a nutshell, is that today's middle-class is not behind it as a political issue. The vast federal support for middle- and upper-middle–class housing is virtually invisible to the public. Few realize (or acknowledge) that the combination of tax breaks, mortgage insurance, lender regulation, the secondary mortgage market, and mortgage revenue bonds are what make homeownership possible for many Americans. "In this era of skepticism about the role of government, political candidates can win votes by advocating that we get government 'off our backs.' In the area of housing, if we followed this advice, a majority of Americans, and the housing and banking industries, would be flat on their backs."[61]

Shockingly, the largest federal subsidy for housing goes to the wealthy in the form of homeowner tax deductions, such as mortgage interest deductions, property tax deductions, and investor deductions. These three tax deductions alone (excluding those deductions that helped fund affordable housing) accounted for a subsidy of $98.3 billion in 2002—more than three times the outlay for housing assistance.[62] Those with the largest homes get the largest subsidies. In contrast, many low- and middle-income homeowners don't have a large enough tax liability to take advantage of the deduction at all.[63] As Dreier puts it: "Federal housing subsidies for the well off are an entitlement. Federal housing subsidies for the poor are a lottery."[64]

Thousands of federally subsidized Section 8 units are scheduled for voluntary renewal of their twenty- to forty-year contracts—and many are opting out, converting to market-rate rents. Other units are disappearing because of condo conversions and demolition. The nation's affordable multifamily stock is rapidly shrinking.[65]

"In many cities, [housing vouchers] go unused because renters can't find suitable housing outside the ghettos," says Dreier. "The result is like giving people food stamps when grocery shelves are empty."[66] To further compound the problem, 2005 was the first time the federal government did not fund all housing vouchers in use.[67]

Although no longer legal, residential segregation persists because of long-standing housing patterns and economic disparities. HUD estimates approximately three million fair housing violations occur every year, and the vast majority go unreported.[68] Today, roughly 50 percent of black and Hispanic poor people report discrimination during their housing searches.[69] Public schools are rapidly resegregating, in large part because of the Supreme Court's 1991 Dowell decision allowing a return to neighborhood schools. The average poor, minority student still attends a poor, minority school, contributing to a relentless cycle of poverty.[70]

We are seeing efforts at urban revitalization of city centers and downtown areas through thirty years of redevelopment efforts. But when the middle class returns to crumbling urban cores, the draws are usually the convenience of urban life, the proximity to work and cultural centers, and the allure of older architecture—not an urge to integrate. A gentrification process is drawing wealthier residents back to urban living and often displacing low-income urban households. Architects and developers have embraced the principles of "new urbanism" and "smart growth" to create livable cities with aesthetic appeal, but often they make no or only token plans for low-income families.

Various Calls for Change

We introduced this chapter by stating that one third of the country is struggling with housing affordability and that homelessness keeps skyrocketing. In more than fifty years of trying different approaches to meet the goal set by the 1949 U.S. Housing Act, we have failed to provide "a decent home and suitable living environment for every American family." In this section we look at regional and federal strategies that can help in meeting that 1949 goal.

Regional Strategies

While states and cities lack the financial resources to close the "double whammy" gap between housing costs and incomes, they can play a huge role in other ways. In a century of experiments, we have learned some things that work. We know that it works, for example, to include the poor throughout the city rather than isolating them. Some of the following regional housing strategies can effectively accomplish this.

Smart Growth Regional Planning

Cities scrambling for revenue hope housing problems will go away and often assume that somehow the larger region will absorb the lower income needs. Yet even businesses are beginning to recognize the link between high housing costs and employee recruitment, productivity, and retention.[71] Affordable housing must be a priority in regional planning and closely linked to income and jobs.

Also, density must be addressed. Often blamed for frustrations such as traffic jams and crime, well-planned density can actually relieve these problems rather than exacerbate them. Increased density serves more households per dollar spent on infrastructure such as roads, water, and power. Density can actually deter crime. A bedroom community, which is basically abandoned during the workday, is more vulnerable to crime than a vibrant, densely populated, mixed-use, mixed-income, mixed-dwelling type, well-designed neighborhood.[72]

Destruction is certain for you who buy up property so others have no place to live. Your homes are built on great estates so you can be alone in the land. (Isa. 5:8, NLT)

Inclusionary Zoning and Density Bonuses

The Center for Housing Policy defines inclusionary zoning as allowing "the development of affordable housing to become an integral part of other development taking place in a community." In practical terms this has usually involved local zoning ordinances requiring the inclusion of a percentage of affordable units in all new housing development. Density bonuses are incentives that states or cities offer to developers. A municipality might offer a developer the right to build as many as 25 percent more units than normal zoning laws allow in exchange for including affordable units in the development. These tools create a mix of incomes in the same development. Often, a municipality with an inclusionary zoning ordinance will offer a density bonus to make the requirement financially palatable for the developer.[73]

Affordable Housing Trust Funds

Funding is one of the biggest challenges of affordable housing. Trust funds serve as a valuable source for part of that funding. Housing trust funds can generally be defined as a government fund financed from an alternative source that is earmarked for affordable housing production. For example, jurisdictions can direct a portion of real estate transfer and recording taxes, property taxes, or development fees for this use. (The "Community Organizing" model in chapter 15 is based on this model.)

Land Trusts and Ground Lease

In a land trust, a nonprofit corporation owns the land, but low-income homeowners own the housing on the land. Without having to pay for land, often the most expensive part of housing, the homes become affordable. Land trust models can support a mix of land use options, all participating in a model of permanent affordability. City governments across the country are initiating the land trust model as a way to preserve their affordable housing stock and fight gentrification.[74] (Chapter 14 is based on this model.) A similar model is being used by universities and other public institutions such as school districts. Affordable homes are built on the institution's land and then sold to the local workforce. This enables institutions to make money by leasing their land (using a ground lease) while providing affordable homes for their employees.[75] The homes remain permanently affordable, with limited equity earned by the owner.

Second Units

The allowance of second dwelling units (sometimes called "granny flats" or "maids quarters") on properties zoned for single-family detached homes requires no government subsidy. Benefits include added income, increased sense of security, increased tax revenue for local governments (without housing subsidy expenditures), maximized land usage, an increase in rental stock, a mix of incomes in the neighborhood, and circulation of local money to small local contractors (as opposed to outside developers who are often employed to build larger complexes).

Rent Control/Rent Stabilization

This is a widely used, if controversial, method of maintaining housing affordability in urban areas. Rent control, despite popular misperception, does not mean that landlords cannot increase their rents.[76] Critics of the policy have blamed rent control for lackadaisical building maintenance and actual abandonment by landlords demotivated by their lowered income. Studies are hard-pressed to back this up, however. A federal government study in 1978, following a big push for rent control in the early 1970s, showed that eight cities reported major abandonment problems. Of those eight cities, only New York had rent control laws in place.[77] This demonstrated that abandonment occurs with or without rent control. New York City, with the oldest program in the country, studies their rent control very closely. In Manhattan, rent-controlled units outnumber unregulated rental units six to one. The city has shown that within the five poorest Manhattan sub-boroughs, the rent-controlled units built after 1947 are in "much better shape" than the unregulated housing.[78] When rents are adjusted at the rate of inflation, landlords still have a steady net profit, while the value of their property appreciates.

Manufactured Housing[79]

This solution to increased homeownership opportunity is more of a phenomenon than a planned strategy. Low-income consumers themselves have chosen manufactured homes as a viable option. From 1993 to 1999, easy credit fueled a 25 percent increase in manufactured housing sales to low-income buyers. However, because of changes in credit terms and availability, current sales for manufactured housing are lagging below this model's potential.[80]

A Federal Strategy: More Vouchers, More Units

Some of our readers might question whether a federal strategy is needed. One might think that with all the wonderful examples in this book, increased church participation could help solve this problem. But many of the success stories you will read here were made possible, in large part, by some form of government funding. The problem is too big, and the expense too great, to create quality, well-managed housing without some subsidy. Dreier says,

> America's housing crisis is fundamentally about affordability: the gap between housing costs and household incomes. It requires money to fill the gap. Only the Federal Government has the resources to address the problem, even if Federal policy is implemented at the State, metropolitan, and local levels...Some form of

government support is necessary to make housing economically manageable for the poor, as well as for growing segments of the middle class.[81]

So what should the federal strategy be? As mentioned earlier, all of HUD's housing subsidies combined serve only 25 percent of the people in need. A housing subsidy program serving all eligible low-income households would cost about a third of what we spend on Medicaid annually. We need programs, such as the voucher system, that help relieve the high concentration of extremely low-income households in high-poverty neighborhoods.

Because there is insufficient affordable housing in every state, another component of the federal strategy, then, should be to preserve existing affordable housing and increase the affordable housing stock—both rental and homeownership. Future developments should be mixed-income housing—the model preferred since the Gautreaux lawsuits. And such housing should not be developed only in urban areas. Suburbs and rural areas must be opened up to mixed-income development.[82]

Numerous other strategies are being developed, tested, and debated. Room remains for many more creative, effective approaches to addressing the vast and complex housing hardship that we've never truly fixed.

A Challenge to the Faith Community

The church has a distinguished heritage of providing leadership for the great social movements in this country. Radical antislavery activists came out of what are today conservative seminaries. Jonathan Blanchard, the founding president of Wheaton College, was, according to the *Dictionary of American Biography*, a "violent abolitionist" and claimed that "every true minister of Christ is a universal reformer, whose business it is, so far as possible, to reform all the evils which press on human concerns."[83]

In the 1880s, the Salvation Army began day-care centers, provided free legal aid, and worked to keep first-time criminal offenders from prison, where they might become hardened convicts. One of their most significant efforts was joining journalist W. T. Snead to expose the selling of young girls into prostitution. The report dramatically changed public perception of these girls from wanton women to victims of horrible social conditions.[84]

The Roman Catholic Church was actively involved in labor reform movements and advocating for the poor. Dorothy Day, cofounder of the

---

If a brother or sister is naked and lacks daily food, and one of you says to them, "Go in peace; keep warm and eat your fill," and yet you do not supply their bodily needs, what is the good of that? So faith by itself, if it has no works, is dead. (Jas. 2:15–17)

Catholic Worker movement in the U.S., wrote articles in *The Catholic Worker* newspaper to inspire the clergy to social action.

Jesus met pressing needs, and so must we. Many churches have followed Jesus' lead by meeting the needs of struggling, low-income families. The stories you will read in this book are stories of congregations creating affordable housing. In so doing, they have unleashed the body of Christ to dream God-sized dreams. Churches across the nation have discovered the thrill of watching God bring about miracles in the form of award-winning affordable housing and changed lives.

Will you join them? Will you courageously take a stand and become a YIMBY (Yes In My Back Yard)? Will you call for healthy neighborhoods with a mix of income levels? Will you explore the possibilities of becoming an affordable housing advocate, developer, or manager? Will you consider your part?

Ownership, Land, and Jubilee Justice

A Biblical Rationale for Affordable Housing

LOWELL NOBLE WITH ED MAHONEY,
BERT NEWTON, AND JILL SHOOK

Dr. John Perkins, an African American born and raised landless and poor in Mississippi, loves to say the following:

Give a person a fish and he eats for a day. Teach a person to fish and he eats for a lifetime. That's a lie! The real issue is: Who owns the pond?

"Give a person a fish" equals charity. "Teach a person to fish," emphasizes job skills. But if the one fishing does not own the pond, she can be denied the right to fish in the pond. As a young man, Perkins recalls doing backbreaking labor all day for a man who wanted to pay him fifteen cents for his day's labor. He wanted to refuse it, but did not dare to. The man owned the wagon, the mule, and the land. All John had was his labor and dignity. Perkins elaborates in a talk with volunteers at the John Perkins Center for Reconciliation in Jackson, Mississippi: "Justice is an economic issue. Justice is a management issue. Justice is an ownership issue. Justice has to do with equal access to the resources of God's creation."

After General Grant won the battle of Vicksburg during the Civil War, he took over the Jefferson Davis plantation, allowing freed slaves to farm it, loaning them the supplies. They worked hard, had a good crop, made a profit, and paid back the loan. So Grant repeated and enlarged the experiment the next year with the same good results. The following year when the Civil War ended, as an act of reconciliation between the North and the South, the plantation was returned to the Davis family. This left the freed slaves landless in an agricultural society; they did not own their own pond/land and lost control over their future.[1] History teaches that without justice/ownership soon even new-found freedoms are lost. Segregation[2] and sharecropping replaced slavery—a system just a few notches above slavery.[3] Yes, Lincoln freed the slaves (liberation), but neither he and his followers nor Congress followed emancipation with justice/ownership— the promised "forty acres and a mule"[4] never materialized. Freedom without justice is not enduring; freedom and justice must go together. And, often, land ownership is justice.

Manning Marable, an African American historian, observed in *The Great Wells of Democracy:*

> Let us suppose that the general redistribution of abandoned and confiscated plantations had been carried out…There were approximately 350 million acres of land and 1 million black families living in the South in 1865. Forty acres allotted to each African-American family would have been only 40 million acres. This reform could have been accompanied by the general redistribution of lands to poor whites, nearly all of whom had owned no slaves. Had comprehensive land reform occurred in the South in 1865–1866… the history of black America would have been fundamentally different. Jim Crow segregation would not have been imposed on southern society, and there would have been no need for the Civil Rights Movement a century later.[5]

Dr. Perkins has said if we were to simply give poor people money, the wealthy would have the money back the very next day. A family replacing an old sofa, for example, would likely purchase it in a furniture store owned by a comparatively wealthy businessman, or a national or multinational corporation. Because the store was not in their own neighborhood or locally owned, with local employees, that money would cease to circulate to develop their own disenfranchised community. Apart from economic community development and "owning the pond," redistribution of wealth is not effective.

Today, the radical idea of restitution and redistribution of land and wealth is finding expression through community development, community organizing, and numerous other affordable housing models featured in this book.

In Jackson, Mississippi, Voice of Calvary Ministries (founded by Dr. Perkins) helped those living in the Olin Park neighborhood. The area was full of trash, abandoned homes, drugs, nightclubs, and renters of "shotgun" style homes. Homeownership was never considered an option or even a dream. Because of community development efforts, banks started to provide no-interest loans. Now neighborhood families are building equity and take pride in their community.

Today, the Spirit of God is calling the church to fulfill the mission of Jesus to set the oppressed free from housing injustice in our country. Maybe not with forty acres and a mule, but by creating a more just system–better lending products, better zoning laws–and more opportunity for access to land and resources.

In this chapter, we explore our relationship to God, the land, and the oppressed. We explore how these laws and principles that span scripture should guide our response to the housing crisis today. The Old Testament is replete with themes such as the value of the material world, of land, its ownership and preservation, the fair distribution of land, and its redistribution.

Old Testament Foundation: Our Relationship to Land

We are from the earth and will return to the earth. But what is our relationship to the earth while we live here? Beginning with Genesis, God gives us glimpses into the One who has authority over all the earth's resources and who delegates that authority and responsibility to men and women to rule over creation (Gen. 1:28). God stands as the only true owner of the land. It follows then that a more biblical concept of human land ownership revolves around the idea of stewardship. We are to manage the earth and its resources according to the rule of the One who owns it.

> The term "Land" refers to the whole material universe...[I]t is the raw material from which all wealth is fashioned. It includes not only soil and minerals, but water, air, natural vegetation and wildlife, and all natural opportunities–even those yet to be discovered. It is a passive factor of production, yielding wealth only when labor is applied to it...On the land we are born, from it we live, to it we return again–children of the soil as truly as is the blade of grass or the flower of the field. Take away from man all that belongs to the land, and he is but a disembodied spirit. Material progress cannot rid us of our dependence upon land.[6]

In ancient Israel, land was conceived of as an inherited gift to be passed on from generation to generation. The Bible recognized that land could be bought and sold–but not for private gain. "Moreover, the profit of the earth is for all" (Ecc. 5:9, KJV). Land does not make it into the index of most theological texts, but biblical authors were inspired to write extensively about it. The first sins resulted in a cursed land. The first dispute between Lot and Abraham was over land. Obedience brought land blessings, and disobedience brought land curses (Deut. 27–28). Sin brought about the destruction of land and whole cities (Gen. 19; Ezek. 16:49) God enabled Israel to inherit the promised land. Whole books of the Bible are dedicated to Israel's acquisition and subdividing of that land (Num. 34, Josh.). Full chapters are devoted to land use (Lev. 25); property rights (Ex. 22), including protection against "stealing" land (Deut. 19:14; 27:11–16); and laws governing the preservation of homes on the land (Lev. 14:35–54). For example, some very specific "building codes" are given about houses contaminated with an infectious mildew, along with specific instructions on how it was to be removed—reading like a process for lead paint removal today. Even how to enforce this law is recorded. Moreover, the Bible gives women the right to inherit the land (Num. 27; 36), and a "healthy" land was promised if certain conditions were met (2 Chron. 7:14).

Walter Brueggemann's theological work *The Land* provides insight into the central place of land in the scriptures. The Bible, he notes, is primarily concerned with being displaced and yearning for a place: "The yearning to belong somewhere, to have a home, to be in a safe place is a deep and moving pursuit."[7]

> [T]he Old Testament...was concerned with place, specific real estate that was invested with powerful promises...Israel's fortunes between landlessness (wilderness, exile) and landedness, the latter either as possession of the land, as anticipation of the land, or as grief about loss of the land.[8]

When it comes to fundamental issues of justice, access to land and all the laws that govern land are paramount. The promised land is the hope of the landless, literally the gateway to opportunity. Migrations have been taking place for centuries, beginning with Abraham, and up to the boat people of our day. Immigrants come to America looking for the inheritance denied in their countries. A poor family's attempts to borrow from local banks, obtain credit, or qualify for a mortgage are fruitless in most places in the world without a land deed. Sadly, this is often true among Native Americans. Years of renting and home improvements on rented property leaves a family with no return on their investments. Lack of access to land and capital perpetuates poverty.[9]

Old Testament Law: Sabbath Economics Applied

The Sabbath became the primary organizing mechanism for assuring the elimination of poverty.[10] To modern Christians, Sabbath denotes a quaint Old Testament practice we either no longer observe or have interpreted broadly as the spiritual practice of worship and rest. For the ancient Israelites, however, Sabbath entailed a belief that their society, and even creation itself, revolved around the Sabbath. After commanding the Israelites to bring their tithes each week and practice debt forgiveness every seven years, God declared that if they follow these laws, "there will be no poor among you" (Deut. 15:4, NASB). An astounding declaration!

A forty-year miracle of manna sustained their nation at a time when they might have perished in the desert. On the sixth day God gave sufficient food for two days (Ex. 16), teaching them of God's provision, the discipline of Sabbath rest, and a lesson in Sabbath economics. If they collected too much, the extra would rot. God made sure that no matter how much people collected, no one had too little or too much. This lesson of economic equality and trust in God as provider was also applied to land and labor. Once every seven years, the land had a sabbatical, lying fallow for a full year. Israel's sustenance was drawn only from what would naturally grow without tilling or working the land.

After seven sabbatical cycles (forty-nine years), Israel observed Jubilee (Lev. 25).[11] The competitive economy resulted in monetary debt, slavery, and repossession of land. If a family had not previously been able to get back their land, after forty-nine years the law prescribed grace by which the land could be returned to them. According to this legislation, a family's land and houses could not be permanently seized. Land and housing laws were written into the very fabric of Israelite society as part of Sabbath law.[12] These laws provide a more equitable access to the resources by stopping concentrated land ownership or monopolies by landlords, and the resulting division of society into landed and landless classes. Jubilee effectively took the profit out of landholding, leaving no incentive for speculation, removing one of the root causes of poverty from Jewish society.

Although most Old Testament scholars find no evidence that the Sabbatical laws were consistently and comprehensively applied, we can point to glimpses of both ancient and modern applications.

In the book of Ruth, land inheritance plays a key role in the romance. Two destitute women—one a foreigner—stagger into Bethlehem, just recovering from famine. Little opportunity exists for Ruth to find food and shelter for herself and her aging mother-in-law. Ruth would be a familiar character on the streets of any major city today. In God's economy, the destitute find hope when godly people step forward. If Naomi lives long enough, she will get her land back in the Jubilee; or, if she dies and Ruth has married within the tribe of Judah, Ruth's heirs will be able to claim it.[13] In Ruth's case, Boaz fulfills the laws in the Old Testament that command God's people to allow the poor to glean leftover grain from their fields (Lev. 19:9; 23:22). Boaz then steps into the role of the kinsman redeemer who is meant to provide a home to family members (even distant relatives) after tragedy had robbed them of their inheritance. The marriage and provision of land are premised on application of Sabbatical laws.

Nehemiah boldly confronted landowners who were exploiting the poor. Nehemiah demanded they immediately return the excessive interest, the fields, vineyards, olive groves, and houses they had taken. The oppressors repented and engaged in restitution (Neh. 5). The principles of the Jubilee were not minor cosmetic adjustments to the economic system, but instead a major overhaul.

Are biblical principles relevant to modern economic systems? Can efficiency and profit mix with justice and grace? Could Jubilee principles be applied in a non-Christian setting? The answer is a resounding *yes!* We have twentieth-century historical examples to prove it.

The following example is from *A Captive Land,* by a British scholar James Putzel. As a part of the World War II peace settlement in the Pacific region, General Douglas MacArthur grudgingly approved, under Russian pressure, comprehensive land reform programs in Japan, Korea, and Taiwan. Previously in each of these countries, a small number of landlords owned most of the land. Landlords were required by law to divest themselves of most of their land, making the land available to the landless peasants. As owners, the peasants quickly increased production, laying the foundation for future industrial economic growth in these countries.[14] Doing justice makes good economic sense. The planners of this land reform may or may not have been aware that they were applying Jubilee principles.

> It is notable that severe poverty and starvation is not a product of "overpopulation,"…The most densely populated countries of the world [Korea, Singapore, Japan] have less poverty than some of their neighbors, because of more equitable land systems.[15]

Much the same happened in parts of India after independence was gained from the British in the late 1940s. Normally, landlords hold the political power and block land reform. But Gandhi had released so much moral power in society that comprehensive land reform became public policy in parts of India, making it possible for landless peasants to own their own land. Government extension agents aided the farmers, and again production soared. Previously dirt-poor farmers began to prosper; the whole community benefited.[16]

General MacArthur refused to push for land reform in the Philippines after World War II because he was a friend of the Filipino elite.[17] As a result of this failure, Filipino society has often been torn by civil war largely fueled by a poor peasantry wanting access to their own land, which had been taken from them illegally. The peasants had no ownership of the pond. "The United States was also founded with notions of the Jubilee with the inscription on the Liberty Bell reading: 'Proclaim Liberty throughout all the land unto all its inhabitants.'" (Lev. 25:10)[18]

God promises peace and security in the land as a result of obedience:

> For if you truly amend your ways and your doings, if you truly act justly one with another, if you do not oppress the alien, the orphan, and the widow, or shed innocent blood in this place, and if you do not go after other gods to your own hurt, then I will dwell with you in this place, in the land that I gave of old to your ancestors forever and ever. (Jer. 7:5–7)

Old Testament Prophets: Judgment for Disobedience

The rich and powerful violated the Sabbatical and Jubilee principles and began oppressing the common people, which created class divisions in Jewish society. In Hebrew culture, "the possession of land, power, economic security, and social status made a person rich, and the absences of these factors made a person poor."[19] "Few pieces of literature, ancient or modern, come close to the prophetic defense of the poor against the wiles of the rich."[20] God sent prophet after prophet screaming with warnings from heaven, calling the people of God back to doing justice. Along with idolatry and immorality, Isaiah severely condemned oppression, especially by the rich who cornered the resources of God's creation and left little for the poor. Isaiah spoke directly to the unjust housing practices of the day:

> This is the story of the LORD's people.
>> They are the vineyard of the LORD Almighty.
>> Israel and Judah are his pleasant garden.
> He expected them to yield a crop of justice,
>> but instead he found bloodshed. He expected to find righteousness,
>> but instead he heard cries of oppression.
>
> Destruction is certain for you who buy up property so others have no place to live. Your homes are built on great estates so you can be alone in the land. But the LORD Almighty has sealed your awful fate. With my own ears I heard him say, "Many beautiful homes will stand deserted, the owners dead or gone." (Isa. 5:7–9, NLT)

Both Jeremiah and Isaiah clearly denounced the rulers and wealthy elite for building large, luxurious mansions for themselves while exploiting the poor and ignoring the plight of the needy for adequate housing. (See also Am. 5:11–12.)

The land and homes themselves became symbols of all that was wrong in Israel. Hosea proclaimed that the land mourned because of the injustices committed upon it (4:3). Isaiah prophesied that Israel would be like lands overgrown with briers and thorns (5:6). All the prophets warned that Israel could be expelled from the land if she did not turn back to the Lord God and deliver justice to the poor, including the redistribution of the land. If Israel had obeyed the Sabbath laws and the year of Jubilee, they would have been spared God's judgment and their exile from the land.[21]

Old Testament Prophets: Hope for a Housed City

While the prophets cried out for obedience to the law, they also envisioned a return to the land and a renewal of Israel's faith in God. Even as the Babylonians were laying siege to Jerusalem, Jeremiah bought land in his hometown of Anathoth. Jeremiah's purchase provided hope for urban renewal, showing, "Someday people will again own property here in this land and will buy and sell houses and vineyards and fields" (32:15, NLT). He spoke of a messiah who would come and "do what is just and right in the land" (33:15, NLT). Isaiah, too, looked forward to the time when Jerusalem would again be a place of peace and prosperity, when God's people would again have a home. "They shall build houses and inhabit them; they shall plant vineyards and eat their fruit. They shall not build and another inhabit" (Isa. 65:21–22a). Ray Bakke paraphrases this passage, explaining how Isaiah provides a blueprint for an ideal city: "All housing issues are addressed–there is no gentrification. People get to live in what they build, no absentee landlords or housing speculation–a housed city."[22] The words of this passage describe an ideal future on earth, not just in heaven. Ezekiel included the foreigner in his vision of a restored Israel, saying that when the land is divided up, "You are to consider them [aliens] as native-born Israelites; along with you they are to be allotted an inheritance among the tribes of Israel" (Ezek. 47:22b, NIV). Foreigners and indigenous peoples in any nation, including the United States, often have the most difficult time obtaining adequate housing. Language barriers, prejudice, unfamiliar customs and laws, and lack of legal status can hold them in the bonds of poverty:

> In God's sight all people share equally in the image of God, but some people, on account of their physical, psychological, or socio-economic situation, are singled out for an extra measure of the protection of God. They are those whom society has undervalued, ostracized, and often rendered powerless. They are the victims of oppression, discrimination, and exploitation. The rich and the strong are often able to silence them, to make them weak, and to banish them to obscurity. The God of the Bible, however, sees all things and hears even the voice of the poor and the oppressed.[23]

The Gospels: Jesus Addresses Oppression, Proclaims Jubilee

Most American Christians and even some Bible scholars seem unaware that these same themes run through the New Testament. Though the Romans added to the oppression of the Jews in Palestine, Jesus often found himself in conflict with the religious elite who controlled Judaism, Jerusalem, and the temple. The religious leadership controlled the economics, giving them enormous power. But they used the power to corrupt the system. The Roman military campaigns just prior to the time of Jesus devastated the region. Some elite Jews, who often compromised and collaborated with Rome, exploited the misfortune of the Galileans by buying up the land and keeping landless peasants in perpetual debt. Jesus confronted the authorities twenty-seven times in the gospels. For example, Jesus exposed them for "devouring widows' houses" (Mt. 23:14, NASB), most likely referring to some form of predatory real estate practice.[24] These debts, in addition to heavy taxation, robbed the peasants of Galilee of any hope of obtaining their own piece of land.[25]

Scholars concur that the religious-based oppression was worse in Jesus' time than during the times of Amos and Isaiah.[26] There was so much gold in the temple when the Romans sacked and destroyed it in 70 C.E. that the price of gold dropped fifty percent in nearby Syria as it began to circulate.[27] Nothing angered Jesus more than a religious system misusing God's name to exploit people. (See Mt. 23.) When the rich and powerful control most of the resources, it leaves the poor without enough to meet their basic needs. In an agricultural society, that meant that the poor lacked even a plot of land on which to grow food and build a house. Yet in God's economy, everyone has a God-given right to food and shelter.

After forty days fasting in the wilderness, Jesus opened his ministry by claiming as real what Isaiah had hoped for:

"The Spirit of the Lord is upon me,
> because he has anointed me
>> to bring good news to the poor.
He has sent me to proclaim release to the captives
> and recovery of sight to the blind,
>> to let the oppressed go free,
to proclaim the year of the Lord's favor."
(Lk. 4:16–18)

When Jesus read from Isaiah 61 to introduce his ministry he added a phrase found in Isaiah 58:6–"to let the oppressed go free." So what did Jesus mean when he said, "Let the oppressed go free"? How does this happen? Freedom from oppressors has to do with creating justice tied to the climax of Jesus' mission: "to proclaim the year of the Lord's favor"–the Jubilee. The language of this links it to Leviticus 25, the Jubilee year–the solution to the economically oppressed[28] –good news indeed for the poor!

In the beatitudes, Jesus also alluded to the possibility of Jubilee type redistribution: "Blessed are the meek, for they will inherit the earth" (Mt. 5:5), referring to Psalm 37:11, "The meek shall inherit the land." By invoking the Jubilee vision to inaugurate his own ministry, Jesus put his finger on the festering societal wound, pointing out that only by radical surgery could healing and wholeness take place–for both the rich and the poor. With courageous, Spirit-led obedience to the radical mission of Jesus, both the rich and the poor are set free.

We tend to overlook these radical teachings against oppression and focus on passages more comfortable to us and less controversial. Too often we blame the poor, without seeking to understand the government policies and the more fundamental reasons for their struggle. Are people poor because it's their fault? or is society at fault? The Bible teaches both: "Lazy hands make a man poor, but diligent hands bring wealth" (Prov. 10:4, NIV), and "A poor person's farm may produce much food, but injustice sweeps it all away" (Prov. 13:23, NLT). Yet, biblically, the primary cause of poverty is oppression.[29] The Hebrew root of the word for *oppression* means the cruel and unjust exercise of power and authority, usually through the control of social institutions. Oppression crushes, humiliates, animalizes, impoverishes, enslaves, or kills persons created in the image of God.[30] At times, oppression is legalized: "Woe to those who make unjust laws, to those who issue oppressive decrees, to deprive the poor of their rights and withhold justice from the oppressed" (Isa. 10:1–2a, NIV).

Luke's gospel emphasizes God's passion for justice for the poor. But that passion involves love for the rich as well. The involvement of the rich with those on the margins of society will be part of their own salvation, not a salvation of works, but of repentance, conversion, and forgiveness that results in justice for the poor. For most rich, their wealth stands between them and God; they think they are self-sufficient, and that they do not need God or the poor.

Jesus' Teachings: Woe to the Rich!

Jesus said, "No slave can serve two masters; for a slave will either hate the one and love the other, or be devoted to the one and despise the other. You cannot serve God and wealth" (Lk. 16:13). Luke follows this with, "The Pharisees, who were lovers of money, heard all this, and they ridiculed him" (Lk. 16:14). Like the prophets before him, Jesus repeatedly exposes and condemns the religious elite for their neglect of justice, using the strongest possible language in Matthew 23.

In Luke 18, we find Jesus challenging the rich ruler to "Sell everything you have and give to the poor...Then come, follow me" (v. 22, NIV). Sadly, he refused. But in chapter 19 we find the rare example of a rich person abandoning his wealth so he could enter the kingdom of God. Zacchaeus, the wealthy tax collector, met Jesus and repented. Zacchaeus states: "Look, Lord! Here and now I give half of my possessions to the poor, and if I have cheated anybody out of anything, I will pay back four times the amount" (v. 8, NIV). Genuine repentance leads to radical restitution. It seems that Zacchaeus did not sugarcoat the sins of his profession. Tax collectors would often collect more than they should to line their own pockets. As a result, Jesus said, "Today salvation has come to this house" (v. 9, NIV). Like Zacchaeus, Millard Fuller, a wealthy man, sold all to begin Habitat for Humanity, as you will read in the next chapter.

At the end of Luke 19, Jesus drove those selling animals for sacrifice (presumably at exorbitant prices) out of the temple. Jesus shouted about how they had turned God's house into a "den of robbers" (v. 46). Jesus directly challenged the chief priests' power and authority and their system of oppression, so they began to seek ways to kill him. Socioeconomic sins are central to Luke's gospel. In fact, Jesus spoke more about money, oppression, and justice than heaven *and* hell combined. And, often, heaven or hell was connected how we use our wealth. "Woe to you who are rich" summarizes Jesus' teaching regarding the rich (Lk. 6:24). Jesus went on, asking us to love our enemies and to be merciful as God is merciful (6:27–49), urging us to do no less than act as a community in which God, not wealth, rules. Under the reign of Christ, oppression is dealt with and justice is created.

These radical themes run throughout scripture, but our eyes are often not trained to see them, partly because we don't know what to do with their practical outworking. For example, the gospel of John has more references to attempts to arrest, stone, or kill Jesus than do the synoptic gospels. Why? Much of John is organized around feast days at the temple, where Jesus exposed corruption and oppression done in the name of God.

So what is Jesus asking of us? How are we to follow his example? Or do our fears of being labeled "liberal" or "radical" blind us, sapping our courage to wrestle with what the Bible teaches regarding land justice and its implications for today. None of this is easy, especially as the gap between rich and poor widens, even within the American church. But Jesus tutors us as we embrace his holiness, both private and public, to transform our values and our communities as we step out in faith to care for those on the margins.

The Early Church: Breaking Addiction to Riches

What is the mark of the Spirit-filled Christian and church? Some say speaking in tongues. Yet a distinguishing characteristic is what people do with their possessions. Jesus' first disciples seemed to have no question in their minds as to how the Jubilee was to take place. They instituted the Jubilee among themselves in the power of the promised Holy Spirit. Peter, with arguments and exhortations, challenged the early church:

> "Save yourselves from this corrupt generation." So those who welcomed his message were baptized, and that day about three thousand persons were added...All who believed were together and had all things in common; they would sell their possessions and goods and distribute the proceeds to all, as any had need. (Acts 2:40–41, 44–45)

Jesus' promise of Jubilee was fulfilled. They took it upon themselves to practice what Jesus had preached, not waiting for any kind of universal social change:

> There was not a needy person among them, for as many as owned lands or houses sold them and brought the proceeds of what was sold. They laid it at the apostles' feet, and it was distributed to each as any had need. (Acts 4:34–35)

The Sabbath laws were not destroyed, but fulfilled, right under the nose of a selfish, brutal, and hypocritical ruling class. A Spirit-filled church incarnated the Jubilee and took care of the poor. In 2 Corinthians 8 and 9,

Paul discusses the principle of generous giving with a cheerful heart. He refers to the Old Testament Sabbath desert miracle and reflects the biblical principle of equality. Paul writes:

[I]t is a question of a fair balance between your present abundance and their need, so that their abundance may be for your need, in order that there may be a fair balance. As it is written,

"The one who had much did not have too much, and the one who had little did not have too little." (2 Cor. 8:13b–15)

A Spirit-filled church addresses the addictive nature of riches (and its closely related sins of racism and classism). It may be that riches are more dangerous and addictive than drugs, alcohol, and tobacco: "For the love of money is a root of all kinds of evil, and in their eagerness to be rich some have wandered away from the faith"(1 Tim. 6:10). If riches are this dangerous, why do most of us want them? Why are there no "Riches Anonymous" groups in the church? If the American church would heed the biblical teachings on rich and poor, oppression and justice, it could easily eliminate substandard housing in a generation. Unfortunately, biblical justice has too often either been avoided or watered down.

Today's Church: Justice Lost In Translation

For centuries, English-speaking Christians read a Bible that said little about justice. In the older *King James Version* (KJV), the word *justice* never occurs in the New Testament, and rarely in the Old Testament. The Hebrew word *mishpat* is mistranslated as "judgment" about 100 times and translated as "justice" only once. The *New Revised Standard Version* (NRSV) and *New International Version* (NIV) each translate it as "justice" about 100 times. In the KJV, the famous verse from Amos 5:24 reads: "Let *judgment* run down as waters..." In the NIV it reads: "Let *justice* roll on like a river"[31]

In the New Testament, most translators interpreted the Greek word *dikaiosyne* as "righteousness," even though a growing number of scholars, such as Nicholas Wolterstorff, Howard Snyder, David Bosch, Graham Cray, Glenn Stassen, and David Gushee, insist that *dikaiosyne* means both "justice" and "righteousness" or justice/righteousness.[32] There is only one major English translation that captures the strong justice meaning of *dikaiosyne*– the New English Bible (NEB), translated by British scholars. Matthew 6:33 reads: "Set your mind on God's kingdom and his justice," and Romans 14:17 reads: "The kingdom of God is...justice." Graham Cray translates Matthew 5:6, "Blessed are those who hunger and thirst for justice..." Cray comments:

Much of this is entirely lost to readers of the English Bible, because of the false separation made between righteousness and justice, and because "dikaiosune" is consistently translated righteousness in English translations, whereas in the Septuagint [Greek translation of the Hebrew OT] it was often used to translate [the OT word] justice.[33]

In summary, Cray states that the *agenda* of the kingdom of God on earth is *justice,* and the *dynamic* of the kingdom of God is the Holy Spirit. Rarely do theologians make this close tie between the Holy Spirit, the kingdom of God, and justice. Sidney Rooy, in an unpublished manuscript entitled *Righteousness and Justice,* comments on the discoveries his missionary family made as they read the Bible together in Spanish: "Soon we discovered that righteousness and justice are universally translated 'justicia'–our word for justice. Suddenly the Bible was full of texts about justice."[34] It appears that the Romance languages have only one word for justice/righteousness, and the primary meaning in these languages is justice. But most English-speaking people miss the justice emphasis of the kingdom of God.

The Kingdom of God: Christ—the Remedy for Injustice

Justice for the poor in the power of the Spirit incarnates the kingdom of God on earth. The Messianic passages from Isaiah, describing the coming death of the Messiah, are filled with strong language denoting justice as central to the nature of the coming kingdom of God. (Isa. 9:7; 11:1–4; 16:5; 28:16–17; 42:1–4; 61:1–4, 8)

Western Christians usually define the gospel, in essence, as, "Christ died for my sins." This is true, yet one cannot isolate his death from his incarnation–what Jesus stood for, how he lived, those he chose to get close to, and what he valued. Jesus was crucified because of his relentless identification with the people on the margins of society, his refusal to embrace the status quo, and his confrontations with a system that oppressed the poor. Jesus' suffering on the cross is an example for us to follow, as well as the means for our own freedom from personal and societal sin.

Throughout United States history God has used Christian leaders who have identified to the point of death with the sufferings of Christ to bring more just laws and freedoms. For our nation's first fifty-four years, we didn't allow people to vote unless they owned property. Not until 1920 could women vote. Only in 1965 were obstacles such as literacy tests and poll taxes dropped, finally allowing many blacks to take advantage of the voting right given them ninety-five years earlier. Until the Fair Housing Act was passed as late as 1968, minorities could not own property wherever they wished. All the while, our nation clung to a constitution that reads: "With liberty and justice for *all.*"

Dr. Perkins was the Martin Luther King Jr. of Simpson County. Perkins set up new structures–cooperatives–that gave ownership and control to the blacks. Soon they began to own homes. This became a threat to white leaders in his Mississippi hometown. In 1970, the sheriff beat him brutally, nearly to death. However, by the early 1980s the governor honored Perkins for his work. He had the only church in Mississippi in which blacks and whites worshiped together. He's been given seven honorary doctorates for his justice work, has served on a presidential commission on poverty, and has authored ten books—even though he only has a third grade education. God delights to confound the wise and do what seems impossible.

Though we cling to biblical truth, it takes time to realize the Kingdom goals Jesus set forth in his mission and prayers. The time is now. The need is urgent. Love and the power of the Holy Spirit provide the courage for the church to set the pace and the example by demonstrating justice to the wider society. The church must risk having a view that does not tolerate poverty, but works tirelessly for just access to resources, land, and a decent place to live for everyone.

Tangible Structures

While working on this book at Zona Rosa, my favorite coffee shop in Pasadena, people wanted to know its topic. "It's about churches involved in creating affordable housing," I'd explain. And invariably their response would be, "Oh, like Habitat?" People are amazed to learn that Habitat for Humanity is only one model, among many, that churches have embraced as they go about building affordable housing.

Over the past four years, while attending Affordable Housing Seminars, Christian Community Development Association Conferences, and my doctoral courses from Chicago to China, I would ask respected pastors and community development practitioners, "Who are the best out there? Which churches exemplify successful affordable housing ministries?" It was like a giant puzzle the size of the United States. Eric Swanson said, "You have to talk with the Stranskes." Marilyn Stranske said, "You have to feature Nehemiah Housing in New York," and on and on. God was clearly leading as the puzzle pieces began to fit into place.

Once the featured models were selected, people kept suggesting others: Corinthian Point planned community of 452 single-family affordable homes, a ministry of the Windsor Village Church[1] under Pastor Kirbyjon Caldwell in Houston, Texas; West Angeles Church of God in Christ led by Lula Ballton; and the First African Methodist Episcopal Church in Los Angles (FAME) and their Renaissance Corporation founded by Mark Whitlock and led by Peggy Hill. Mercy Housing, having developed 17,383 units of housing, was serving approximately 55,000 people with an average income of $14,568 by the end of 2005.[2] This impressive organization is run by Catholic sisters. Had space allowed, I would have featured the unique model of Urban Homework, led by Chad Schwitters and Cody Schimelpfenig. They address need for quality affordable housing in Minneapolis, while bringing the presence of Christians to love their neighbors and involve youth in the construction. Similarly, groups like the Esperanza Community Housing Corporation (ECHC) founded by Sister Diane Donoghue tap into funding from HUD's Youth Build program, which helps high school students obtain their diplomas as they learn to build homes.[3] This list could go on and on.

A number of these ministries deal with both sides of the "double whammy"–the high cost of housing *and* low wages, offering job training, job placement, and the creation of better-paying jobs. Many help families better manage their resources–breaking vicious poverty cycles.

Beginning in February 2002, several of the authors whose words you are about to read met on a regular basis. We consulted with Jude Tiersma-Watson, professor of Urban Ministry at Fuller Seminary, who coedited *For God So Loves the City*[4] with Charles Van Engen. Together we designed the framework, length, and criteria of the chapters in this section. We would use the following outline and subtitles, which essentially follows the process for best practices:

- The Story (Untitled)
- Daring to Listen
- Developing Partners
- Doing the Work
- Dealing with Realities
- Developing Insights

One day I called the head of the Department of Architecture from my alma mater, California Polytechnic State University–San Luis Obispo. I asked, "Are there additional affordable housing models I may have overlooked?" He essentially said that if we are to get serious about housing our nation, we need each of the models featured in this section and many more.

Habitat for Humanity and Peachtree Presbyterian Church

Listening to the Powerful and the Poor

MILLARD FULLER

Introduction to the Sweat Equity Model BY EDWARD F. MONCRIEF

In the mid-1980s, I was privileged to spend a day with Millard Fuller, founder of Habitat for Humanity. At the time, I was director of CHISPA,[1] a nonprofit housing corporation I had founded. I toured Millard through Salinas Valley's deteriorating farm labor camps, showcasing various new construction projects we had developed. We discussed the similarities of our self-help models. CHISPA was engaged in *mutual* self-help, which employed future owners' "sweat equity" and harnessed public financing. Habitat's *volunteer* self-help model taps "sweat equity" contributed by both the future owners and volunteers, using "the economics of Jesus."[2] Biblical economics are summarized in Exodus 22:25, "In our dealings with poor people, we are to charge no interest and seek no profit." By the time Millard and I met, our mutual self-help housing model had been around for twenty years.

The Beginnings of Sweat Equity

In the late 1930s and early 1940s, on a couple hundred acres of Pennsylvania farmland, American Friends Service Committee (AFSC) helped to organize Penn-Craft. They borrowed the frontier experience of barn raising and created a support system for community building with the area's poverty-stricken and disenfranchised coal miners. The effort began with families helping each other to build their homes.[3] AFSC is the Quakers' organizational expression of their vision that genuine social change "works to transform conditions and relationships both in the world and in ourselves, which threaten to overwhelm what is precious in human beings." It nurtures "the faith that human conflicts can be resolved nonviolently, that enmity can be transformed into friendship, strife into cooperation, poverty into well-being, and injustice into dignity and participation."[4]

In the mid-1950s, a group of Quakers settled in California's San Joaquin Valley equipped with a faith, a vision, and a very practical set of skills and experiences at the right time. Edward R. Murrow, a well-known commentator, aired *Harvest of Shame*, an early television documentary exposing the plight of immigrant workers, living "on the edge of your cities."[5] In Fresno County, George Ballis, a feisty photojournalist, shot telling photos of shabby mining shacks relocated in Three Rocks, where some thirty immigrant farmworker families shared one rusty water faucet. The national media picked up the photos first. Then the Moscow daily, *Pravda*, printed them under the headline, *Capitalists' Treatment of Their Workers*. Despite years of resistance from federal housing officials, suddenly the government became interested in farm labor housing.

In the early 1960s, Bard McAllister, a staff member of the AFSC's Farm Labor Project in Visalia, could be found circulating among the squalid labor camps of Tulare County, seated in some hot and dusty frontyard whittling and listening to the Mexican *campesinos*. His Quaker values taught him that listening, rather than speaking, was a way both to teach and to learn; as he listened, he learned that these immigrant workers dreamed most about homes of their own.

The First Projects

Goshen, Three Rocks, and Cutler saw AFSC's first self-help housing projects. Prophetically, Goshen[6] came to mean "a land of plenty." Families organized into groups of ten or so were taught the needed skills to lay foundations, pour cement, raise walls, string wire, and nail roofing. They worked evenings and weekends, men and women alike, contributing some twelve to fifteen hundred hours of "sweat equity" labor over several months. No one could move in until all of the homes were finished. Low-interest mortgages came from the U.S. Department of Agriculture's Farmer's Home Administration (now Rural Development Services).

From these early experiences, mutual self-help housing was born, institutionalized by the Economic Opportunity Act of 1964. Farmers Home Administration began funding rural nonprofit housing organizations to provide supervision and support to self-help projects across the country. During the 1970s, the pioneering work of the AFSC's Farm Labor Committee (McAllister, Howard Washburn, and Bob Marshall, among others) pushed California to create and fund pre-development financing programs to provide grants and loans to nonprofit development organizations. As a result, the State's rural housing programs for migrant workers became a model for the nation. Self-Help Enterprises in Visalia, the first test case, became the nation's most productive mutual self-help housing developer, assisting over five thousand families throughout the southern San Joaquin Valley since 1965.

During my Salinas Valley tour with Millard, we agreed that each form of these sweat equity self-help methods has its strengths: *Mutual self-help* housing with its emphasis on establishing a community of homeowners among low-income families working together to achieve their dreams; and *volunteer-based self-help* housing involving the broader faith community with families who will own the completed homes.

In 1992, Millard with bold faith proposed a daring initiative: to eliminate all "poverty housing" in Americus, Georgia, and Sumter County, where Habitat is headquartered. Although stunned by his vision, the Habitat Board voted unanimously to accept this challenge. Churches and organizations from all over rural Sumter County, the U.S., and beyond joined in. By the end of the decade, the goal was met.[7] This helped to spawn Habitat's exponential growth locally, nationally, and internationally.

In what follows, you will read Millard's journey and the story of one congregation that caught Millard's fever for exponential growth.

Habitat for Humanity and Peachtree Presbyterian Church

MILLARD FULLER

Jesus felt genuine love for this man as he looked at him. "You lack only one thing," he told him. "Go and sell all you have and give the money to the poor, and you will have treasure in heaven. Then come, follow me." —Mark 10:21, NLT

For many years I listened to the call of money and self before God began to show me what a truly rich life was all about. Beginning in my college days, the driving force in my life was to make a pile of money. It didn't matter how—selling birthday cakes or cookbooks or toothbrushes, renovating real estate, or promoting and selling tractor cushions. I just wanted to be rich. In 1964 I knew I was well on my way. The treasurer of our company walked into my office in Montgomery, Alabama, and informed me that I was worth a million dollars. I wasn't surprised; nor was I satisfied. My next goal was 10 million.

The Poor Rich Man

I was living the life of a rich man. I paid cash for an elegant gray Lincoln Continental with all the luxury options. My wife, Linda, and I kept horses in the country on our three cattle farms that totaled some 2,000 acres. We had a cabin on the lake, two speedboats, and a full-time maid to help with our two children. Linda had so many clothes and shoes that she could not fit them in our closets–and we had a lot of closets.

My affluence came at a price, however, including estrangement from the church. I had been raised in the church and believed in the Christian message. Linda and I even started a United Church of Christ in our home. However, I gave only the leftovers of my time to the Lord. If my business conflicted with church activities, the business always came first. I wanted to serve God, but at my own convenience, without financial sacrifice. One year I made $60,000, and gave the church $40 a month; when my annual salary increased to $100,000, I gave $80 per month–less than one percent. To be honest, working with the church created a favorable impression for my friends and business associates. Particularly in the South, it was important to appear to be a Christian.

My obsession with work caused health problems, but I rationalized– these were simply part of the price to pay for success. I kept pushing. One of those maladies perhaps would have killed me if Linda hadn't precipitated a crisis. Even though I loved Linda deeply, I neglected her. The business increasingly took first place. I was seldom at home, and when I was, I talked about work. Linda tried to get me to understand her loneliness, but I wasn't hearing her. One Saturday evening in November of 1965, she announced that she was leaving me. She said that she was not sure if we had a future together and that she needed to get away for a while to think over a lot of things. She decided to go to New York to talk with a pastor whom we both knew. The next day, I drove her to the airport; she boarded an airplane alone and left.

I had much thinking to do. The week that followed was the loneliest, most agonizing time of my life. I tried to concentrate on work, but it was impossible. Instead of leaving the office at midnight, as I usually did, I had to leave at 5 p.m. to take care of the children. My son looked up at me at bedtime and said softly, "Daddy, I'm glad you're home." Chills ran up my spine as I realized I had become a virtual stranger in my own house.

Linda called on Thursday night and told me I could join her in New York the following Tuesday. In New York we were reconciled and decided to radically change the direction of our lives. We would give away all our money. We had gone too far down the wrong road to be able to correct our direction with a slight detour. We simply had to go back and start all over again, but this time we would let God choose the road for us. Together we embarked on a tremendous journey of faith that gradually helped us rebuild our relationship.

Habitat's Beginnings

We went back home, gathered the children, and drove to Florida to determine what we were going to do when we were no longer rich. On our trip back, we stopped at a Christian community called Koinonia Farm in southwest Georgia. We intended to stay only a couple of hours. There I met Clarence Jordan, a man of tremendous faith and spiritual insight. God had surely led us to this place. We stayed at Koinonia for a month. Each day as I helped with the chores, I talked with Clarence, who showed me what it meant to be a disciple. Also during our stay, I transacted by phone most of the business necessary to liquidate my interest in the company.

At Koinonia we developed the fund for a housing program—the model for Habitat for Humanity. That was not immediate, however. Our family lived in Africa for a time, where we developed a housing program. We learned to live trusting God to guide us. Eleven years after our marital crisis, I placed the sign in a window in Americus, Georgia, proclaiming the opening of Habitat for Humanity. This is God's work. Habitat for Humanity is a Christian ministry created to witness to the gospel of Jesus Christ. Churches, therefore, are natural and primary partners.

In more than ninety countries around the world, Habitat for Humanity International has built over 200,000 houses. In each home lives a family who has experienced the blessings of hope and the incredible outpouring of love. Through donations of money, labor, and in-kind goods and services, Habitat builds houses and sells them at no profit, with no interest. In addition to making a down payment and monthly mortgage payments, homeowner families invest hundreds of hours of their own labor—sweat equity—into building their houses and the houses of others. This labor reduces the cost, increases the pride of ownership, and fosters the development of positive relationships.

In this chapter you will find the story of one of Habitat's most amazing church partners, Peachtree Presbyterian Church in Atlanta, which has built 142 Habitat houses in Atlanta since 1988–143 and 144 will be complete in 2006. They have also built twenty-four homes in Hungary and four in Northern Ireland. The faithful supporters at Peachtree heard the voices of both the powerful and the poor that inspired them to make the largest commitment of any church to Habitat for Humanity.

The Peachtree Story: A Challenge from the President

Peachtree Presbyterian Church is the largest Presbyterian Church in the U.S.A. This congregation includes some very affluent and influential people, among them early political supporters of former President Jimmy Carter. Some of those old friends arranged for him to speak at Peachtree during their stewardship campaign. When he stood at the pulpit and looked at the congregation, he commented on the lack of diversity. He challenged Peachtree Presbyterian to reach out into the community and to serve a broader group of people.

Daring to Listen: A Determined Pastor

Dr. Frank Harrington, the senior pastor at Peachtree when President Carter spoke, was greatly concerned over the lack of people personally involved in ministry. "He saw right away that Habitat was a means of connecting a lot of people and for developing relationships," said Elijah Moore, former board president of Atlanta Habitat for Humanity. Frank loved projects and how the church could make a difference. As a visible sign of God's love, Habitat for Humanity fit his theology to a "T." Lynn Merrill, former Peachtree member and coordinator of many Habitat projects at the church, said that Carter's challenge inspired the congregation, but it was the dynamic pastor's urging that made the Habitat partnership a reality.

She explained that one evening before a meeting Harrington approached her as chair of the missions' council. "He wanted me to make the motion to commit $100,000 to Habitat. I was aghast. We had not even discussed this as a committee. He said, 'You are not hearing me. I want you to make the motion to commit $100,000 to Habitat.' Obediently, I did!" Harrington's strong personality was an integral part of the success of the Peachtree partnership.

The church leadership approved the $100,000 commitment to Habitat to purchase land for twenty-one houses and build a test house. This would help the Atlanta Habitat affiliate practice building an entire house in seven days–in preparation for the 1988 Jimmy Carter Work Project, an annual Habitat blitz build, drawing volunteers from all over the world. The Carter project is held in a different location each year; Atlanta Habitat hosted it in 1988.

Developing Partners

Every aspect of a Habitat project is built on partnership–partnership with God, with sponsors, volunteers, and homeowners. Often this partnership with homeowners–offering families hope–inspires volunteers and donors to support the work of the ministry. "In 1989 we built a house with a woman who lived in a neighborhood where she was constantly afraid of gunfire," remembered Merrill. "She and her children would lie in the bathtub in an attempt to stay away from the spray of bullets. Stories like these kept us involved. People at church would say, 'We've got to do this.'"

The homeowner of the second house Peachtree sponsored had a drug problem and began to fall behind on his payments. His family began to disintegrate as well. The man turned to the Peachtree volunteers when he was ready for help. His Peachtree friends helped him get into rehab, and he is now an advocate for fighting drug abuse. Merrill noted that although he lost ownership of the Habitat house, he did turn his life around. "It was not exactly what we hoped for," she said, "but we saw him changed in a different way."

Doing the Work

Organizers put the word out in the congregation for volunteers–for construction helpers, people to make lunches, help with devotions, and more. Everybody wanted to help! Walter Waddey, a Peachtree volunteer, said he knew God was calling him to work on the test house despite the fact that construction was scheduled during the most important financial week of the year for his company. More than 50 percent of their annual business was put on the books during the last week of the fiscal year, and Waddey wanted to take that week off. His boss was incredulous. But a week before the project, a scheduling change meant the big financial week no longer conflicted with the construction schedule. "I just looked at my boss and smiled. I told him I guess I was supposed to work at the Carter camp," Waddey said.

Atlanta Habitat selected Evelyn Jackson to be the homeowner of the test house. Jackson had a limited education, had been married at fourteen, and worked as a housekeeper. She lived with her mother and father, her two children, and other family members. In applying for a Habitat house, she realized that she shouldn't be sharing a bedroom with her preteen son. "I think the [Habitat] affiliate saw us as a congregation that could help her succeed," said Merrill. "I can remember meeting Evelyn at the site and digging the footers for the house in the Georgia clay—some of the hardest work I have ever done. I can remember her saying, 'Why are you doing this? You don't even know me.' I told her she was giving us the opportunity to live out our faith." The two women have maintained a relationship over the years. "We have married our children and buried our parents together," Merrill said of her forever friend. "Evelyn has taught me courage, kindness, thoughtfulness, and willingness."

When the Jimmy Carter Work Project was formally announced in a press conference, everyone gathered on Jackson's porch. Merrill said she was jaded for a moment when President Carter arrived in his limousine, "but he had on his work boots and wanted to walk the property that he would be working on. He won me over for life," she confessed. "He reached out with such kindness. So many people wanted to help," explained Merrill. "Not only did it give them a chance to help someone, but people got to know and work alongside other church members whom they had never met. It erased any lines between people in the church. The airline president was sweating alongside the average Joe."

Building Excitement

"The momentum was strong," said Merrill. "There was never any question that we would build another house after the Carter project." In fact, after Jackson's house was dedicated, church members formed a steering committee to direct their next steps.

"We got involved in everything from soup to nuts," reported Waddey. "We helped with site selection and finding homeowners. We even got involved in projects where we were not building. Looking back, I am not sure how I would have reacted to us if I had been an affiliate leader, but we wanted to help. Our goal was to revitalize a neighborhood. We drove around town, looking for the right place. We selected a neighborhood called

Reynoldstown and committed to sponsor six houses a year for the succeeding five years."

Once those five years passed, Peachtree kept building. "We tried to keep a house going all the time," said the Rev. Chuck Mann, former senior associate church minister. The congregation developed new strategies and eventually started building up to ten houses a year. Mann adds, "We also had a lot of fun!"

Keeping the Momentum Going

The plan was not necessarily set up to be long-term, but Habitat volunteer families enjoyed helping homeowner families. These turned out to be long-lasting relationships—a plus for everyone! They set up permanent liaisons between church members and the homeowners. Sunday school classes, which took turns sponsoring houses, invited homeowners to speak. An energetic singles' group provided a great deal of support.

Peachtree demonstrates a fundamental principle of fund-raising. Money follows involvement. They had lots of people involved and constantly brought in new people. That keeps a little group from getting burned out. A broad base of support limits the formation of small little cliques that get burned out and tired. Also, key to maintaining involvement was the presence of Peachtree members on the Atlanta Habitat affiliate board of directors. That helped church members understand what was going on with the ministry as a whole.

Changing Lives

After becoming deeply involved with Habitat, Waddey learned of changes in his company. He began asking himself what he would do if he did not have to worry about money. The answer: He would work for Habitat for Humanity. Like myself, the road was not direct, and the timeframe was not immediate; but Waddey made his way to Habitat. "One Friday night," Waddey said, "a very clear voice came to me from God, saying, 'You've got to quit what you are doing. Follow your bliss and go to work for Habitat.'" Waddey and his wife sat down with their children and explained that they were going to have to get by with less. "I don't know how we are going to do it," he told them, "but I have faith that it will work."

Merrill's husband, Alan, also changed careers as a result of Habitat involvement. "He was an MBA with Kimberly-Clark who loved to work with his hands," said Merrill. "He had to get involved with Habitat, or he would have nothing to talk to me about," she laughed. Following their daughter-in-law's illness and his fifty-fifth birthday, he proclaimed that life was too short. He was going to do something different. He took early retirement and became a carpenter, "something he would have never done without Habitat," Merrill said.

Passing on the Challenge

After Peachtree became deeply ensconced in its Habitat commitment, I was invited to speak at Highland Park United Methodist Church in Dallas. Like Peachtree, Highland Park is also one of the largest churches of its denomination. The congregation had built seven houses at the time of my visit. I thanked them for building the seven homes, but then described Peachtree's work and asked why the Presbyterians were so far ahead of the Methodists. I challenged them to build one hundred houses, just as Peachtree had done. On that Sunday morning, when the senior pastor was not present, the congregation got excited. The pastor later wrote me that Highland Park agreed to build one hundred houses!

Dealing with the Realities

The Peachtree/Habitat partnership has experienced growing pains and challenges over the years. However, their commitment to live out their faith and to make a long-term change in the lives of individuals has allowed them to develop a steady rhythm of serving God by serving others.

A Changing Environment

Rising house costs have meant a reduction in the number of houses the church could sponsor. Peachtree had steadily increased its commitment from $95,000 in 1994 to $200,000 in 2000. When sponsorship costs soared to $45,000, money didn't go as far, but Peachtree kept supporting Habitat at the same level. The combination of concern over rising house costs and the availability of a volunteer workforce led the congregation to budget $150,000 in 2004 to build three houses. Ironically, while the number of houses was reduced, inexplicably the number of volunteers went the other direction. Members of the congregation were signed up on waiting lists to work on the homes.

"We as leadership at the church have to acknowledge a changing environment," said Johnny Myers, staff liaison to community ministries at Peachtree. "We have to adjust and go where we feel God is leading us. Particularly after September 11, we had to make some cuts in our budget, including some in our own programs; but we maintained our Habitat support."

I see Habitat's work as worldwide, but Pastor Harrington was heavily focused in Atlanta. That was his parish. I am as interested in a remote village in China as a slum in Atlanta, but Frank wanted to work on something he could get his arms around. I had to respect that. Dr. Vic Pentz, the new pastor at Peachtree following Harrington's death in 1999, led the congregation to extend its Habitat mission to Ireland and Hungary. In 2001, the congregation adopted the community of Dunavarsany, Hungry, where they fund construction and send teams of workers to build. "People lead in different ways," said Barbara Hickman, Chair of Community Ministries. "Frank gave Peachtree a vision to tend to its own backyard. Vic opened the gates wider...challenged the congregation to go out globally and see much more than just our own area—while also tending our backyard."

Hickman said she envisions the day when the children of the original singles' group will become the volunteer force for new Habitat projects.

An Uncommon Situation

The Peachtree story is often told in an effort to inspire other congregations, but their circumstances are unlike those of many smaller churches. For them, Habitat was almost like its own business. Volunteers created a detailed database that reflected who was contacted when and what they said. The Atlanta Habitat affiliate had little success replicating the Peachtree model. Large churches identified Habitat as a Peachtree ministry, and they chose to serve in other ways. In many communities, coalitions of small churches, unable to imagine building a Habitat house on their own, pool their resources to fund and build homes. One very successful model has been an Apostles Build, in which twelve churches serve together in the way that Jesus' disciples served.

Not every church can make the same commitment as Peachtree, Presbyterian or Highland Park, but we can use their experiences to talk about commitment. Their efforts were trailblazing. Often when I speak to other churches that are smaller, I tell them to do the arithmetic. If Peachtree, a church of 12,000, could build ten houses a year, I ask them how many they should be doing.

A Personal Toll

"One of the problems in getting so involved in a program like Habitat was that I lost the spiritual side of being at church," said Merrill. "Coming to church to me meant making sure that everything was happening correctly in my Habitat project. It was not about worship." Merrill and her husband have left Peachtree and have joined a much smaller church, but she continues to serve Atlanta Habitat as a board member. Others have stepped in at Peachtree to guide the house building projects there.

Discovering Insights

Frank Harrington told me that Habitat was the most exciting thing his church was doing. It had an amazing effect on the congregation. Other churches are seeing the same result. The Rev. Pat Driskell, pastor of First Cumberland Presbyterian Church in Lubbock, Texas, said, "A Habitat partnership is definitely a two-way street, but there are multiple lanes coming back to the church."

My dream, from the outset of the ministry of Habitat for Humanity, is for our work to be a new frontier in Christian missions.[8] We desire vital and dynamic partnerships with churches to do what no individual congregation can do alone. This work is a new mission field, where people can see the tangible benefit of helping those who are in need. We cannot be content to shine the light of Christ's love within our churches. God calls us to go out in to the world and love others into the Kingdom.

Jubilee Housing

Producing a Hundredfold

SUSAN P. ORTMEYER AND JILL SHOOK

Introduction to Church of the Saviour's Inward and Outward Journey BY MARIAN BRAY AND JILL SHOOK

To understand Jubilee Housing, one must know something about the good soil from which it grew–the Church of the Saviour. The inward journey of this affordable housing story rises to the surface long before church founders Gordon and Mary Cosby had even met.

At age fifteen in 1932, Gordon Cosby and his brother wrangled an invitation to preach one Sunday at a seemingly abandoned two-room church in the backwoods of Lynchburg, Virginia. That Sunday a dozen men, women and children listened to Gordon. His text: Revelation 3:15–16: "'I know your works; you are neither cold nor hot. I wish that you were either cold or hot. So, because you are lukewarm, and neither cold nor hot, I am about to spit you out of my mouth." That sermon was one that Gordon was to preach again and again in a hundred different ways. Appreciative "Amens" punctuated its first delivery.[1]

Gordon and Mary's first church, Ballston Baptist Church, in Virginia, was situated in a tiny village. During this time as a new minister Gordon enlisted in the U.S. Army. The crucible of World War II shaped Gordon. As chaplain of the 327th Glider Infantry Regiment, 101st Airborne Division, Gordon sometimes gave counsel to men who could die in a matter of hours, and every one of them was aware of it.[2] A few days after the D-Day invasion, soldiers were preparing for a 2 a.m. assault. Gordon visited as many men as he could in the moments before the assault. It was a cold, drizzly night, though it was June. He could not see the faces of the men with whom he talked. Crawling into one of the foxholes, one of the men said to Gordon,

"Chaplain, I'm glad you're here. I have a premonition that I'm going to die tonight, that I will meet God before the night is over, and I don't know [God]… Don't give me any stuff about philosophy or theology. I just want you to talk with me about God."[3] When Gordon checked the casualty reports the following day, sure enough, that soldier had been killed.

Gordon could not be present to minister to his entire "flock" scattered across France, so he worked within each small unit to train lay leaders who could provide responsive support and prayer. He traveled from unit to unit, training and encouraging these lay pastors. This structure profoundly shaped Gordon's future church polity.

"When I came back, I had one thing in mind. We wanted to give God an opportunity to see what would happen in a community of committed people," recounts Gordon. He continues:

> This would not be community which is withdrawn and which pulls out of society, as we know it, but would be a community that lives among people. The commitment of our lives would be deep and our bond would be so real that the Holy Spirit would have opportunity to create a community of faith. From this would come a belonging that would be something different, something God could use in a marvelous way for the extension of the Kingdom.[4]

Small Groups—the Inward Journey

As Gordon envisioned his church, he became increasingly convinced that the greatest impact on the world comes about because of small groups of highly committed, disciplined people focused on outward ministries. Quaker theologian Elton Trueblood, who became a close friend of the Church of the Saviour, encouraged this small group vision with an inward and outward focus.

Gordon says, "You've got to have some structure for continual deepening. You have to be accountable somewhere."[5] He continues:

> When we plant ourselves into the common life of a small group of people intent on listening to Jesus and following wherever he leads, we will find our hearts flowering, opening to the needs of the afflicted, the oppressed, the poor. Those who we quietly despised for their lack of hygiene, their lack of education, their lack of willpower, their lack of being more like us, we will begin to love—really love—in the way that Christ loves each of us.
>
> Being with the suffering poor is not optional. Jesus himself said that whatever we do or fail to do for the hungry or sick or imprisoned or destitute, we do or fail to do for him.[6]

Evangelism is central to their mission.

We have to remember though, that we evangelize all the time. We may be true evangelists, or we may be false ones. *But whoever we are is affecting people all the time.* That's just the nature of people—we affect one another. The church is evangelizing all the time; it's always communicating something…In this deepening that we are talking about, Jesus is being known or not known all the time. So every one of our missions of compassion is evangelism. That's sharing the Word, embodying it.[7]

The concept of hearing God's "call" is central to the tradition of Church of the Savior.[8] According to Gordon, God calls each of us to ministry that is simple, impossible, and for the sake of others. Church of the Saviour believes (and teaches often) that every person has the capacity to do the impossible, with God's help and the shared efforts of others.[9] Church of the Saviour's commitment to spiritual growth (the inner journey) and mission (the outer journey) required every member to be in a mission group where their call would be confirmed. Rather than grow larger and more centralized, Gordon's vision was to stay small and multiply congregations.[10] Each little church developed a distinctive style of worship, preparation for membership, and mission. The level of commitment and emphasis on the inward and outward journey are the common threads.[11]

The Outward Journey

The outward journey has taken on many expressions. Like the tiny mustard seed, these small congregations have produced a hundred fold. Eighty independent ministries have been birthed over the years. But the first was *Jubilee Housing*, the soil from which all others grew.

One Family's Path to Self-sufficiency

Jubilee Housing and other ministries of Church of the Saviour changed Ethel and her family's lives.

Ethel and her son rented a two-bedroom flat. One day the owner, who had always charged fair rent, said she needed the flat for a relative moving to town. Ethel and her son would have to move. She learned of the possibility of renting an affordable apartment in the Adams-Morgan neighborhood through Jubilee Housing. She filled out an application and waited on pins and needles for the approval of the six-person committee (many of whom were themselves residents).

She did indeed receive approval and moved into Ontario Courts. Some time later, when she was in labor and on the way to the hospital, she got as far as the ambulance at the curb in front of the apartments and delivered the child right there.

Ethel moved to a larger Jubilee apartment and lived there for almost seven years. However, she always dreamed of owning her own house. When she read a flyer telling of a new homeownership program called "Manna," she immediately signed up to be in the "homebuyers club," a cooperative effort of FLOC and Manna—both ministries started by Church of the Saviour members.

In the "homebuyers club," Ethel learned how to budget and save. At first, the most she could save was twenty-five dollars a month. But after a year and a half of hard work and saving, her bank statement proved she was worthy of a loan, and she was able to buy a home.

Ethel's older son would play basketball with the Good Shepherd program. When she moved to the Shaw neighborhood, she began attending New Community Church. Her younger children became part of that church's after-school program called ASAP—After School Advocacy Program.

Jubilee Jobs receptionist Sheila was Ethel's Bible class teacher. Sheila wanted to go back to school to become a librarian, which left her Jubilee Jobs post open. Terry Flood gave Ethel a chance to fill it, and January 2005 marked twenty years that Ethel had faithfully served as the receptionist at Jubilee Jobs.

The job has brought exciting opportunities to Ethel. She accompanied Terry on a visioning trip to South Africa, where they visited various job and employment agencies. Ethel has worn an African dress ever since.

Thanks to Jubilee Housing, Manna, and Jubilee Jobs, Ethel lives with her three children, now twenty-eight, twenty-one, and eighteen years old, in her own home. Home insurance and Washington, D.C., taxes continue to increase, making it difficult to make the payments. But together, she and her children gratefully and consistently meet their monthly expenses.

Jubilee Housing: Producing a Hundredfold

SUSAN ORTMEYER AND JILL SHOOK

"Still other seed fell on good soil, where it produced a crop—a hundred, sixty or thirty times what was sown. He who has ears, let him hear."—Matthew 13:8–9

Church of the Savior, like a tiny seed, is committed to following Jesus' call on their lives. Many churches exist that are larger in numbers, but few have had as great an impact on housing ministries in our county. Obedience to Jesus led them to begin Jubilee Housing.

On November 1, 1973, a handful of Church of the Saviour members—Terry Flood, Barbara Moore, Bill Branner, and Carolyn Banker—who knew nothing about housing, decided to purchase two dilapidated fifty-year-old apartment buildings, and thus Jubilee Housing was born. With the buildings having names like The Ritz and The Mozart, who would have thought they had over 940 housing code violations and were teeming with frustrated, poor residents? But for these Church of the Saviour members, these deteriorating buildings and their residents would transform their lives, their congregation, and Washington D.C. It took 50,000 hours of volunteer time and $500,000 in grants to clean out the rats and garbage and to repair all the code violations to create ninety affordable units in those two buildings. Since those humble beginnings, like the tiny seed that fell on good soil, Church of the Saviour and its offshoot, Jubilee Housing, has produced a crop a hundred, sixty or thirty times what was sown, with eight renovated apartment buildings providing housing for more than 800 people, setting an example for housing ministries across the country.

All of Jubilee Housing's buildings are located in the Adams-Morgan neighborhood of Washington, D.C, which is now an upscale, trendy neighborhood. With soaring rents surrounding them, Jubilee has maintained their rents at 40 percent of the market rate. Housing costs in Washington D.C. are among the most expensive in the country. Jubilee's goal for poor and vulnerable families is not simply survival, but the redistribution of the resources needed to make life meaningful and purposeful. Not just an opportunity to live, but also a reason for life.

Jubilee Housing today is undergoing a renovation thanks largely to some of the ministries Church of the Saviour initially helped to create: Enterprise Foundation and Washington, D.C.'s Housing Production Trust Fund.

Daring to Listen[12]

The Potter's House

After a disappointing out-of-town speaking engagement in a lifeless church, the idea to open a coffee house first came to Mary and Gordon Cosby. They stayed in a motel with one vacant room above a tavern. The noise kept them awake most of the night. They contrasted the camaraderie they had heard in the tavern with the somber mood in the church they visited, and the idea of a coffee house began to emerge. Church members then confirmed the call. They envisioned a coffeehouse where nonreligious people could ask religious questions.

In the late 1960s, when church members were looking for suitable quarters for the coffeehouse, most wanted it to be in the fashionable Georgetown area of Washington D.C. None had the poor in mind. In ten months of looking, they found nothing, so they settled for an empty store on Columbia Road, at the time one of the worst areas in our country's capital, but the best place for the Potter's House coffee shop to open.

After the riots of 1968, most middle-class D.C. residents avoided the Columbia Road area, feeling that it was too dangerous. What used to be elegant housing for the well-to-do had slowly deteriorated into slum housing for the elderly and those too poor to move elsewhere.

At first, none of the church members gave much attention to the ghetto streets behind the Potter's House, hidden from their sight. However, the experiences of civil rights actions in Selma, Alabama, and the Vietnam War gave them new understandings of oppression. They became involved with medical aid to wounded Vietnamese children. The more they listened and worked with the children, the sharper their own community's issues came into view.

The Potter's House is where Jubilee Housing and many of its associated ministries began. The Potter's House is "where the needs were first perceived, the dreams first dreamt, and the new visions formulated."[13]

Hearing the Call to Begin Jubilee Housing

The newspapers began to give more and more space to the worsening housing crisis in the city. People silently suffered and grew poorer and poorer while they struggled to pay slum landlords exorbitant rents for wretched apartments with rusted-out plumbing, falling plaster, and scurrying rats.

No up-to-date statistics existed on abandoned or substandard houses and apartment buildings. However, according to one District of Columbia government official, if housing were condemned for all code violations, 50,000 people would have had to be displaced. The shortage of low-income housing had become so great that for the first time in the history of the capital, thousands of people who were unable to pay high rents had become "squatters," breaking into abandoned buildings, living there rent free.

Church members began to see with different eyes the boarded-up apartment building a few doors from the Potter's House. According to Terry, "When the Church of the Savior opened The Potter's House, due to its location, they could not get away from human suffering."[14] On Thursday evenings at The Potter's House, Terry, Carolyn, and Barbara focused on the massive problem of housing in the District. It seemed to them that the best way to eradicate the creeping blight and decay of the city was to purchase housing in the area, to work with the tenants to upgrade it without raising rents, and then to begin a program of education, literacy, recreation, and counseling that would engender hope and spread to the larger community. The more they talked, the larger the vision grew, expanding to include citywide transformation engaging the whole city.

Carolyn secured a real-estate license and began to investigate the deteriorating structures in the streets behind the Potter's House. She finally managed to track down the absentee owner of two apartment houses, the Ritz and the Mozart, which seemed in desperate need of attention. They turned out to belong to a wealthy octogenarian living alone in a hotel room. He was much too shrewd to reveal how eager he was to be rid of the buildings, and Carolyn was much too shrewd to reveal that the group on whose behalf she was negotiating had no money.

The new mission took its name after the biblical Jubilee Year, which was established to "proclaim liberty throughout the land to all its inhabitants" (Lev. 25:10, RSV). Gordon sums it up in these words: "Jubilee, in its original Biblical meaning focused on the outsider–the weak, the defenseless, the outcast. It was a social idea designed to prevent the creation of a permanent class of poor people. Land lost because of economic misfortune was returned every 50 years–the Year of Jubilee. Thus the ones outside could start up again. They were given the tools for a comeback."[15]

Developing Partners

Early Partners: Jim and Patty Rouse

Jubilee Housing may never have been born without the important partnerships in the business world. Jim Rouse, a wealthy philanthropist, developer, and CEO of Rouse Company, was familiar with Church of the Saviour through a church membership preparation program. In 1972, Terry, Barbara, Carolyn, and Bill asked Jim for advice about creating low-income housing in the Adams-Morgan neighborhood. They had no development or construction experience and very little money. Jim listened politely, but lovingly discouraged them from doing it. He said it was unrealistic; their group was too poor and too small. They ignored him and put down a nonrefundable deposit on the buildings.

As Gordon preaches, "the most helpful experiments are accomplished by people who are too naïve to know what they are getting into. The wise and experienced know too much ever to accomplish the impossible."[16]

When Jim saw how stubborn they were, he chose to support them in spite of his own wisdom. Though it seemed ridiculous, he could not help but be impressed with the relentless passion and determination he saw. So he bought the first two buildings and leased them back to the church for the amount of the mortgage payment. He helped with $625,000 to complete the transaction and $125,000 toward the cost of rehabilitation. Lily Endowment provided a matching grant. And the church raised the rest.

Jim's initial participation in Jubilee Housing was the start of a lifelong association with Rev. Gordon Cosby. Jim and his wife, Patty, were married at the Church of the Saviour. While Jim was building one of our nation's first planned cities–Columbia, Maryland–he asked Gordon to be on his advisory team for planning Columbia's churches. In 1982, Jim founded The Enterprise Foundation, which today is one of the largest nonprofit agencies in the country focused on affordable housing. The Enterprise Foundation has provided $6 billion in equity, loans, grants, and technical assistance to nonprofit organizations across the nation that build and revitalize local neighborhoods. They have built 175,000 homes and apartments and helped over 40,000 into jobs.[17]

Doing the Work

When Jubilee acquired the Ritz and the Mozart in 1973, the buildings were some fifty years old and had deteriorated badly. Jubilee was served with a daunting list of 940 housing code violations. The Ritz had sixty apartments and the Mozart thirty, so it was not feasible to move the families to other apartments while theirs were being rehabilitated. Church members asked the families to help renovate their apartments while they continued to live in them. Since the only alternative was to try to find quarters in the city that might be even worse, they said yes. Volunteers from other churches also helped with the work.

Christmas at the Ritz and Mozart

Gordon asked his congregation to devote some of the time usually given to preparing for Christmas to help with the renovation of the apartments. Young and old, skilled and unskilled responded. The more hardy souls were put to work scrubbing the halls and shoveling out garbage. Others were assigned to painting, carpentry, and plastering. One member who owned a paint and wallpaper store donated hundreds of rolls of wallpaper; a store was set up in the basement so that tenants might come in and select the wallpapers they wanted. A congressional assistant was appointed to run the "store," while an electrical engineer, accustomed to spending his free time playing golf, was assigned to supervise the task of replacing defective light fixtures. People who never in a million years would have seen the inside of a slum apartment were engaged in the renovation of one. Workshops in paperhanging, glass cutting, and plastering were scheduled. An assistant at CBS was given the job of scavenging for paints and materials.

Church of the Saviour had stumbled onto the appropriate way to celebrate the Christmas season. They gave each other gifts of paint rollers, overalls, and books with useful titles, such as *The Boiler Room: Questions and Answers.* They took their children to the lighting of the Christmas tree in the lobby of the Ritz. By the time Christmas came around again, word had reached the Vale Technical Institute, which runs an automotive trade school outside Pittsburgh, Pennsylvania. The students responded by locating a forsaken bus and using their skills to restore its engine and interior. They gave it a sleek yellow finish, printed *Jubilee Community* on both sides, and delivered it to the children of the Ritz and the Mozart with a Santa Claus at the wheel.

Jubilee Acquires Cresthill and other Buildings

In April 1975 Jubilee acquired another apartment building, the Cresthill, near the riot corridor of Northwest 14th Street, for $10,000. Tom Nees, the pastor of the First Church of the Nazarene, and a group from his congregation who had worked for fifteen months in the Ritz and the Mozart, assumed responsibility for the new building.

Cresthill's nickname in the neighborhood was "the city dump" because of trash that had accumulated behind the building over an unknown period. Not only was the exterior of the building knee-deep in trash, but the large basement area was full of uncollected garbage. The roof of Jubilee's new building was so far gone that the new owners allowed the top-floor tenants to pay no rent. In exchange for free housing, they agreed to put out buckets when it rained and not to call the inspector. The hot water and heating systems were in the same state of disrepair. During the winter months, the forty-eight apartments had hot water only three hours each day, but tenants raised no complaints, lest they be pushed into the ranks of the city's thousands of homeless.

The Cresthill was, however, more than a sprawl of unlighted halls and deteriorating apartments. Many of the residents had lived there for a long time and had shared a lot of life together. Perhaps because of their plight, they knew a sense of community in the building. The average income of most of the families living in the Cresthill, like that of those living in the Ritz and the Mozart, was below the poverty level. Moreover, 58 percent of the adults were unemployed or on public assistance, and of the 42 percent who were working, many were working temporary construction jobs or day work. The resident managers had worked against overwhelming odds to make the building livable. They listened to the Cresthill's new owners and believed that the people of Jubilee might be genuinely concerned persons. They called on all the tenants, explained the change in ownership, and shared with them Jubilee's vision. As a result, the tenants helped with trash removal and supported Jubilee when it presented a proposal to a local community organization. This kind of participation established relationships quickly and enabled the work to move ahead more rapidly. With the support and confirmation of his congregation, Tom Nees resigned his position as pastor of the First Church of the Nazarene. With some members from that congregation and the tenants of the Cresthill, he began a new inner-city church committed to offering decent housing at submarket rents. The entire Nazarene denomination and many of the Cresthill tenants backed the effort.

After the Mozart, Ritz, and Cresthill were acquired, other buildings followed: Ontario Courts, Marietta, Sorrento, Fuller Courts, and the Euclid.

Other Programs Emerge

By the summer of 1975, an innovative program simply called *Stretch* was underway. It began with a hearty breakfast that the children themselves learned to prepare in an apartment left vacant for their use. Grits, eggs "any way you want them," sausage, bacon, pancakes—all were on the week's menu. The meal was served in the coffeehouse room, where the piano was located, to provide a time of singing and reflection on the day before the children went to activities in the basement rooms. Math labs, reading, leatherwork, art, and carpentry workshops were among the activities.

In addition, Janet Caldwell would bring children from Jubilee housing to Dayspring, a 200-acre retreat center founded by Don McClament in the 1970s. When the yellow Jubilee bus broke down, Janet had to quickly arrange alternate transportation, enabling many more people to become involved with the children.

Seeds grew into a network of Church of the Saviour ministries that today demonstrate the value church members place on children as they evoke potentialities, giving children a rootedness to sustain and nurture every aspect of their lives.

Sometime between 1973 and 1975, Pat Sitar, manager of Jubilee Housing, took a class on "The Call." Considering her love for children, she envisioned a program for the children in Jubilee housing. Pat went to Vermont. At the Western priory, in a barn by a beautiful lake, God spoke to her about starting Good Shepherd. The voice was so clear that she thought the man sitting next to her was telling her to begin Good Shepherd. Today *The Good Shepherd Ministries* provides daycare for young children, an after-school center, a teen learning center, a music center, sports programs, and summer activities. *The Patricia M. Sitar Center for the Arts* also serves at-risk children and youth as they explore music, dance, drama, writing, and visual arts. It is housed in Jubilee Housing's Ontario Courts.

Once Church of the Saviour members were involved with so many children and their parents in the neighborhood, God began to call them deeper to consider new structures to bring about Christ's mission of caring for those on the margins of society.

Seeing the number of underweight babies being born and medical problems due to poverty moved Ann Barnet, a doctor and a member of the Eighth Day Faith community, to begin *The Family Place* in 1979. Additionally, *Columbia Road Health Services* provides health care to many of D.C.'s most vulnerable residents. When church members saw minor health conditions escalate for the homeless because they had no place to recover, they began *Christ House*. *Mary's Center* is a maternal and child health center, and the *D.C. Health Care for the Homeless Project* operates clinics in shelters and a mobile medical clinic for the homeless. *Joseph's House* offers housing and hospice for men with AIDS and *Miriam's House* offers the same for women with AIDs. Driving down Columbia Road, one is struck by the dramatic public art of bronze statues in front of this array of tall stately buildings that house most of these ministries. The way these art objects depict Christ's tender love for children and the vulnerable takes one's breath away.

Terry Flood, cofounder of Jubilee Housing, found her passion during the 1981 recession. She began by cold calling from the Yellow Pages searching for jobs and connecting people to job openings. As the ministry grew, Terry's call was confirmed. In the last twenty years, Jubilee Jobs, at no cost to the poor clients or to their employers, has helped some 15,000 unskilled or semi-skilled hear the words, "You're hired," and begin the journey toward a living wage.[18]

Conversations continued after church and at the Potter's House. Church members became more acutely aware of how the lack of affordable housing affects a disproportionate number of low-income elderly with longer life spans than the past. A program called *Sarah's Circle* was started in an acquired building to provide affordable housing, friendship, meals, education, and health programs, and support services to seniors in a caring atmosphere.

Since 1986 *Samaritan Inns*, in another acquired building, has worked with hundreds per year of those who are homeless and addicted. Over 90 percent of those who successfully complete the lengthy three-phase program move on to live their lives as taxpaying citizens, drug-free role models, reliable employees, and caring parents.

People began to arrive from across the country to see what God was doing through the small Church of the Saviour congregation. Moore began *Ram's Horn*–where visiting groups interested in Jubilee Housing could catch a vision for Church of the Saviour's inward and outward journey and the growing array of Jubilee Ministries. Today a similar ministry is arranged through the Festival Center, where people learn at the *Servant Leadership School* about Church of the Savior and Jubilee Ministries. The school, established in 1989, explores dimensions of servant leadership and equips leaders for inner-city mission, both spiritually and practically.

Today's Renovations and Partners

Thirty years after the Rouses helped with the purchase of the first buildings, the Ritz and the Mozart, Jubilee's aging buildings were again in need repair.

Terry described the current reality, "In 1973, the cosmetic aspects of refurbishing the newly acquired buildings could be done by volunteers. But today, with heaters needing to be torn out and a whole new heating system put in its place–such expensive development can only be done by experts, but at a cost beyond Jubilee's resources."[19] A Capital Needs Assessment conducted in 2002 determined that it would cost more than $8.5 million to replace the outdated and undersized building systems. On further investigation, it became clear that the wisest and most cost-effective path would be to thoroughly modernize the buildings and living spaces through comprehensive renovation of its seven buildings. Plans call for new mechanical, electrical, and plumbing systems; architectural and structural improvements; complete living unit renovations; significant redesign of common areas; installation of new security systems and air conditioners. In addition, new program spaces, such as computer labs, other classrooms, and a wellness center were planned for Jubilee Housing residents. The total development budget for all seven properties is nearly $26 million. While committed to keeping its rents low, Jubilee Housing has until now used private fundraising and has avoided government funding. But to achieve a renovation of this size and scope, Jubilee Housing has had to reinvent the way it approaches financing affordable housing.

After a year of considering the options, Jubilee Housing decided that for the first time in its history, it would seek government assistance in the form of Low Income Housing Tax Credits and money from Washington, D.C.'s Affordable Housing Production Trust Fund. Calling on the city to invest in the capital improvements was a win-win proposition for all involved—especially with an economic boom in the Adams-Morgan neighborhood. This infusion of funds would significantly curb annual operating deficits, allowing Jubilee to focus more of its time and resources on providing expanded opportunities for life-improvement for the resident community.

Volunteerism has again burgeoned around the complicated task of providing temporary relocation support for households. Jubilee's emphasis on resident involvement has not changed from earlier days. Residents give input into the design. Also, a residents' building committee has been involved in prayer, getting petitions signed, and advocating for tax credits and for money from the city's trust fund.

Tax Credits and Enterprise Foundation

Bart Harvey, who took over leadership of the Enterprise Foundation for Jim Rouse, advised Jubilee to consider tax credits. More than coincidentally, it was Bart who helped Jim lobby Congress in favor of creating the Low Income Housing Tax Credit program many years before. This program allows companies with significant tax liabilities to invest equity capital in affordable housing developments in return for "credit" against that tax liability.

Gordon Blackwell and Juanita Waddell played a key role in applying for tax credits. After a career of more than thirty years of developing affordable housing across the southeast, Gordon was preparing for retirement and offered his services to Jubilee at no cost. His friend Juanita, another seasoned affordable housing developer, helped Jubilee fashion its application for tax credits and trust fund resources. With the benefit of these partners, and the prayers of the wider Church of the Saviour community, Jubilee Housing prepared a 250-page tax credit application. On the eve of submittal of the application, a group of residents appeared at the office to offer their support. Many of the residents had led a petition campaign within the buildings in support of the application and now asked to gather in a circle of prayer around the application that would help decide their fate in the coming months. They laid their hands on the application and asked God to supply—and God did![20]

Manna and the Housing Production Trust Fund

With roots in Arkansas, Jim Dickerson came to Church of the Savior to learn and experience firsthand its unique approach to membership and the basic structures that gave it such life, energy, and commitment. He soon began New Community Church, and at the same time, using a loan from a Christian friend and his own home to guarantee the loan, Jim founded Manna. Manna initially helped one homeless family into a home and then rolled that money over many times. The loan fund is now two million with more than 850 homes sold to those in need of affordable housing. In addition to providing affordable homeownership (including its Home Buyers Club and Individual Development Account programs), Manna is engaged in redevelopment and renewal of neighborhoods, community organizing, tenant organizing, living wage campaigns, and preservation of existing affordable housing threatened by landlords' opting out of expiring long-term contracts.[21] Jim Dickerson was the founding member and president of a citywide coalition that gathered two thousand people to persuade officials to fund the Washington D.C. Housing Production Trust Fund.[22]

As mentioned earlier, the Washington D.C. Affordable Housing Production Trust Fund is now a key source of funding for the Jubilee Housing renovation project. Even though the trust fund is a dedicated source of income, residents have to fight every year to prevent local politicians from dipping into those funds for other uses. Each year residents show up at city hall to make sure that this funding source remains secure. Jim Knight, current executive director of Jubilee Housing, notes that residents' involvement in the process is inspiring: "This year, several residents shared their stories of transformation at a press conference with the mayor—these folks would never have done this before…as we step out in faith, asking for what we need…leaders are being developed."[23]

Renovations will take about three years to complete, and the total price tag will approach $26 million. While the tax credit and trust fund resources will provide most of the needed capital, Jubilee must raise nearly $2.5 million through private sources to deliver the full vision of expanded services for the resident community. Renovation began in August 2004, with the Ritz and Mozart to be among the first four buildings renovated.

Dealing with Realities

Avoiding Paternalism

In the early years, building trust with the residents was a challenge. Church members were questioned concerning paternalism: "How do you avoid being labeled paternalistic? Isn't it likely to be said of you, 'Here comes whitey from the suburbs with all the answers on how we should run our lives!'"?[24]

In response, one member astutely diagnosed the problem of paternalism:

> I don't know which comes across with more negativity—racism or paternalism. I have heard both sides. I think they are equally unwelcomed. Paternalism is more to be feared perhaps because it

is more insidious... paternalism is masked from ourselves and for that reason it is one of the biggest problems we encounter.[25]

The same member added, "Reflection is essential. We have to take time to stop and ask, 'What is really going on here?'...So that we are not bulldozing through, assuming that our objective is the right objective. We have to wait until we sense that what we are doing is in some way of the Spirit."[26]

The answer also comes from staying closely connected to the people living in the buildings. As another member stated:

> We have learned to get into the middle of the problem and to see it not as a problem that we solve, but one that we share in...Their problems are the same as ours–for we all share in the human condition. We come up with acceptable solutions not because we are better or know better, but because we have worked them out together with those who are more involved than we.[27]

Part of Jubilee's effort to find a way out of paternalism was the initiation of wide support programs based on tenant participation. In the beginning, meetings were called, and a tenant on each floor was elected to serve on a council of moderators. At first the response was enthusiastic, but before long participation began to fall off.

Part of the difficulty grew because Jubilee had not fully worked out its own identity. Some of the members saw themselves simply as landlords, obliged to provide attractive and livable quarters for the residents. Others saw themselves as part of a biblical "liberation movement," the goal of which was to raise leaders from among the poor themselves. Each of these concepts was valid, yet needed to coexist. Housing code violations had to be corrected and payments made, for neither the city's housing agency nor the banking institutions were going to wait while the tenants, together with Jubilee, hammered out a new vision and mode of existence. Over the years new structures emerged that provided the tenants a larger participation in the decision making. The hope was for tenants to eventually own the buildings, but after arguments, tears, and repentance, that did not happen. Even today, negotiations continue to transfer The Cresthill to some form of tenant ownership.

Radical Realities

More than fifty-five years ago, Gordon Cosby dreamed of a church that would be radically different. It would focus on Jesus, the call to sacrificial service, and a balance between the inward and outward aspects of faith. "It would require its members to be deeply trained in both theology and Christian formation–as if their very life depended on it."[28] Gordon says,

We weren't clear on anything at the beginning! Except that we wanted authenticity. We talked in those early days about "integrity of membership." We wanted to be real. We wanted to be faithful to the real Christ, and we wanted to embody as best we could the meaning of the New Testament church. So that hunger was there. But we had to learn step-by-step many of these things we have been talking about. Each one of the steps was very painful, and we lost people at each of those steps as it became clearer.[29]

Gordon's commitment to multiplying congregations of small, highly committed membership proved to be seed that fell on very good soil, producing a hundred, sixty or thirty times what was sown (Mt. 13:8).

Discovering Insights

It remains a persistent reality that to provide truly affordable housing in tight housing markets requires remarkable will to do so and the benefit of a wide variety of funding sources. Individuals, foundations, and congregations continue to give generously to make possible the work of Jubilee, in addition to Jubilee's partnership with the city. The enormous outpouring of volunteer hours in the early days has been matched by amazing generosity of groups like Pinnacle Development Partners, Hickok Warner Cole, and Clark Construction—all top firms in their fields—doing the work for far below normal rates.

Early on, Church of the Saviour had a hand in establishing the very programs now helping Jubilee Housing move into the future. Jubilee has come "full circle" and is now benefiting from organizations and governmental policies designed by the initial visionaries who helped dream and make the ministry a reality in the first place. It is imperative that housing ministries like Jubilee expand and continue to succeed, for the need for affordable housing in D.C. and across the nation has never been greater. In 2002, the wait for Section 8 vouchers in D.C. was essentially indefinite, with 26,000 applications backlogged. Even for those in the "highest-risk category"— families labeled homeless—7,000 applicants were waiting for vouchers.

Coming Home

The early gatherings at the Potter's House became mini-revival meetings, where each gave small testimonials to movements of grace. At one meeting, Mary Powell, who had worked for a whole week in a vacant apartment, got up and said:

Yesterday the little girl who is going to live in this apartment came down. She was a fifth grader and really cute…Her room was going to be painted yellow, and she and I sat down together, and I asked her the kind of yellow she wanted in her room and then we mixed the paints until it got to be just the color she wanted, and then we put it on the wall together.[30]

Sammie Jones, who had refurbished a whole apartment with a friend, followed Mary Powell's testimonial:

After I had walked up four flights for about the sixth time, Mrs. S. said, "When are you going to rest, girl?" And I said, "I don't know." And she said, "Come on in and I will give you some beef stew." So we sat down to delicious beef stew in her apartment. We were giving to each other. It was a miracle to me because I had never expected that this would happen. I had expected to feel good about doing something else for someone, but I did not expect to make friends and have people do things for me.[31]

Ram's Horn Feasts

In Jubilee Housing's second year, tenants and church members began to gather every other week at the Potter's House for an evening that began with a common meal followed by prayer and celebration.

The meal was usually served by the children of the Ritz and the Mozart, who had formed a Ritzart Baking and Catering Service and begged for chances to use their new arts. The occasions came to be called the Ram's Horn Feasts, after the ram's horn that was sounded to herald the beginning of the Jubilee Year. It was actually a blast from the ram's horn that sounded when the walls of Jericho were about to fall.

At the Ram's Horn Feasts we do a lot of talking about houses, and community building, and a world that is divinely marked for salvation. The other night, after the simple meal had been eaten and the tables cleared, we each drew the floor plan of the houses where we had lived as children, so that we might know each other better, and understand better how houses had shaped our own histories for better or for worse.[32]

When they had made their rough sketches, they gave each other "tours" of their sketched out rooms:

Hyib's house was a one-room thatched dwelling in a compound in Africa…Esther's house was a two-story farmhouse in Virginia where every room was graced by the memory of a gentle and teaching father. Then there was Louise Stewart's house, which was a one-room log cabin. "My father was shot in that room when I was three," she said. When asked "Why?" she simply replied, "It was over ten cents. My father was shot for ten cents."[33]

The community that gathers for the Ram's Horn Feast is made up of a great diversity of persons–the wounded, the old, the maimed, the halt, the educated and not so educated. Some are successful; some are so-called "dropouts." A few like to speak in intellectual terms, and a few like to speak in tongues. Some are from churches housed in storefronts, and some are from churches with impressive towers. They meet to celebrate their common humanity and to read and ponder scripture and to wait for the empowering of the Spirit. They believe that God acts with men and women whenever they move out in love for their neighbor. Ultimately, they believe that Jubilee is about community and belonging for everyone. Gordon Cosby spoke to this eloquently: "A society is ultimately judged by its attention to its weakest members, those outside with their potential unused and lost forever…The overall goal of Jubilee is to bring the poor inside…The Jubilee Vision is made real in that great moment when one outsider comes inside and is forever home."[34]

An Ex-Prison and an Abandoned Hospital

BOB LUPTON AND MARY NELSON

Introduction to Adaptive Reuse Model BY JILL SHOOK

My dad was a volunteer fireman in my hometown of Yorba Linda, California. Memories of the old fire station still jerk at my heart strings. When I moved to Pasadena, I watched several old fire stations–no longer in use –adapted into other uses. The tall, broad, arched garage entrances are still visible. These are models of adaptive reuse. Adaptive reuse protects our built heritage and preserves glimpses of our national story–all the while building a future for generations to come. It changes buildings' functions to accommodate the changing needs of our communities. Some definitions include the reuse of salvaged materials epitomized by the Watts Towers in Los Angeles.[1]

Today, reuse is a movement in the world of architecture. Examples are everywhere. Ghirardelli Square in San Francisco, among the first, showed the commercial potential of reuse and has been widely imitated. "Developers saw a vast 'nostalgia' market, and an alternative to the standardized shopping malls."[2] In Moscow, Idaho, an old railroad grain elevator has been adapted into a garden store and residence. Abandoned factory buildings in North Adams, Massachusetts, have been transformed into one of the foremost contemporary art museums.[3]

The benefits are numerous. The restoration of older vacant buildings decreases crime, increases property values, maintains the character of our cities, bolsters our civic pride, promotes tourism, and honors the sentimental value of older structures. Since the process is labor-intensive,[4] employment increases, strengthening the physical and social fabric of the community. Plus, reuse of materials keeps our landfills from filling so quickly.

73

Conservation of our cultural legacy cannot be minimized, but neither can the conservation of the Earth.

Authors Janice and Donald Kirk sum it up well:

> In Genesis the first thing God said to humans is basically, "Here's the earth, take care of it" (Gen. 1:28–29) with the command repeated in the next chapter, "The Lord God placed the man in the Garden of Eden to tend and take care of it" (Gen. 2:15)."[5]

The Kirks' book provides a powerful biblical basis for environmental concern. It asks us to care for "the environment with an attitude of integrity for life on earth–using but not abusing, enjoying without destroying–so the earth may become a place of praise to God."[6]

Ray Bakke's book *Theology as Big as a City* provides a theology of God's redemption of both people and places. Bakke says, "[Y]ou are never more like God than when you are living in relationships with God's people and working in partnerships for the re-creation and redemption of God's world."[7] Such redemption is God's specialty:

> I will cause the towns to be inhabited, and the waste places shall be rebuilt. The land that was desolate shall be tilled, instead of being the desolation that it was in the sight of all who passed by. And they will say, "This land that was desolate has become like the garden of Eden; and the waste and desolate and ruined towns are now inhabited and fortified." Then the nations that are left all around you shall know that I, the LORD, have rebuilt the ruined places, and replanted that which was desolate; I, the LORD, have spoken, and I will do it. (Ezek. 36:33b–36)

When we turn desolation into a garden of Eden by adapting and reusing, we partner with God's dreams for our cities. This restorative redevelopment is often referred to as "green" construction–it conserves the energy to extract, process, and transport building materials–preserving the resources and energy that once were used to create our cities.

Ever since our country adopted building codes and began loaning money mostly for new construction, the reuse of older buildings has been cost prohibitive. Now, however, tax credits and land value are making adaptive reuse possible. The availability of utilities and public services already on the site also lowers site preparation costs. One company in Downey, California, decreased site work costs by 50 percent by reusing their old building.

Linking landmark events and historic buildings to renewed uses–such as the old fire stations in Pasadena and the amazing adaptive reuses of the Atlanta Stockade and Beth-Ann Hospital featured in this chapter–represents a way of salvaging a piece of our heritage deserving historic preservation. But there are times when the numbers don't balance out and even the purest preservationist cannot justify such redevelopment.

In the following narratives, Bob Lupton shows how faith led him to adapt a prison to new uses, and Mary Nelson relates the adaptive reuse of a hospital. They could not justify such outlandish redevelopment, yet, armed with their faith combined with proven skills and reputations as seasoned affordable housing developers, they knew God was doing something in which they had the privilege to participate.

An Ex-Prison

BOB LUPTON

Where there is no vision, the people perish. —Proverbs 29:18, KJV

On a hill looking down into the heart of Atlanta sits a monstrous stone and concrete structure, a vacant, barred hulk, a reminder of a darker time in the city's history. Known as the Atlanta Stockade, it was a place of gross inhumanity in the years following the Civil War, a prison that housed both hardened criminals and those too poor to pay fines for petty offenses. Men, women, and children as young as ten were indiscriminately crowded into large cells in which beastly behavior went unchecked. Some years the venereal disease rate among inmates was as high as 90 percent. Frequent public complaints claimed that family members sentenced there had simply disappeared, never to be heard from again. The official record documented only one death in the prison's entire history—a man who had tuberculosis. Not until the 1950s, thirty years after the prison had been closed down, did highway excavation across the property turn up the skeletal remains of some fifty bodies with no record of who they were or how they got there.

In 1927, after decades of controversy, the city fathers decided to rid Atlanta—new queen of the South—of the Stockade stigma and voted to demolish it. But the building had been built too well. It had been constructed using a "brand new" technology known as steel reinforced poured concrete. Manufacturers claimed this material would become increasingly harder over time—perfect for prisons since it would only become increasing impregnable as the years passed. The engineering tolerances were not tested at that time, however, and they substantially overbuilt the structure. Some of the walls were four feet thick; and the roof, all poured concrete, was sixteen inches thick. Demolition bids were prohibitive, so the building was abandoned. Vandals destroyed and burned everything that was combustible; but the concrete shell was indestructible, and the barred windows, like hollow eyes, looked down into the heart of the city.

Daring to Listen

After nearly a century of decay, signs of life began to stir about the old prison property. Renny Scott, an Episcopal priest who lived in the community, suggested that this might be a good location to shelter homeless families. The very thought of housing our most vulnerable citizens in a prison seemed inhospitable! Yet Scott persisted. We at FCS (Family Consultation Service) Urban Ministries agreed to at least invite a group of architects to tour the facility and determine if it could be made to feel homey.

Seven architects from several design firms arrived one morning to explore the old monstrosity. All had seen it from the expressway and were intrigued by the gothic architecture, but none had ever visited. Climbing over rubble and trash and feeling their way along dark, graffiti-covered halls, they emerged into an open, three-story atrium at the center. "Could this cold prison be made to feel warm and inviting?" we asked. When I offered them an "ancient" set of original blueprints uncovered in my research, it was as though I handed them the Dead Sea Scrolls. Obviously, such a remarkable, historic landmark would be an architect's dream. They envisioned windows and light, textures and color—a world of creativity that I could not see. They saw columned porches and a grand entryway, charming loft apartments and spacious common areas. Over the next hour and a half I listened to an animated discussion about how this symbol of injustice could be transformed into a symbol of compassion.

Then one of them asked me about our budget for the project. I told him that money was not an issue, that, in fact, we had in excess of three thousand dollars currently on deposit! Their laughter echoed off the walls of the atrium. It was clear that these men had never built anything by faith before. They assured me that they had not. If they were to offer their God-given talents to the accomplishment of this vision, I gently nudged, we could raise $150,000, maybe $200,000 right here, today in donated architectural fees! They said they would get back to me on this.

Over the next couple of weeks, I learned a very important distinction: the difference between the *chaff of bright ideas* that gets wisped away by Monday morning's busyness and the *kernel of vision* that is implanted in the soil of the human spirit. When God drops a kernel of vision into one's spirit, it begins to germinate, to heat up, and takes on a life of its own. And when it pushes its way up into the conscious attention of the bearer, it cannot be ignored.

Developing Partners

When the seven architects reconvened two weeks later, God had planted such a vision in the soil of their spirits. They had discussed the matter with their firms and agreed, unanimously, that the design community should take on this project pro bono! With one important condition: The project would require a very close working relationship with the general contractor, since nothing in the conversion would be standard or code. Design decisions would have to be made daily, on site.

"Who is your general contractor?" they queried.

"Who do you know?" I replied. When their laughter was once again under control, they set about making a list of the general contractors. They would invite the city's twelve largest contractors to a breakfast in the warden's office at the Atlanta Stockade—that grabbed everyone's attention! Not one of the "generals" wanted to miss this intriguing event. When the morning arrived, the architects had built a makeshift ramp over the debris for easy access, swept a path through the soot, broken glass, and needles, and placed lanterns along the dark corridors to illuminate the way to the warden's office. A gourmet breakfast, served on linen and china, was spread for the contractors. And standing prominently on an easel in glowing lantern light was a large, full-color rendering of the vision of the Stockade—transformed.

These twelve major generals are some of the city's fiercest competitors, who bid against each other every day in a dog-eat-dog environment. When they emerged from the warden's office, pledging to pool their resources to undertake a joint effort pro bono, history had been made! The generals, following the lead of the architects, locked arms, divided the project up twelve ways, and set about recruiting their subcontractors and suppliers. The architects committed the money to pay a full-time on-site architect; and the contractors did the same, hiring an experienced project manager.

Doing the Work

Coordinating donated services and materials from scores of companies was a Herculean challenge. Fourteen electrical contractors volunteered, along with six mechanical firms and a generous assortment of demolition, masonry, interior design, carpentry, drywall, painting, and landscaping companies. Plans were adapted to accommodate a donated industrial heating and cooling system. Special techniques were required to apply a new exterior sealing product provided by the manufacturer. To meet code, an elevator had to be installed. Cutting and coring through walls intended to be impenetrable proved the largest physical challenge. But there were others. Legal and insurance issues were complex. Each company, if it provided services free or at cost, had to provide liability insurance and workman's compensation coverage for its workers...an exorbitant sum! The "generals" appealed to their insurance brokers who for years had written their construction policies and convinced the insurance industry to do what it had never done before—create a comprehensive package to cover all participants and pick up the cost of the policy!

Project estimates climbed to $3.2 million, a cost far beyond the capacity of our small nonprofit ministry at FCS. But momentum was building. First local, then national, news media picked up on the historic transformation with a series of colorful articles. Atlanta Mayor Andrew Young presided over a "bar breaking" ceremony as workers with cutting torches opened "a window of freedom." HUD secretary Jack Kemp came to a luncheon held in a graffiti-covered prison ward and proclaimed the project an exemplary model of private sector initiative. Tom Brokaw even showed up with his filming crew. Churches, foundations, and businesses jumped on the bandwagon; and eleven months from the time construction began (and almost four years from the inception of the idea), the Atlanta Stockade was converted into sixty-seven beautifully furnished loft apartments without our ministry's incurring a penny of debt!

The Stockade was given a new identity: GlenCastle. Free from debt service as well as property taxes (a legal firm took on the task of removing the facility from the property tax roles), the rents were established at a rate minimum-wage earners could afford, with utilities included. At the time of this writing, the facility remains full and generates adequate cash flow to pay all operating expenses, including professional property management and maintenance, and is still the most affordable, unsubsidized housing in the city.

Dealing with Realities

It would be misleading to portray the experience as either easy or trouble-free, inspiring as it is. Zoning issues and building code barriers frustrated the progress, with no small amount of arm wrestling applied by our seasoned professional team. Design disagreements erupted over the size of units and handicap accessibility. Differences of opinion arose over austere vs. plush involving the amenities. Then, too, construction had its challenges. Immovable staircases were too steep; ventilation had never been a concern; water pressure was insufficient to supply the required sprinkling system. The mayor generously offered city services to run sanitation lines up to the prison, but the city bureaucracy proved to be so cumbersome and inefficient that the offer was graciously rejected. Our greatest strength proved to be the well-respected, highly experienced construction experts. No problem was too difficult to solve or negotiate. These professionals brought the skills and standards of their trades and produced a product that was excellent in every respect. Not only did they create a facility that elicited pride in participants and residents alike; but they also reduced operating and maintenance costs in the long run, due to the quality of their materials and workmanship.

I would also be wrong to create the impression that funding for the project happened miraculously and without effort. Admittedly, the historic significance of the building and the emotional marketing sizzle inherent in a conversion of this nature made funding the project far easier than raising routine operating dollars. However, even with substantial pro bono investments of architects, contractors, subcontractors, and suppliers (which totaled over $1 million) more than $2 million in cash had to be raised. We hired a very capable development consultant who produced promotional materials, planned fund-raising events, created foundation proposals, designed a direct mail campaign, lined up speaking engagements for staff, issued press releases, and managed the entire process. Conducting feasibility studies, acquiring property, organizing committees and task forces, planning the campaign, and securing enough commitments to afford reasonable assurances to large donors that the project had a good chance of succeeding all took nearly three years of preparation before actual construction began.

Certainly, seemingly miraculous occurrences took place. For instance, the senior executives of Chicago-based Amoco Oil, on their own initiative, appealed to the corporate foundation to give an unheard of $300,000 as seed capital to launch the project. Neither before nor since has Amoco given such a sizable gift to a nonprofit organization, even in their home city. It was our first corporate gift and served to legitimize the project in the eyes of other corporations and foundations. Many divinely ordered coincidences reassured us that this was in fact a vision authored by the Spirit. Hearing the story, nationally recognized gospel singer Larnell Harris wrote a song about this "Castle of Hope" and performed it on the prison site before a group of astonished participants. Two wealthy sisters saw their great-grandfather's name on the vine-covered prison cornerstone and became instant benefactors. Many churches and Sunday school classes, never before involved directly in urban ministry, joined the effort. Such "coincidences" were not uncommon. They could not be planned nor counted on, nor could anyone lay claim to them. But they came with the expenditure of enormous amounts of energy on the part of staff and volunteers.

Renny Scott and I assumed the role of guardians of the vision. Occasionally, the project attracted opportunists who saw it as a means for personal gain. While no one was opposed to participants receiving legitimate credit that would obviously have public relations value to their companies, some self-serving entrepreneurs attempted to position themselves politically and leverage their association with the project to gain business. As guardians of the vision, we insured the mission remained focused on compassionate service and that everyone involved was either volunteering or providing goods or services at cost. On one occasion, we applied to the state for historic tax credits that we intended to sell to raise construction money. As soon as the word got out that someone stood to gain through the purchase of these tax credits, the spirit of service noticeably changed. When we discovered what was happening, we cancelled the application. Maintaining the purity of the vision became an essential leadership role.

Another opportunity dropped in our laps and seemed ideally suited for GlenCastle. Congress had just passed the McKinney Act to address the national problem of homelessness. The city offered us the entire $3 million Atlanta allocation to underwrite construction costs and ongoing support services for residents. We were ecstatic! It was the very sum needed to underwrite the project. But as we read through fine print, we became uneasy. First, the money had to be used to house and treat homeless men only—a significant departure from our vision to provide families a secure and affordable place to get back on their feet. Also, restrictions on the expression of religious faith raised concerns. Ours was clearly a Christian ministry, and though we were not heavy-handed in our approach, we valued the freedom to engage in discussions of faith as appropriate. It became increasingly apparent that the vision would have to be significantly altered if we accepted these funds. The decision was agonizing, but we declined the funding and went back to the drawing board.

(I should add that policy changes introduced by the Bush administration's Faith-based Initiative have significantly eased restrictions on faith-based organizations, allowing—even encouraging—ministries to apply for government funding. Though still not permissible to proselytize using public dollars—a wise and fair regulation—faith groups now have far greater freedom of expression and programming.)

Discovering Insights

Having adequate capacity and resources to complete a project certainly makes the undertaking far less stressful. However, by limiting vision to available resources, one will not be depending upon divine intervention. Divinely authored vision—the kind that extends one far beyond one's own abilities—requires a frightful level of risk-taking. It is fundamentally different from strategy planning and goal-setting. It requires letting go of the security of predictable outcomes and venture into uncharted waters with little more than an inaudible internal voice as a guide. Such vision is not a product of human creativity. It is divinely conceived and implanted in the spirits of those willing to trust miracle over plan.

One final note: I frequently receive credit for the accomplishment of this amazing transformation. While this feels very good to my ego, and I often simply accept such accolades with graciousness, I know quite well that this was a vision for which I can take no legitimate ownership. Here I am not being humble; I am admitting a reality. Some would ask me: What leadership skills, what ministry experience, what construction expertise, did you have that prepared you for this project? In truth, very little. I am by profession a psychologist. I am not an ordained minister, not a real estate developer, not even a very organized manager. I was simply in a place where the God of history decided to move. Our small urban ministry, while stable and credible, had neither the funding sources nor administrative capacity to take on a mission of this magnitude. These were things that God brought to us as needed. I am humbled and exceedingly grateful that God used our ministry as a conduit and that I was given a leading role in this drama.

Scope of FCS Urban Ministries Housing Initiatives

FCS Urban Ministries, a nonprofit community development organization, partners with depressed neighborhoods in Atlanta's inner-city to restore health and vitality. In addition to hands-on ministry with youth, families, and seniors, FCS develops revitalization plans with communities and implements housing redevelopment strategies. FCS is committed to mixed-income housing. To that end, the organization has built 200 affordable single family homes, developed a 67 unit cohousing village, created three mixed-income subdivisions, converted a prison into 67 affordable loft apartments, rehabilitated a 60-unit public housing project into a privately managed rental community, participated in the creation of a 640-unit urban golf course village, is a partner in a 192-unit affordable town-home development, and is planning a 800+ unit housing community in one of Atlanta's worst slums. For more information, see the Web site at: http://www.fcsministries.org/ministries.htm

A Closed-down Hospital Campus

MARY NELSON

If you put an end to oppression, to every gesture of contempt, and to every evil word; if you give food to the hungry and satisfy those who are in need, then the darkness around you will turn to the brightness of noon. And I will always guide you and satisfy you with good things. I will keep you strong and well. You will be like a garden that has plenty of water, like a spring of water that never goes dry. Your people will rebuild what has been in ruins, building again on the old foundations. You will be known as the people who rebuilt the walls, who restored the ruined houses. —Bethel's mission statement, from Isaiah 58:9-12

"St. Anne's needs miracle",[8] the Crain's Chicago Business newspaper headline screamed. Bethel New Life, a faith-based community development corporation on Chicago's west side, had just purchased a closed-down, 9.2–acre, 437–bed, seven-building hospital campus in the heart of its inner-city, riot-torn community. The entire square-block hospital campus is in the heart of a once thriving working-class White community now turned African American. Riots in the mid 1960s caused major disinvestments and the decline of the economic base of the community. St. Anne's Hospital was unable to deal with the financial demands of the ever-increasing Medicaid patient mix and finally had to close its doors, unable to sustain the economics. What do you do with a closed-down, no-longer-viable hospital campus in the midst of a divested inner-city community? The health care needs were even greater, but reopening the hospital was not financially viable.

Our community-based board of directors and members of Bethel Lutheran Church (the community church out of which Bethel New Life emerged) struggled with the questions of capacity, financial viability, and vision for the rejuvenation of this boarded-up campus, which was fast becoming an eyesore in the community. Today, the adaptive reuse of this former hospital campus is a national model, with 125 units of subsidized housing for seniors, 85 units of assisted living, adult day services, a health clinic, an 80–person child development center, and the transformation of the former chapel into a cultural and performing arts center, small business center, and headquarters for Bethel New Life's administrative operations. More than $30 million was brought into this credit-starved community to complete the campus reuse. Now the campus really is "new life" in an intergenerational and community-based way.

Daring to Listen

Bethel Lutheran Church was rooted in its working class community when it started in 1903. When other churches fled in the four years of riots in the mid-1960s, the white-turned-black church stayed in the community. Bethel's pastor, who came at the start of the disturbances, gave leadership to the dwindling white congregation. We became a community reaching out to meet the needs of our low-income neighbors. Bethel soon became a primarily African American church with a blend of Lutheran liturgy, gospel music, and altar calls that some laughingly labeled "that Lutheran Baptist Church." The small band of now-African American congregants understood the need to be a presence in the community rather than attend to only the internal life of the congregation. This gave birth to the development of Bethel Christian School and Bethel New Life—nonprofits that are ministry arms of the church. The church grew from its original small group to a 600–member congregation. Thus, with larger numbers, Bethel could dare to dream about the hospital campus conversion.

Our mission reminded us of God's vision for the human community—with justice and compassion we would give witness through building again what was in ruins. The promise that God would keep us strong and well—despite the difficulties of the days—spurred us on.

The vision and promise of God had to be strong to overpower the voices of the financial community who turned down loan applications, the foundation community who thought we had bitten off too much, and the skeptics in the community who thought this was another pipe dream that would end in disaster. Bethel Church and the Bethel New Life boards prayed and attended lots of meetings as the staff scrambled to keep the finances going–making applications for grants from the government and private foundations, and furthering the vision of the possibilities. At a critical juncture, we had to ask the Sisters of Ancilla Domini, the former owners of the hospital, to self-finance the purchase since all the banks had turned us down (how do you finance a closed-down inner-city hospital campus with no foreseeable sources of income?). It was the encouragement of the four neighboring community groups who believed in us–knowing we were the only ones big enough to make sure that this campus did not take down the whole community–and the assistance of our local politicians and others that gave us courage. A group of the above went in a van to visit the Mother House of the Sisters and make the audacious proposition: If the Sisters wanted their closed hospital to be a positive force in the community and carry on the mission and ministry of the Sisters, then they needed to figure out a way for us to finance the purchase. God was working in the situation, and together we were able to make the purchase financing work. The headline in the Chicago business newspaper about a miracle being needed was correct. It *took* a miracle–and twelve years of hard work.

Developing Partners

While the church congregation prayed and hoped, the Bethel New Life board and staff did their homework. Dreamy plans for services and for health care for the elderly and children abounded. Banks had turned down financing, and logistical questions of the insurance costs (carrying costs) of building engineers and security guards almost sunk the plan to develop. But the board (a majority of whom were Bethel Church representatives), true to the mission statement of Bethel, voted to take the risk and buy the campus. Then the real work began: developing financing, dealing with issues of the security guards, working with the right stationary engineers, and resolving insurance problems–primarily management of the closed-down buildings. Fortunately, we inherited a lease with the State of Illinois for temporary use of some parts of the campus, which covered the carrying costs and some payment on the mortgage. In the meantime we tried to put together funds for rehab and reuse of the major parts of the campus.

It took gutsy leadership and persistence, creative financing, help from a lot of partners, and determined faith that when obstacles and impossibilities seemed to block the way, God would "make a way out of no way." Prayers on the part of the whole community opened the doors and bolstered the spirits along the way. The Beth-Anne project consisted of putting together a package, piece by piece, over twelve years. And it worked. The pieces and the funding came together. God was gracious; and a local bank had enough confidence in us to loan us the carrying costs while we did the development. We obtained major funding from the U. S. Department of Housing and Urban Development (HUD) with assistance from the U.S Department of Health and Human Services (HHS).

Doing the Work

First we set up the Small Business Center, and then we tore down the oldest part of the hospital building and built in its place a new child development center and connecting lobby. We ran into a snafu *after* we had torn down a section of the old building. Despite our having checked to ensure that the building was not listed on the state's historic building list, we were informed that it was "potentially" historic. Only after a meeting at the offices of the National Trust for Historic Preservation in Washington, D.C. (and six months of aggravation) were we able to get that straightened out with a waiver of the issue. Three years of working with the HUD resulted in the start of the conversion of the upper floors of the main hospital, where we built 125 units of subsidized housing for the elderly. When the building was dedicated, we celebrated God's enabling. Seniors moved from their dark and dank hovel-type housing, neglected by absentee landlords, into this place of pride and joy. We named the campus Beth-Anne, combining "Bethel New Life" with the "St. Anne's Hospital" as a way to show the partnership. Sister Kathleen Quinn Ancilla Domini, said at the grand opening, "My heart rejoices. I have beautiful memories here, and now I see 'new life.'" A representative of the Evangelical Lutheran Church in America said, "Keep it up. *Be* for *us*, the conscience of what *we* need to be in this city. Thank you for your example."

Next came the conversion of the historically significant chapel into a cultural and performing arts center, a place to celebrate the cultural heritage and artistic skills of our African American community and to enable youth to use their energy in creative ways. It was especially hard to find financing or funding for such a venture; it seemed secondary to the community's drastic need for decent housing and jobs. It literally took an "act of Congress" (an actual line item inclusion in a federal appropriations bill) and a capital fund drive, with help from a host of individuals, churches, and foundations, to complete this portion. Bethel Church always led the way in support– even though we didn't have much more than a widow's mite compared to what we needed. The pastor also helped encourage our suburban church

---

Senior resident Pat McCoy was in a nursing home, ready to give up on life, when friends pushed for him to be a resident at Beth-Anne. Today he hovers outside all summer long, tending the flowers and plants with love and care. He actually gets up out of his wheelchair to water and nourish the plants that symbolize new life in a most visible way.

partners to work with us. Some churches invited our Bethel Church gospel choir to sing, and then asked for special offerings; others sponsored events to help raise funds.

Today at the cultural center, youth and adults train in music, and produce dramatic performances, creative mosaics, and paintings on the exterior walls. Youth have left the stamp of their creativity all over the campus with mosaics of life and love for their community. One of the most moving artistic results is a clay tile mosaic built into the ragged edges of an area where the old building was torn down. It says, "*Increase the Peace*" and shows an urban scene of children playing in a gushing fire hydrant, with a boom box in the corner and the sun shining brightly. During the summer the youth were working on it, there were many shootings and deaths of friends, neighbors, and relatives. So they bordered the scene with tombstones bearing the names of those who had been killed, along with a plaque that read, "*In loving memory of those who died too soon.*"

Finally, funds were assembled to redo the first floor for the main Bethel New Life administrative offices and adult day services. We even included a space for a small sundry store that the seniors operate. It has the most wonderful popcorn machine, and each morning our hallways are filled with the tempting smell of freshly popped corn. So on the same campus we now have the elderly, children, youth in the cultural arts, a medical clinic, and administrative offices—clearly a community within the community.

After moving into our new offices on the campus, we focused on the last development piece, the north wing. We were committed to the low-income elderly who would benefit from assisted living and remaining in community—without having to move to a nursing home. It took fusing together subsidies from HUD elderly housing and the state's Supportive Living Program (services) to rehab the north wing into eighty-five units of assisted (supportive) living. We spent over two years trying to figure out how to make the economics work, enabling affordability of the assisted living portion. This unique combination of subsidies makes affordable assisted living possible.

God's nudge to never give up, to be about the work of justice and compassion, and the prayers and hopes of so many people kept Bethel people persistently putting the pieces together.

Dealing with Realities

Obstacle after obstacle stood in our path. We were threatened by many factors: conflicts between funders, the challenge of adaptive reuse of the

---

"Living at Beth-Anne is like living with family. They're going to have to kick me out before I move."—Robert Alexander

campus, and environmental problems. If such efforts were easy, the marketplace would be making them. It is difficult to make affordable housing for a low-income population work. There are many obstacles, turndowns, disagreements, and frustrations. The New Life board and Bethel Church members and staff did not agree on the plan for the former hospital campus, but we prayed about it together and agreed to take one step at a time, moving with what was possible for each piece (starting with the day-care center), allowing opportunities for the next step to evolve out of the process. Our faith was the glue that held us all together when differing ideas, races, and classes would pull us apart. We disagreed, but when we got down on our knees and prayed to God for guidance, we came up with the reminder of God's vision for the human community—of the things that count.

Our deed from the Sisters had a restrictive covenant that said no abortions could be performed on the site. When we got to the HUD closing for the seniors housing, the lawyers said that we couldn't close on the loans and start on the construction because of this covenant. We were astounded. How likely was it that seniors would be getting abortions? After months of trying to get the government to waive this regulation, we finally got the Sisters to agree to remove the covenant in order to receive the $10 million financing.

During another part of the development, it was indicated that we had too much nonresidential space in the building, and the funds could not be used for that. Finally, an adviser researched the alternatives—either convert the space into a two-unit condo, or Bethel could sell the air rights to floors 2–6 to the Residence Corporation. We were way beyond our depth of knowledge, but with help from advisers and others, and persistence, we sold the "air rights" to the Residence Corporation.

We found that each setback created a greater determination, each victory a celebration of God's enabling. God's vision for the whole community—the sustaining energy—is what makes it work. When the banks turned us down for a direct loan, Bethel Church lifted the issue up during Sunday services. The Wednesday prayer group specifically prayed with each visit to a bank. It was through this power that the idea came to approach the Sisters to ask for help with the financing to buy the campus. Our pastor accompanied the team that spoke with the Sisters. There was always the sense that if this was in God's plan, we just had to keep pressing on to find the "way out of no way."

Our church has mortgaged itself five times on housing loans that the bank would not give us unless we had some collateral. That was our five loaves and two fishes. We owned our church building free and clear. We risked "that thing we loved" in order to make it happen. There were gutsy tough decisions to risk finances, reputation, and the future, for the bigger mission. It was the clarity of God's call that enabled the struggling congregation of Bethel Lutheran Church to be willing to mortgage its church building as the only asset we had to collateralize Bethel's first major housing rehab loans. The first time was a leap of faith as we demonstrated our commitment to the work of community. It became easier and easier each of the next five times (for housing deals that were risky, had gaps in value versus loan, etc.) the congregation took that risk. It was like the Children of Israel in the desert, who could look back and see how God had made a way, then trusted him to move forward. It took *"guts"* for the Bethel board and church to take the risk of buying a closed-down inner-city hospital campus, without the funds, or a clear plan for how it could be used to help create a healthier, sustainable community.

We were thankful to have a local bank, First Bank of Oak Park that shared in our vision. They had confidence in us and were willing to take the risk. They loaned us funds to cover the carrying costs of these developments until they became operational and had their own sources of income. Just now, twelve years later, we have restructured the basic financing into a long-term mortgage on the property. We thank God for creative bankers, willing to figure out a way to make it work.

God gives the energy to keep going despite the difficulties. God bolstered us by the prayers and encouragement of the church, and cheered us on by the moments of joy when something long struggled with was resolved and when we celebrated the dedication to God's glory of the next project. Our dedications included all the officials from the various government offices and the elected officials, with comments from potential senior residents, and prayers along with balloons, ribbon cutting, and a reading of our Isaiah 58:9–12 mission statement. At the dedication of Beth-Anne Residences, U. S. Congressman Danny Davis said, "Bethel took St. Anne's Hospital and created a multiple complex—and rather than an eyesore, here is an asset and that has been the genius and ability of Bethel to just dream and then to make those dreams real."

Discovering Insights

What have we learned? The lack of affordable housing is a crisis the church must address, yet we must also be about developing the whole community, especially education and economic development. To do housing or any kind of community development, we have learned that the asset-based approach is best. More details of lessons learned are described in the Asset Based Community Development (ABCD) book entitled *Community Transformation: Turning Threats into Opportunities* (ACTA Publications). Even though most people see only the needs of our low-income community, we have learned to link the strengths of the community: people, local associations, local institutions, physical assets of the campus, and our own "widow's mites." Jesus asked a key question when he told the disciples to feed the 5,000—"What do you have?" Elisha asked the same question to the widow who was left with so much debt that her children were going to be sold in order to pay the debt (2 Kings 4:1–7). Elisha asked her, "What do you have?" God kept that small amount of oil she had pouring until she had enough to pay her debt and live on the rest. She went to the neighbors to ask for more jars, and we too have gone to our neighbors, the local associations and businesses, to partner with them to build the assets. So God made a way out of no way. When we looked at what we had and started pouring, God began to make it happen.

As we looked at our neighborhood, we realized that we had a lot of good natural caregivers in our community, people without high school diplomas, but people who were already caring for grandmas and uncles and neighbors down the street. We also realized we had a lot of elderly in our community, and that they were assets. They were strengths, not problems; they were opportunities. So we began an enterprise to provide in-home care services for elderly, where people could be trained to do in-home care services while elderly could be cared for in their community and in their homes. Now more than 250 paid caregivers from the community are caring for their neighbors.

We've got to be smart about what we do. When Esther wanted a certain thing out of the King, she was smart. She dressed up in her best clothes put on perfume; she enticed and she lured that king with a banquet feast and waited for the right timing to ask for what she wanted (Esth. 5). We've got to be smart about what we do, and we've got to figure it out. We don't want a drugstore in our community just to have a nice drugstore, where all the profits go out into somebody else's hands and the jobs are somebody else's jobs. If we're going to do Christian community development in our communities, we need to keep focused on the right issues. We need to know why we are doing things; we must be willing to risk and be smart about it. We don't need to be replicating what the marketplace is going to do anyway; we need to do what they won't do. In real estate they say location, location, location. We need to take the toughest location, where the marketplace says, "we can't make it work there" and figure out how to make it work by God's grace and enabling.

We've got to be smart and creative in financing. We need to be strategic, as well, whether it's mortgaging our church buildings or finding new ways to put capital together. When we were trying to get into doing limited partnerships before the tax credit days, we developed two capital pools; one was called Sharing and Solutions through Investments. We asked people to invest with us on two promissory notes, and we would pay them back. It was a risky thing. We had another one called Shelter for Shelter (or may we have your interest?). And that's where people invested with us at zero interest, and we invested the money, got the interest, and used the interest for down payments for people in new houses. We must be smart. One of the big new areas where there will be 2.5 billion dollars worth of investments in low-income targeted communities is the New Markets Tax Credits, something that a group of us spent the last four years working on. Many companies and individuals will be making these dollars available in our communities.

We must be smart in regard to diversification of financing. It takes a lot longer to assemble, but there are advantages. Public and private funders "leverage" one another's support, and a wide range of funders helps spread the risk around. Also, diversification means Bethel is not dependent on just one or two funders for the entire project.

Diversification of social capital is also important. As we learned about looking at the assets, we used what people already know and built on it. The community constituency must remain part of the process, and we must value what they know and think. We always made sure that the project involved the community and was *wanted* by the community. The community and church members were stakeholders in the ongoing viability of the effort. Community participation is worth the effort. For example, when we needed a zoning variance, the neighbors came with us to the zoning hearing to show support for this change.

We can't do it by ourselves. We need partnerships. We need to know that the doors are open now much more for working with governments and faith-based initiatives. We need to get smart in how to do that. Many states and cities now have faith-based initiatives, so we must look to those as well as federal partnerships. And we also need to create partnerships in our own neighborhoods. Bethel has been really fortunate to have a partnership with Argon national laboratories, a technology laboratory. Their goal is technology transfer, and our goal was to help them figure out how to make their technology work in our community. We were both partners in trying to figure that out and make it happen. We now have energy-efficient housing, some location-efficient mortgages, and a whole variety of other things.

If we are going to partner with others, we need to put our egos aside. If you want a lot of people to come on board with you, you have got to give away the credit—the mayor and the city government are always looking for support and want their name on successful projects. The federal government is no different if you partner with them. And sometimes other churches get jealous of what you do, so you just give away the credit. Number one, you thank God for what is happening in your midst, and then you give away the credit.

We have to do our homework. When Bethel church started Bethel New Life, and we went to the other churches in our neighborhood (this is more than twenty years ago) we asked them, "Why don't you go with us and do some affordable housing?" Many said, "Well, we don't know how. We don't have any money, and it takes too long." And it's that way for many of our communities and many of our boards who say, "We don't know how. We don't have the money, and it takes too long." In Mark 6, in the feeding of the five thousand, that's just what the disciples told Jesus when he said, "feed them." They said, "We don't have any food or money. Where are we going to get it?" They had the very same excuses that all of us run across as we are doing it. We need to apply our faith, do our homework, and figure it out.

Sunday morning worship becomes our fueling station, our supplier of energy to never give up and to look for alternatives, and our source of encouragement from the family of God to stay the course. Without the faith factor, we would have given up.

We learned many lessons from the hospital adaptive reuse Beth-Ann project. And many factors contributed to the success of this and other projects that Bethel New Life has done. What helped us develop the vision and persistence to carry on in the face of so many obstacles? Clearly the heritage of parents and family built the foundation. For one, my brother, who was the pastor of our church, decided all those years ago that if we didn't do something about housing, there wouldn't be a neighborhood left to be the church. When the church decided to mortgage itself as the only collateral that we could find for the loans to begin this housing ministry, he was the one who gave the effort leadership, and he was the one who, when we came to the tough decisions and the risky moments said, "By the grace of God do it!" His favorite saying from the pulpit was, "You ain't seen nothing yet!" God is always making a way and opening the doors and making it happen.

Pastor Nelson has since gone to be with the Lord. We were truly partners in ministry. He and I also have to credit our very audacious mother for the example she showed us. She was a pastor's wife who stood up for her rights to be a homemaker in the time when women were beginning to go out in the workforce making incomes. She had a Bible class in a penitentiary every week. When she began to realize that the women were released on Saturday afternoon with twenty dollars in their pocket (and there were no halfway houses forty-five years ago in the Washington area), our home became the halfway house. She then went to pester people in the halls of Congress to get the monies to establish halfway houses.

It was my mother, who was so concerned about first-strike weapons and the nuclear arsenals that were building up, who wrote to her congressman, who stood at rallies and spoke up against these weapons because she said she loved her country and wanted her country to be doing what was right. It was my mother who, in exasperation that none of these things made a difference, at the age of seventy-eight, with a heart condition and cancer, put her body in a little boat, in front of a Trident nuclear submarine in those cold Puget Sound waters and was arrested. (A Trident submarine is five football fields long and it has enough atomic nuclear warfare on it to destroy the world seven times over). I was proud of my mother, seeing her in handcuffs and coming before that judge. Late that evening, after the bond hearing, they released her on personal recognizance. Since the Daughters of the American Revolution had named my mother "American Mother of the Year," the newspaper reporters wondered why she would commit civil disobedience. Without a moment's hesitation she said, "I did it for the children of the world." That is the kind of heritage that keeps me pushing on and kept me going in those twelve years of adapting the hospital campus into what we have today.

"St. Anne's needs miracle," the newspaper headline said. We have indeed witnessed a miracle of God enabling a congregation, a board, a lot of advisers, and a staff to turn a closed-down, inner-city hospital campus into a thriving community of children, adults, and the elderly living together to the fullness of new life.

Scope of Bethel's Housing Ministries

Bethel is known for its cutting edge initiatives in affordable housing, community building on assets, creative continuums for elderly and formerly homeless families, and environmentally smart community efforts. Bethel has developed some 350 units of multifamily housing (with creative financing, including sweat equity cooperatives), three seniors subsidized independent living buildings and one assisted living building (273 units) primarily with financing through the HUD, 84 units of supportive housing for formerly homeless families in three buildings, and 176 single family homes in focused area developments. Some of these homes were sweat equity efforts, enabling the very poor to become homeowners. In addition, Bethel developed the award-winning adaptive reuse of a closed-down inner-city hospital's 9.2-acre campus. For more information, see Bethel's Web site: http://www.bethelnewlife.org/about.html

Build a Community

A Congregation's Journey into Afforable Housing

REV. DR. DARELL T. WEIST

Introduction to Congregation-owned Land Model BY JILL SHOOK

I met Rev. Dr. DarEll Weist while attending a course on making your dreams a reality, an intriguing title for a class on how to start a nonprofit organization. Michael Mata, the professor, invited Weist, pastor of the First United Methodist Church (FUMC) of Los Angeles, to speak to us about the dream God had given him and how it became a reality—the story you are about to read.

The dream—really God's dream—was possible in part because of the congregation's assets. When developing the 1010 Development Corporation, Weist put together a talented board of church and community members, with Stewart Kwoh at the helm. Kwoh said, "The FUMC L.A. has been blessed with assets such as land."

Like First United Methodist, other churches have caught a vision to use their land for affordable housing. One interesting example is Lake Avenue Church in Pasadena. They proposed to build affordable units above a parking structure on their land. The structure would have served the dual purpose of church parking for its 5,000 or so attendees on weekends, and as parking for Metro line riders during the week (the Metro line runs within a stone's throw of the church)—if it had been approved.

A congregation in northern California had families knocking on their convent door to find shelter. They knew God was calling them to address the issue of affordable housing. However, unlike First United Methodist, this small congregation, the Sisters of the Holy Family, knew that God also was *not* calling them to build or manage housing themselves. As I sat in the convent interviewing Sister Elaine Sanchez, she explained the structure they set up to provide housing in a way consistent with their mission to families and the poor. They did their research and found a nonprofit developer and property management company who shared their vision: Mid-Peninsula Housing Coalition (MPHC). Selling this developer their six acres adjacent to their convent set them free from legal obligations for the management of the project. Once the project was approved, their part was only that of a religious community of women loving their new neighbors.

As with Weist, this journey took Sister Elaine into the public and civic arena, where her faith was tested and witnessed. Because their property was smack in the middle of the upscale Mission San Jose neighborhood in Fremont, opposition from the city council and the neighborhood extended the approval and the predevelopment process to seven years. Fears abounded. As each objection was countered, new objections arose. Statistics didn't influence the governing bodies. Instead, Sister Elaine's group finally wore the politicians down from a legal standpoint. They had to approve the project or face a lawsuit.

Strengthened by their chosen partners standing with them through those long seven years, they were finally granted approval for their proposal. Sister Elaine sums up her journey with John 5:30, "I can do nothing on my own...because I seek to do not my own will but the will of him who sent me." These became words of comfort as well as a source of pain, uncertainty, and struggle as she followed that place where the heart of God beats within her. This process also deepened the Sisters' commitment to their mission. Today the city council recognizes their effort as having created one of the best examples of affordable housing in the area. What once stirred heated debate and political strife also earned the prestigious Gold Nugget Award for its design of the 101-unit development for families and seniors. Now the city looks to the church to sit on committees that deal with affordable housing issues.

DarEll's life, like Sister Elaine's, has not been the same since God called him into affordable housing. DarEll makes it clear: "Affordable housing is a ministry to the community, first to the people who need it, and secondly to the community who needs to embrace it."[1]

A Congregation's Journey into Affordable Housing

REV. DR. DARELL T. WEIST

"Build houses and settle down...seek the peace and prosperity of the city...Pray to the Lord for it, because if it prospers, you too will prosper."
—Jeremiah 29: 5–7, NIV

The Detour

On the way to my car, I detour through Hope Place and Villa Flores to stimulate my recollection of what God has done. Hope Place encompasses

Hope Village's sixty-six units of one- to three-bedroom family housing and Villa Flores's seventy-five units of senior housing.

On the podium deck I see little Jesus–a six month old, born at Hope Village. His mother, Lilian Rivera, watches him play in a raised grassy patch. Her three older children play on the jungle gym with Ruth and Beliu–twins enrolled in the children's learning center in Hope Village. Alemtsehay, the twins' mother–born in Ethiopia–reads a textbook for her college courses. I watch Nester and his friend play table tennis. Anne, a Korean, waves as I pass by.

The south elevator lifts me to the upper garage, housing the social service delivery arm of South Park Neighborhood Center. In the computer lab, Miriam teaches a group of Hispanic day workers from Villa Del Pueblo, family housing down the street. Walking by the children's learning center playground, I see four children still waiting for their parents–representing four ethnicities and three languages. As they intently play with a truck in the sandbox, I note that "*vroom*" is "vroom" in any language.

Crossing the red stamped asphalt alley, Pembroke Lane, I enter Villa Flores Senior Housing. My eye catches three seniors enjoying the S. Mark Taper Desert Garden. They wave as I pass the multipurpose room where Mrs. Kim leads seniors in line dance. In the lobby I encounter eight well-groomed Hispanic women, two in wheelchairs with their attendants, chatting and sipping coffee–their afternoon ritual. As I approach my car, my heart sings as I consider the global community that God is building.

This is the kind of community that First United Methodist Church, Los Angeles (First Church), is called to serve. Here, we see glimpses of the biblical descriptions of Isaiah 65:17–25–where there is hope and justice for all of God's children. Isaiah's holistic vision of what life should be like became my biblical mandate of God's vision for the city.

Daring to Listen

First Church is one of the oldest Protestant Churches in Los Angeles (1854), and one of America's "megachurches" from the 1910s to the 1940s, with 5,000 members. When the Red Cars–L.A. area public transport–were dismantled in late 1940s, the church plunged to 200 members. The huge 3,500-seat sanctuary, with its Tiffany panels, fabulous organ, and forty classrooms, became a liability. The unreinforced masonry would not withstand a southern California earthquake. For sixty years it stood on the corner of Hope and 8th Street. When it was sold in 1983, the church purchased two office buildings, with a sanctuary and church offices carved out of the first and second floors. The rest of the space housed a child day-care center and an incubator for social justice nonprofit organizations and advocate groups such as Farmer's Market, The Homeless Health Care Project, and Asian Pacific American Legal Services.

As the newly appointed senior pastor, on that first Sunday in 1989 I looked over the multicultural remnant–average age of seventy–and said to myself, "What one thing can I do to ensure that there will be a First Church in twenty years?" I had a leadership responsibility for the present and future health of the congregation. I could have answered in a number of ways, but the word that came to me was, "Build a *community—a neighborhood—*and then from the *neighborhood* you will build a *congregation.*" What a big surprise! I thought that I was to build the *congregation,* but the word was to first build a *community.*

The large block where we now met as a church had vacant space and our five-story and two-story buildings. At the other end of the block sat the four-story National Cash Register office building being adapted by Telecu into forty units of housing for the disabled. First Church owned one third of the block; the Los Angeles Community Redevelopment Agency (CRA) owned the rest.

In 1989, building any kind of housing, even affordable housing, in downtown Los Angeles was novel. Market rate condos had been built in the last ten years, but had a difficult time selling. No one wanted to live downtown. South of downtown, Sister Diane Donoghue with Esperanza Housing was starting to build affordable housing. To the west, the First African Methodist Episcopal (FAME) and West Los Angeles Church of God in Christ were initiating their affordable housing projects, but none near downtown. Despite South Park being declared the future bedroom community of downtown Los Angeles, almost nothing had happened to make that a reality—especially for workers. To the contrary, older dwellings were being torn down, displacing longtime residents to make way for office buildings and parking lots.

This was a novel idea for another reason. As a United Methodist, I had been a local church pastor, a campus minister, a church bureaucrat, and a missionary theological teacher, but never an affordable housing developer. I had no background or training in urban planning or building design. To the contrary, I was born on the prairies of North Dakota! However, I did have good administrative skills.

The congregation said, "Pastor we are fine the way we are. Don't bother yourself about it; it all sounds too risky, too much work." I sensed they were just scared, and I could not get away from the vision: "*Build a community, build a neighborhood; and then out of the neighborhood build a congregation!*" Other pastors had a similar response: "You don't know anything about building; why would you put yourself through that kind of pain?" But the vision persisted. After much prayer and discernment, I decided that I needed a mentor.

Developing Partners

With fear of rejection, I talked to Robert Harris, Dean of the School of Architecture at the University of Southern California. I feared he might say, "That's a nice idea, pastor, but this work is difficult. It is only for professionals. I suggest that you hire someone with the real knowledge to do the work. You leave that to us, and you just continue preaching." Instead, he sympathetically listened and said, "I have just the teacher for you—John Mutlow." The next day I met with Mutlow, a USC professor, and told him my story. He didn't laugh. Rather, he took me seriously and invited me to his class that worked with architectural and design issues. I had a live project, so I became the class resource. As I explained the vision, they provided feedback; and I learned. Before the end of the semester, he said, "DarEll, next semester we should master plan the block."

I said, "John, we don't own the whole block, only one third."

"This means you have development rights," he informed me. "The Los Angeles Community Redevelopment Agency, who owns the rest, doesn't know what they want to do with it." So I was off and running with another learning experience.

About halfway through that semester, the area project manager for the CRA/LA said to me, "CRA would like to master plan the block."

I told him, "What a great idea!" (The same vision was coming to a number of people at the same time.) However, I added, "We don't have the $60,000 to pay the architect who would do the master plan."

"Oh," said the CRA project manager, "We have the money, but no one to staff it." I told him that my executive assistant and I would be happy to staff it. Another learning experience! The master plan included 445 units of housing—48 percent at market rate and 52 percent affordable—with a day-care center, a social service neighborhood center, a church building, a meditation garden, offices, and parking.

During that semester, Mutlow said we needed to talk about a HUD 202 Senior Housing project. Thus he introduced me to a whole new community of resources: architects, financial consultants, engineers, contractors, CRA project managers, building inspectors, real estate agents, management companies, and other nonprofit and faith-based developers— a host of people wanting to help God's vision come to life on our block.

As these partnerships developed, Mutlow and others introduced a world of funding possibilities: foundation grants, tax credits, HUD allocations, grants from the Community Development Department, HUD pass through grants from City Housing Authorities, tax exempt bonds, bridge loans, money from the Federal Home Loan Bank, etc.

Early in this process, I created a 501(c)3 development corporation: the 1010 Development Corporation. The fragile multiethnic congregation at First Church had no ability or prior experience to say either yes or no to developing affordable housing. If pushed, they would say no. However, since this was a ministry of the First Church, seven members of the board of directors are from the church and six from the community at large. The church needed ownership and a positive relationship with the project. The community directors came from USC, UCLA, Bank of America, Metro-politan Transit Authority, a contractor, and a future resident of the senior housing. The 1010 Development Corporation brought the congregation, the stakeholders, and the residents into conversation, providing skilled advisors to build 141 units of affordable housing.

In my case, I did not ask for approval from the congregation, but for permission to explore the project with the development corporation. The congregation had all kinds of questions, "Where is all this money coming from? If the project goes bankrupt, will we lose our church? Will we like the people who move in?" Many of the questions had no answers until we worked through the project. For example, most of our affordable housing was financed with tax credits, meaning we have a limited partner or tax syndicator that owns 99.9 percent of our project for fifteen years. To most congregations this sounds like a very bad deal; and ours was no different. But the community board of directors gave the church directors the courage to risk when decisions were beyond them. Now they see how building a community is creating a future for their congregation, and they are grateful.

Doing the Work
Villa Flores

Our development team—initially an architect and a financial consultant—helped us define how much housing we could build on our land and if we could get it financed. Having a contractor come on board immediately was essential. The contractor and architect teamed up to design and build our project within its budget. Value engineering helped us find less expensive and even better design elements. The diversity of development team members from different companies greatly enhanced our project.

Mutlow suggested we begin with Villa Flores. In planning this seven-story, seventy-five unit senior complex, our earthquake solution was unaffordable—our first crisis! Redesigning the subterranean footing and placing apartments on the ground floor proved cheaper and better. But questions arose: "Would that be safe?" The solution: storefront-type window space to provide security where plants and other decorations enhance the building. Pages of questions emerged in our weekly construction meetings: "The carpet color?" "The make and type of refrigerators?" "Where a bathroom emergency outlet should be placed?" "Should the bedrooms have ceiling fans, and the multipurpose room a full kitchen?" We were creating space for people to live well.

Halfway through construction, it hit us that funding for the Mark S. Taper California Desert Garden was overlooked. The garden required extra light soil, since it would be above the subterranean parking garage, making it expensive. Delighted, we found a foundation that understood our mission, feeling honored that we would ask them to help. After thirteen months, the construction was complete! We received our occupancy permit early on an October afternoon of 1998. By 5 p.m. that evening, ten qualified residents were sleeping in their apartments!

Hope Village

One year after finishing Villa Flores, we began building Hope Village, our family housing. It was on the fast track. Challenges abounded. Our building, one story too high for a certain category of residential funding, forced us to redraw plans mid-construction. After one of our weekly construction meetings, I wanted to see the cable TV and phone jacks. Perusing the partially built units, we were suddenly inspired to have cable and phone/data outlets in each of the 150 bedrooms. Our tenants deserved computers and Internet access, and they are now very grateful!

Dealing with Realities

Enriched Housing

In market rate housing, amenities are things like swimming pools, beauty salons, weight rooms, etc. But amenities for affordable housing are enriched social services such as computer labs, ESL classes, nutrition classes, etc. At Hope Place we have these enriched services, plus our day-care center, food distribution, senior and youth programs, and a weekly parish nurse. These instill skills, new life, and new hope as our church continues the tradition of social service in Lost Angeles begun in 1890.

These amenities, along with our community choir and regular barbecues for the tenants of Villa Flores, Hope Village, and Telecu Plaza (housing for disabled residents next door) foster natural relationship with church members and among tenants. God is creating a community! As a result, the neighborhood is a safer place. As residents take responsibility for each other and our beautiful buildings, pride is instilled. Our attention to upkeep causes residents to treat the project with respect, thus preserving our property value.

The Risk

It requires gutsy faith to sign loans and obtain grants for $25 million dollars. Even though it is not personally our money, it nevertheless affects a dearly loved organization. Depending on other professionals to carry out our mission and dreams is not how congregations normally function. We depended on a host of advisors; even now, we depend on a property manager. But even management must be managed. I now help other congregations build affordable housing. Two congregations quit in the middle of the planning stage. The commitment and risk were too much.

Prayer Life

Decisions big and small for which the congregation had little or no background were more than we could imagine. We developed our prayer life, giving us confidence that we were following God's agenda. Prayer calmed me numerous times when I knew this task was beyond me, when I doubted myself. Prayer allowed us to find out-of-the-box solutions. God created a new community and changed lives—especially my own. The congregation grew in their prayer life and their understanding of God's dream for the city.

Leadership Skills

My gifts in administration were used to help realize the dream. Understanding the rules and the limits of multiple funding sources required someone who could manage a complex project and guide the congregation in the learning experience. I wanted my congregation to see beyond their own church to people who they never thought would be a part of their congregational family. But I initially had to step out, asking the congregation not to put up roadblocks. Once the buildings were up, the church adopted them as their own—after they understood what it meant to create our community: namely, that affordable housing is not a profit center or a way to balance the congregational budget. (In a good year, a small amount of residual receipts remain after all the reserves are satisfied and bills are paid.) And it means that with public funds we must be willing to take the tenants God gives us, those who qualify with background checks, by income level, and family size. We have excess applications, so tenants are chosen by lottery. God has a marvelous way of giving us good and interesting tenants…

Imagine a fourteen-year-old Hispanic doing his Chinese homework! He says he will be trilingual in about two years: English, Spanish, and Chinese. As part of the team of neighborhood youth from Hope Place, he painted a 35-foot mural of "Heroes and 'Sheroes'" installed on the fence at Hope Village. He participates twice weekly in our after-school youth programs.

Our Korean harpist teaches private harp and piano lessons to our children, and music at our children's learning center. She occasionally plays for First Church's worship services. Harp music is regularly heard from a studio offered rent-free out of gratefulness for sharing her talents!

Discovering Insights

I discovered that God often gives only the vision we need at the moment. The rest comes as we work it.

I discovered that church culture tends to be in risk-avoidance—at all levels of church administrative bodies—local, regional, or national level. Initially, I received little or no support from bishops, program staff, or fellow pastors. They wanted to see the whole vision; God had only given me part of it. When the buildings were completed, their attitude changed to one of support; but they had to be convinced.

I discovered a whole group of professionals in the community. Many of them were uninterested in our Sunday worship services, but believed in the dream. They were proud to be part of God's work for the city and ready to give many hours. This is a ministry to this creative group of professionals.

I discovered many people willing to serve as mentors. They helped me ask the right questions, gave me the right books to read, and helped solve difficult problems.

I discovered that God would make available the resources to do God's agenda.

I discovered that building affordable housing is a spiritual journey. My prayer life, my relationship with God, and my understanding of God's mission in the world has grown.

I discovered that God's community is multiaged, multilingual, multicultural, multieconomic, multireligious, and among the disabled. The congregation's ministry is within that community.

Building a community of people on our block is just the beginning. It is then out of this neighborhood that a new congregation of God's children will come.

Change from the Inside Out

A Tenant Takeover

PAUL A. SMITH

Introduction to Tenants Taking Ownership BY Shane Claiborne

Together with creation we groan for liberation from decay (Rom. 8). Philadelphia is groaning in the ruins of an industrial city–700 abandoned factories, 200,000 lost jobs, 15,000 empty lots filled with trash, 25,000 vacant homes…and a ten-year waiting list for Section 8 affordable housing, yet with more abandoned houses than homeless folks. One neighbor just received her Section 8 voucher and said, "Now that I have a job, a family, and a house, the city is ready to help. I could have really used that back when I applied…fourteen years ago." Our neighborhood is hard, beautiful, and never dull.

I live in a community called The Simple Way, located in Kensington, statistically one of Pennsylvania's poorest neighborhoods. Here we practice resurrection, believing that life is more powerful than death, that grass can pierce concrete. We plant flowers inside old TV screens and computer monitors. We run a community store where folks can share things. We help kids with homework, and they help us imagine a better world. We feed hungry folks. We grow into properties that have been decaying, houses left abandoned groaning for life and beauty.

It isn't easy running a 501(c)3 "anti-profit" organization out of our houses, with no paid staff and no way to compartmentalize our "service" or "charity" work from our lives, families, and homes. But it is what we believe in. Like Mary and Martha, the gospel of the early church was lived out of people's homes. We believe visions of reconciliation and redistribution will never make their way into our church until they are realized in our living rooms and dinner tables. The sacred had to be decentralized, found in ordinary things like bread, wine, or turnip greens. Since hospitality is a cornerstone of our way of life, a strong passion for housing is natural. From the beginning, our community has been bound up in the struggle for affordable housing.

The Kensington Welfare Rights Union (KWRU) started as a group of homeless mothers sharing their welfare checks and taking care of each other's children. In 1995, about forty of these families moved into an abandoned cathedral in North Philadelphia as an act of survival and a refusal to remain invisible. Soon after they moved in, the Archdiocese announced they had 48 hours to get out or face arrest. In the verdant suburbs of Philadelphia, some of us read their story in the newspaper in the Eastern University cafeteria. We scarfed down our dinner, piled in a car, and headed into a city neighborhood we had been told never to go near. After weaving through the streets of row houses and abandoned buildings, we came upon the monstrous cathedral, St. Edwards. A banner on the front read, "How can we worship a homeless man on Sunday and ignore one on Monday?" The families embraced us; children grabbed our hats and invited us into their struggle. Our lives have never been the same.

We went back to our college inspired and disturbed, aware of the ticking clock. We ran through campus, distributing flyers saying, "Jesus is getting kicked out of church in North Philly," with invitations to an impromptu meeting. Expecting no more than a dozen of our crazier friends to show up, we were shocked when over one hundred people gathered. The next day dozens of us poured into "St. Ed's," casting our lives with the families. It became a media spectacle. Reporters made it look like the Catholic Church was kicking homeless people onto the street (since the Church *was* kicking homeless people onto the street). The 48-hour deadline passed, and public support for them only grew stronger. The families remained for days, weeks, months.

The struggle sparked a powerful movement on our campus. Each time city officials came to evict the families, we ran through campus honking our air horn, piled into a cavalcade of cars, and headed down to St. Ed's. We became known as the YACHT Club (Youth Against Complacency and Homelessness Today). Some boaters mistakenly called on occasion…We didn't hesitate to invite them to sell all they had and give it to the poor. The Spirit was tearing through our college campus like a wildfire. We took over chapel services, inviting students to join the movement. The president of Eastern gave her bed to the families in St. Ed's.

Every week dozens of us went to Sunday services at St. Ed's, where we sang old hymns and freedom songs. Gospel choirs came, and we danced in the aisles. Catholic clergy led liturgies. Kids and homeless mothers preached the gospel. We served communion: old apple cider and stale bagels. Many of us experienced true communion for the first time. There came a point at which many of us said, "Let's stop complaining about the church we see and *be* the church we dream of." I literally found God amidst the wreckage of the church.

We dreamed ancient visions of the Early Church in which, "There were no needy persons among them," because everyone shared their possessions. We thirsted for the kingdom of God, and we knew that it could come "on earth as it is in heaven," as Jesus said. We were not interested in a Christianity that only offered these families mansions and streets of gold when they got to heaven, when all they wanted was a bed for their kids *here*...and many Christians had an extra one.

The adventure of St. Edward's ended with the families of KWRU holding a press conference. As people viewed the news, many donated housing, city agencies were persuaded to provide housing, and friends made sure everyone was taken care of. This was a project of survival, never intended to be a permanent solution (with one bathroom and no heat!). The homeless thanked everyone for the powerful movement of allies who stood with them in their struggle, then marched to the mayor's office, saying, "You have no idea what it is like to walk in our shoes." They took off their shoes, leaving them in a pile outside the mayor's office, with the invitation to come and see what life was like in their shoes.

The legacy of St. Edward's is far from over. Shortly afterward, a group of us from the YACHT Club moved into Kensington and began The Simple Way. Nearly a decade later, it is still our home. KWRU is now an international movement of poor and homeless families fighting to end poverty. KWRU taught us the difference between managing poverty and ending it, valuing solidarity over charity. We learned that we are not a voice for the voiceless, for no one is without a voice. We realized many people talk about the poor; but few talk *to* the poor, and even fewer join the voice of the poor. Most of all we learned that love takes risks, gets you in trouble, and sets you free (though you may end up in jail).

The families of KWRU have taken courageous steps to bring attention to the housing crisis in Pennsylvania, erecting shantytowns all over the "City of Brotherly Love." And we have helped families move into abandoned housing, over and over—and we have gone to jail, over and over. Is it illegal for a homeless mother to house her children in a vacant property, *or,* is it wrong for the city to have vacant properties when families are in need of housing? As Augustine said, "An unjust law is no law at all." So KWRU now has "reclaimed" houses all over North Philadelphia to assure that families are cared for. Sometimes they last a week, and sometimes they last for years. Often allies who believe that these are human rights, even if the government does not yet recognize them as such, turn on the utilities. Police show up in court and argue that charges they brought against us should be dropped because our cause was just. We even had a judge say, "If it were not for people who broke these unjust laws, we would not have the freedom that we have. That's what this country is built on, from the Boston Tea Party to the civil rights movement. These folks are not criminals...they are freedom fighters."

I am reminded of the words of Dr. King: "There is nothing wrong with a traffic law which says you have to stop for a red light. But when a person is bleeding, the ambulance goes through those red lights at top speed... Disinherited people all over the world are bleeding to death from deep social and economic wounds. They need brigades of ambulance drivers who will have to ignore the red lights of the present system until the emergency is solved."[1]

On one occasion, a police officer took us to jail for standing with homeless friends facing arrest. He searched me, found my Bible, and said, "I'm going to have to hold onto this...It's a dangerous book." He smiled, but I thought–it *is* a dangerous book. For hundreds of years this book has gotten people in trouble, locked up, executed.

As my dear mother says, "Christianity was never meant to be safe. We are just promised that when we walk into danger, God is with us." Well said, Mom. Perhaps the most dangerous place for a Christian is in safety and comfort, for we need to follow the way of the one who left all comfort, born a baby refugee, and wandered Galilee a homeless rabbi.

You are about to read another story of courage and risk–by another group of people who would not be silenced, in another abandoned building, across the country from North Philly...also practicing resurrection. Here is the resurrection story of Paul A. Smith.

Change from the Inside Out—A Tenant Takeover

PAUL A. SMITH

"He has shown strength with his arm; he has scattered the proud in the thoughts of their hearts. He has brought down the powerful from their thrones, and lifted up the lowly." —Luke 1:51–52, RSV

In the community room, festooned with streamers and balloons, a hundred guests mingle, waiting to surprise a new high school graduate. "Where will Cristina be going to college?" someone asks. The question is so natural and normal. Its very normalcy suddenly makes me aware of the depth of transformation that has occurred here. My eyes fill with tears of gratitude. It wasn't always like this...

The basement community room, now painted bright yellow, with an immaculately polished floor of reds, greens, and yellows, was a dark, smelly cavern with broken pipes dripping sewage onto a rat-infested mound of trash. Few kids ever graduated from high school. It was "normal" to go to jail, become pregnant, or be wounded in a drive-by shooting.

In those days, anyone who demonstrated leadership potential left the neighborhood. But now, Teresa and Maria, with several others, have become citizens of the United States. "Pedro" stopped drinking and reunited with his wife when he discovered his vital role in the community. "Moises" attends church regularly. Of the eighteen households who received housing assistance, only one retired gentleman still qualifies with a low enough income. What I savor the most is how close we have become. We have worked together, disagreed, cried at funerals, and danced at weddings. Somehow we became a community. How did this happen?

Daring to Listen

In 1987, four seminary students, inspired to prepare for ministry in the slums of the developing world, decided to rent a one-room apartment in an inner-city, immigrant neighborhood in Los Angeles. The Cambria Apartments, with its large courtyard filled with children, proved an ideal place to learn ministry skills. Soon others joined. Some were called to serve overseas as missionaries, but several of us were called to stay. We affiliated with InnerChange, a division of Church Resource Ministries. We came as learners, not experts with an agenda. Convinced that if God had called us to this neighborhood, then God was already at work among our neighbors, we determined to listen, pray, and seek out the leaders he was preparing. We built relationships through kids clubs, yard sales, youth outings, tutoring, sports, helping neighbors navigate the legal and medical systems, and "just hanging out." Living in the same building, with shared experiences, built bonds of trust and understanding. God blessed this relational strategy, although nothing could prepare us for the surprising way the ministries would unfold.

We prayed as commanded in Jeremiah to "seek the peace and prosperity of the city...Pray to the LORD for it, because if it prospers, you too will prosper" (Jer. 29:7, NIV). And there was much to pray for: In front of the Cambria Apartments addicts smoked crack, prostitutes solicited clients, and gangs exchanged daily drive-by shootings. As you entered the building, an overpowering stench assailed you. The carpets hadn't been changed in seventy-five years. (During the reconstruction, we discovered newspapers dating from World War I used as padding!) Many of the apartments had been subdivided, lacking a bathroom or kitchen. Jury-rigged sinks and hotplates served for kitchens, while families shared a filthy bathroom at the end of the hall. Plaster was falling, and the plumbing was failing, despite the efforts of the manager—a rough man who held things together as best he could. Roaches were everywhere. One side of the building was rotten and moldy. (When we took up the carpet, a worker fell through the floor!) Yet things got worse before they got better.

In 1992, our neighborhood was impacted by civil unrest following the Rodney King trial. A number of stores, including a building across the street, were looted and burned. In our building, the manager was fired. Gang members and drug dealers squatted in vacant apartments, roaming the halls freely. A succession of nonresident managers completely failed to take control of the situation. In this state of affairs, our evangelistic Bible study hosted by InnerChange gave several tenants a chance to gather, discuss the deteriorating conditions, and consider options. During those first attempts to negotiate with the landlord, pressuring him to make improvements, nobody realized that the future leadership of a tenant movement was sitting together in the living room.

Each person brought different gifts. Teresa Marcial, a social leader in the neighborhood, quickly grasped complex issues that had to be negotiated, and represented tenants with praise. Josefina Guzman, a compact extrovert bursting with energy, was effective in marshalling the other tenants. Maria Contreras, the bespectacled group skeptic, was the oldest of the leaders, unafraid to call people to account or to shoot down far-fetched ideas.

Seeking help for Cambria Apartments, residents contacted tenant organizers and public interest lawyers who advised us of our rights and helped us develop a strategy. Meanwhile, the city attorney's slum housing task force prosecuted the landlord for criminal violations of the building and safety code. The owner eventually pleaded no contest to ten of forty counts, including cockroach and rodent infestation and inoperable smoke detectors. In June 1993, he was fined and ordered to remedy the situation. Despite the judgment, he continued to "bleed" the building—collect rent without making repairs. To further pressure the owner, attorneys from the Legal Aid Foundation of Los Angeles helped the tenants organize a rent strike. Rather than pay the landlord, we deposited our rent in an escrow account.

In response to the city's legal action and the rent strike the landlord abandoned the building. Utility shutoff notices arrived, and trash piled up. Tenant organizer Enrique Velasquez of Inquilinos Unidos ("Tenants United") coached us into direct action by asking, "What are you going to do about it?" So the tenant leadership went door-to-door collecting money from each apartment to pay the utility bills, while other tenants rounded up pickup trucks to haul away trash. Every Saturday morning, residents swept and washed down the hallways, courtyard, and trash area. Enrique's passion to confront injustice with action energized us. After several months, Enrique broached the idea that we should consider buying the building. At first the idea appeared preposterous, but he introduced us to partners who could help.

Developing Partners

When the idea of purchasing the building was first considered, many of the key players of the development team were already in place—most importantly, a dedicated core of tenants. The other parties—lawyers, organizers, developers, government officials, contractors, and financiers—represented the tenants, worked for the tenants, or partnered with the tenants. The project depended on a group of residents with recognized leadership who were willing to endure conflicts, threats, and meetings several nights a week for five years.

Without partners, the best efforts of the tenants would have been in vain. The organizers helped the tenant group gain cohesion through direct action. The lawyers developed structures for the organization, and the city attorneys prosecuted the landlord. Astonishingly, this team did not come together due to strategic planning. In fact, no one can recall how these essential partners became involved. Apparently tenants independently contacted the different organizations. The assembling of such a dedicated and talented team was a gift of God.

Legal Aid Foundation of Los Angeles (LAFLA)

After organizing the rent strike, the Legal Aid Foundation of Los Angeles (LAFLA) assisted the tenants throughout the project. Elena Popp, a no-nonsense, bilingual LAFLA attorney, facilitated the transformation of a group of tenants into a nonprofit corporation. She gave us practical training (on holding meetings, making decisions, and negotiating) and legal help in incorporating as "Comunidad Cambria,"—essential to receive funding, acquire property, and execute contracts. While Elena guided tenant meetings, her colleague, Francesca Baxa, played a quieter role, drafting and negotiating our many contracts.

Southern California Mutual Housing Association (SCMHA)

Enrique Velasquez introduced us to two professors of urban planning from UCLA—Neil Richman and Allan Heskin—committed to empowering residents. They had been looking for a group to pioneer a tenant takeover in Los Angeles. They brought a network of helpful contacts: former students now working for the City of Los Angeles Housing Department, interested in funding a tenant takeover—if a sufficiently committed group of tenants could be found. Professor Heskin was also president of the Southern California Mutual Housing Association (SCMHA)[2], an organization able to coordinate the entire project. So we hired SCMHA as our development consultant. Their project managers Josefina Aguilar (at first) and Georgina Tamayo (for the bulk of the project), met regularly with our tenant leadership, wrote funding proposals, assembled the development team[3], processed paperwork, and supervised the purchase and rehabilitation of the building. Georgina Tamayo, in particular, mastered the art of knowing which decisions the tenant board needed to make, translating complicated issues into understandable terms.

City of Los Angeles and California Equity Fund (CEF)

SCMHA helped us obtain the seed money[4] needed to pay the bills while the development team prepared our application for major financing from the City of Los Angeles Housing Department.[5] The funding came in two phases. First came money to purchase and operate the building while developing construction plans and budgets. Once satisfied with our plans, the city council, supported by Councilman Mike Hernandez, approved construction funds. Early in our struggle, he had visited the building, listened to the residents, and promised to help. Comunidad Cambria applied for Federal Low Income Housing Tax Credits. A group of investors, the California Equity Fund (CEF), purchased the right to use those tax credits by forming a limited partnership with Comunidad Cambria. Funds from CEF repaid half of the city financing.[6]

Our Role as Partners

From the beginning, this was a tenant-led project. Members of InnerChange living in the Cambria Apartments supported the tenant leadership by participating as tenants, rather than as technical advisors. As the project unfolded, we saw that our skills—the ability to read contracts, spreadsheets, and plans with an intimate knowledge of the building and its residents—complemented the gifts of others within the building, who led a cohesive tenant organization.

Doing the Work

Controlling the Property

After the landlord abandoned the building, the first task was to get control of the property. A group of drug dealers moved in, claiming to be the new management, attempting to collect rent, and giving vacant apartments to their drug clients. Despite harassment and intimidation by this "new management," the tenants' rent strike held. At this point, tenants who had not yet participated in the tenant movement stepped up involvement or left the building. The tenant group slowly asserted control by paying the utilities and organizing the building clean up.

Since the landlord was not paying the mortgage, ownership of the building passed to an out-of-state heir of a previous owner. Faced with losing money and a lawsuit from the city, she put the building up for sale. Week by week, the price dropped. Negotiating through a third party to conceal our identity, the tenants made a deal with the owner October 1993. While financing for the sale was finalized, she agreed to hire our chosen property management company.

Immediately, we began the legal incorporation process. The city expressed concern over the capacity of the tenants to run the organization responsibly, so as a compromise the initial board of directors consisted of three elected tenant leaders, three representatives of community organizations, and one member appointed by the city. It turned out that the tenants always formed a majority due to their consistent attendance. In addition, the outside representatives regularly deferred to the residents. After several years, we modified the structure to contain six residents and three outside representatives.

At the time of our first elections, November 1993, two of the three from our Bible study won election. The officers were: Theresa Lopez, a native of Los Angeles; Teresa Marcial (president); Maria Contreras (secretary); and Theresa Lopez (treasurer). Only Theresa Lopez spoke English fluently, but, due to her children's involvement in gangs, the others did not trust her. In August 1994 she resigned to avoid a conflict of interest. To everyone's surprise, when the obvious candidate did not attend the election, I was unintentionally elected. Initially I was perturbed, since my intent was to only support others as leaders. Later I realized that by being elected to the board of directors, I was in a position to effectively support the tenant leadership.

We determined how much rent each tenant had been paying before the strike and which apartments were occupied by squatters, and then the tenants voted to end the rent strike. After the sale was finalized on May 31, 1994, those who did not pay rent were evicted. Thankfully, we evicted the remaining drug dealers for nonpayment of rent—much safer and easier than attempting to document their illegal activities. Nevertheless, one gang leader, who grew up in the building, asserted his right to visit his mother. Once inside, it was all too easy for him to open a back door and let in the rest of the gang. Our unarmed security guards did not dare stand between him and his mother. When the gang threatened to burn down the building, we issued fire extinguishers to every tenant, showing that we would not be intimidated. Still, nothing seemed to work to dislodge the gang.

One day in September 1994, I felt inspired that "this kind comes out only by prayer." I invited any interested tenants to pray. During the next meeting, a tenant leader was attacking me for interjecting my religious beliefs into the project when a friend whispered in my ear that the police had just arrested the key gang leader. We instructed the security guards to escort the remaining gang members out of the building. Stunned by the arrest of their leader and having no excuse for staying in the building, they left peacefully. The next day, we painted over gang graffiti during a tenant work project planned weeks earlier. Surprisingly, when the Cambria Apartments were renovated, the gang considered the building a source of neighborhood pride and did not tag it.

Developing Plans

As we struggled to take control of the building, one committee wrote bylaws and house rules; another prioritized emergency repairs. The architects designed construction plans for a major rehabilitation and reconfiguration of the building while consultants worked with the tenants on the overall financial plan.

We had to decide our ownership goals. Should we build equity or reduce rent? Own our individual units or own the building collectively? For the residents, ownership meant control of the building. We fought the landlord to improve the building, confronted gangs and drug dealers to have a safe place to live. Ownership was the ability to make decisions about our environment—from the color of the paint on the walls to the rules of conduct in the halls. Acquiring equity was not a high priority, so our consultants worked with us, planning how each household would be eligible for membership in Comunidad Cambria as long as they lived in the building. The members would elect residents to the board, which would control the property.[7] Members would not buy or sell their interest in the property; they would simply have a vote in the corporate leadership. Residents would pay just enough rent to cover operation and long-term maintenance of the building.

Taking control was also a priority in the architectural redesign. The apartment complex was anything but secure! Its courtyard opened onto the street, and each apartment had a back-door service entrance via ten unlit, rickety stairwells—ideal hiding places for gangs and the homeless. The architects proposed enclosing the courtyard and converting the back stairs into additional space for apartments. In their zeal to make the building secure, they accidentally eliminated all access to the trash bins. Because the tenants were involved in the design process, we caught this mistake and decided on a single secure back door. We also replaced the plumbing, electrical systems, doors, windows, and cabinets. Even the lead paint was stripped from the walls.[8]

Using many of the existing walls, we reconfigured the floor plan to yield forty apartments, ranging from studios to four bedrooms in order to accommodate the needs of existing tenants. A family of ten crammed into a one-bedroom apartment now lives in a four-bedroom one. A wheelchair-bound student now has wide doors and a special bath. Thanks to a lift at the entrance of the building, she is no longer trapped in her apartment and can go to college.

Dealing with Realities

Owning Slum Property

As soon as we acquired the building, we became slum landlords, despite our efforts to make emergency repairs. In October 1994, the city attorney showed up with inspectors. They were mostly sympathetic, understanding our plans to rehabilitate the building. The electrical inspector, however, felt that nothing short of a new electrical system would be safe. We would be prosecuted unless we evacuated or made prohibitively expensive temporary repairs.

We planned to move out during construction, but lacked the thousands of dollars per month required for relocation expenses—the difference in rent caused by the relocation—unless the tenants qualified for low-income housing assistance. A housing program administrator dashed our hopes by outlining all the obstacles to receiving assistance. We sat there, stunned. But then Prof. Richman asked, "What would happen if tenants were living in a building that was declared uninhabitable?" His response: "They would immediately qualify for emergency assistance." In one stroke, our two greatest problems resolved each other! However, emergency assistance was slow in coming. One week before we were required to move, only one emergency application was approved. Lawyers and housing program administrators were processing applications in the courtyard on move-out day while volunteers from suburban churches carried furniture around them!

After our departure, the empty building was at risk of vandalism. We caught a couple men with a shopping cart stealing the sprinkler system for scrap metal. Continuing irresponsibility on the part of the security company drove one tenant, Ignacio Martinez, to check on the guards twice each night for the three years that we were out of the building.

Contractor Woes

In the spring of 1995, we selected a general contractor. After he met with the architect, he revised his bid upwards. As a result of the 1994 elections, the rules for tax credit financing changed; we had to reconfigure the building to increase the number of three bedroom units. Once again, the contractor raised his bid, although the new design incurred no extra expense. Finally, just before Christmas, believing that everything was worked out, at our scheduled meeting to sign both the loan papers and the contract, to our astonishment, the contractor didn't show up! That first week in January 1996, we received a fax from the contractor. "The prices on my bid were guaranteed through the end of 1995, the new prices are…," raising his price $200,000. Locked into our financing, we asked him, "How do you propose that we can complete the project?" He outlined a stripped-down building, with no carpets, blinds, refrigerators, stoves, or community room—all with a contractor we didn't trust. We suspected that he had "low-balled" us—intentionally bidding low to get the contract, then raised his price.

In a despondent mood, the board met; nobody could think of alternatives. I thought, "Lord, I can't believe that you led us through everything for it to end like this!" Stalling for time, I proposed contacting an absent member of the development team by speakerphone. And I prayed. When the call finally went through, to my own surprise, I asked, "What about Sanderson?" Allen Sanderson, a general contractor, had helped us work up the plans in the first place. We eliminated his bid because it did not meet all our selection criteria. Nevertheless, it was competitive with the latest offer. Within a week, he was our contractor. The next day, as I told my InnerChange teammates about this episode, I started weeping. I could hardly believe that I was so passionate about carpets, refrigerators, and stoves. Slowly I realized that it wasn't about the furniture. It was about dignity. It was about someone trying to take advantage of my neighbors because they were poor. We weren't aiming for anything extravagant, just basic clean, safe housing that people need in order to function. Our decisions had been tempered with realism and practicality.

For me, this was a turning point. A committment to work together to address our common problems had been my reason for participation in the tenant movement. But I doubted the project would succeed. As I wept, I experienced the depth of God's love for my neighbors–a love expressed in such mundane things as carpets, blinds, and refrigerators. With growing confidence, I knew that God would provide every need and overcome every obstacle–a testimony of God's concern for the dignity of the poor.

Team Tensions

My conflict with the other tenant leaders was painful. Our different values and leadership styles came to a head as the building neared completion in early 1998. The other tenant leaders feared we could lose what we had worked so hard to achieve. They worried about accepting undesirable tenants, maintaining order, and losing the building to the city or investors. My actions aggravated their concerns.

One day, a stranger approached us, asking if we knew how to rent an apartment. To the consternation of the other tenant leaders, I cheerfully gave her the telephone number to call for an application. They felt I was overly trusting of a suspicious character. I, on the other hand, trusted that our application process would distinguish suitable tenants on the basis of objective criteria such as credit reports. My assumption that the system would work (or that we could correct it if there were problems) revealed my white, middle-class background. I also irritated the tenant leadership by approaching a tenant who was having trouble completing her paperwork, reminding her of the deadline, and offering to help. The leadership felt that if she couldn't be responsible, they didn't want her in the building, despite the fact that she had attended tenant meetings for five years.

This conflict reflected a fundamental disagreement about how the project should treat the weaker members of the community. I have come to see the value of strict leadership. Most of the tenants have responded to the high standards demanded. The rent is paid on time. The building is immaculate. But I grieve for those who chose to leave our community rather than conform, and I long for a more gracious atmosphere.

As painful as these conflicts were, through them we truly came to know each other. We have a mutual respect and understanding based on a shared history. We still struggle from time to time. One or two leaders consider me too soft to those on the margins and not sufficiently concerned with security and order. Meanwhile, I have come to appreciate that the type of leadership needed to seize control of a chaotic and violent situation is not always delicate in its use of power.

Discovering Insights

Development Takes Time

Tenant-controlled development of low-income housing is rare. I can see why! It is time-consuming and difficult, yet it transforms the participants and produces housing suited to the neighborhood. Our collaborators were sometimes impatient with our consensus-based decision-making, not understanding why key decisions had to wait for a tenant meeting. We operate differently than does a development corporation with a CEO. But it works. InnerChange was involved in prayer and community building for five years before anything happened with the Cambria Apartments. We ministered from the conviction that "God cares about the practical details of your life," and we provided a safe context for people to talk with each other. We could neither predict nor control how this would bear fruit. Once tenants focused on the condition of the building, it took an additional year and a half to learn how to work together, for leaders to emerge and develop credibility, and for initial actions to produce results. Even after we decided to buy the building, the acquisition and rehabilitation of the Cambria Apartments took far longer than anyone anticipated. At each step, we developed new capacities.

Other groups have attempted to replicate Cambria by sending community organizers into a building for a month. It doesn't work. A tenant movement cannot be manufactured from the outside. It must be an "inside job" initiated by committed tenants with bonds of trust. Organizers are important, but they build on what is already present.

Bridging the Cultural Gap

Bridging the cultural gap between the tenants and the many professionals who helped us proved a huge challenge. We had to operate on two levels at once—in the neighborhood and in the larger legal and financial context. The tenant leadership established hands-on control of the building by knocking on doors saying, "Your portion of this month's utility bill is ten dollars. We'll expect to see you Saturday morning for the clean-up." We established financial and legal control of the property by negotiating for its purchase with a loan of over one million dollars. Few people—such as our project manager, Georgina Tamayo, who grew up in an immigrant housing project, were capable of working on both of these levels. Our progress depended on such people. After the departure of our first project manager, several SCMHA staff struggled with the role until Georgina took the position. Although she had less housing experience, her cross-cultural skills made her far more effective. Also, the Legal Aid attorneys were extraordinarily skilled with cross-cultural communication.

Since I was a tenant, my role as a bridge person was distinct from that of Georgina and the LAFLA attorneys. Due to the InnerChange strategy[9] to move into the neighborhood, I arrived as a culture learner, unable to speak Spanish. In tenant meeting after tenant meeting, I slowly learned the language and began to understand my neighbors' values and concerns. Now I conduct meetings in Spanish, while my neighbors take pride in having taught me what I know. Over time, I developed a sense of how solutions proposed by the technical staff would play out in the neighborhood.

Because we had bonded as peers, the tenants felt free to debate solutions, accepting some of my ideas and rejecting others. Yet I underestimated the difficulty of watching my neighbors make decisions with which I disagreed. Sometimes content to be outvoted, I realized that healthy development of the group required me to lose from time to time. But on other occasions my deeply cherished values or goals were challenged; the process was agonizing! At times I almost wished that the project were not tenant-controlled; that we could just do things my way. However, I am humbled to realize how much would be lost were that the case.

Ownership Transforms

Tenant involvement often results in good development decisions. But even bad decisions are part of a growth process that can strengthen the project. Once I wanted to fire a company that was not performing. The motion failed by a single vote. We decided to give the company more time. I felt this was a terrible decision. After some reflection, I realized that the board didn't know how to evaluate the company's performance, so we developed evaluation criteria and communicated it to the company. Learning to evaluate and communicate expectations was more valuable than simply replacing the company.

The Cambria project has changed our community and everyone involved. Before we started, the teens used to say, "Nothing will ever change here." Now an atmosphere of hope extends beyond our walls. Shortly after the Cambria Apartments were completed, the owner of the house across the street decided to fix up his property and move back into the neighborhood saying, "now there is hope for this street." Other landlords soon followed suit, repairing their buildings. That Christmas, for the first time in years, someone put up a string of lights. The following year, the entire street was ablaze with Christmas decorations. The fear and darkness that had oppressed our street is gone. When it attempts to return, we confront it with a reservoir of hope and a critical mass of committed residents.

Cristina's graduation party is now long past. She and I chat in the courtyard with each other at a birthday party. Life swirls around us. Children excitedly play tag. A couple of men hang a piñata from the avocado tree. I ask Cristina about college. Then she surprises me, "I've decided that I want to be an architect." Hope. Dreams. New Life. A safe oasis for children to play. A vibrant community. This is what we work for–a taste of God's design for life.

The Point

RAY STRANSKE AND MARILYN STRANSKE

Introduction to Mixed Use and Mixed Income BY JILL SHOOK

Today, city cores are being revived. People are repelled by the "big box" and strip malls that tend to isolate and alienate society. People flock to vibrant town centers, searching for the soul and "heart," if you will, of our cities. When I moved to Pasadena in 1990, its old town was blighted. Today, Pasadena's old town teems with vibrant street life. Many dynamics have created its urban revival, not the least which is the de-segregation of land uses—a mixed-use model. Residents again live over shops and can walk out to get their morning coffee.

While riding my bike around Pasadena, I've discovered at least six somewhat dilapidated, tiny storefront grocery stores smack in the middle of residential neighborhoods. Some are still in operation, grandfathered in from a day when mixed land use in residential neighborhoods was legal. Throughout history in ancient towns of Greece, China, and walled cities of Europe, land uses have been mixed. Owners lived above or behind their corner grocery stores, watch repair shops, barber shops, and so on. Within a single block you would find residences, commerce, entertainment, lodging, and civic and cultural institutions.

> With what's been built in the last 50 years, we forgot how civilization and cities worked for 2,000 years...[T]here's a reason the butcher, the baker and the candlestick maker lived around the corner from each other.[1]

The Legacy of Mixed Use

During the industrial revolution, industrial land use became incompatible with other land uses. So zoning laws emerged, no longer allowing uses like tiny stores in the middle of a neighborhood. Zoning laws also reinforced economic and racial segregation. With the proliferation of cars and roads (roads began to be used solely for vehicles—not shared with pedestrian or bicycle traffic) and larger single-family homes, we initiated a more horizontal planning approach—a spreading of cities and an emptying of city cores.

With no city planning experience, "in 1961, at the height of urban planners' crusade to obliterate all the charming, lovable parts of American cities,"[2] Jane Jacobs wrote a book influencing a generation of city planners and architects: *The Death and Life of Great American Cities.*[3] She celebrated what nearly everyone else called slums and eyesores. These included the close-knit urban neighborhoods under assault by superhighways and high-rise housing projects and "the seemingly small things that make a city work well for its residents: the presence of people deters crime; a mix of shops and housing makes a neighborhood both convenient and lively."[4] This higher density model achieves greater energy and land use efficiency. For example, parking spaces used by residents at night have a dual use for shop customers during the day.[5] Often mixed-use models include an integration of "life-cycle housing," enabling children to afford that first apartment and grandparents to live close enough for their family to watch them.

Mixed use is a more emotional, cozy model—it creates a village, a sense of family in a day when many families are fragmented. Jacobs loved the hubbub of city life in her Greenwich Village, New York, neighborhood so much that she fought hard against its destruction by a proposed highway. God, too, loves our cities and longs for their integration and restoration. In many places the Bible records tears, anger, and dismay—emotions deeply engaged over cities and places. "The purpose of God is not to return to the garden but to go on to the restored city," says Ray Bakke.[6] We may live in a suburb lacking character, charm, and a city center. Still, God may want to use us to help a city find its "soul" and vitality. Integration of the needs of people met though well planned places is the basis of the mixed-use model.

Two other major influences profoundly shape the mixed-use model: postmodernism and the environmental movement. Postmodernism embraces "complexity over simplicity and inclusiveness over exclusiveness"[7] – all those messy complexities that make urban life so interesting. Jonathan Cohen describes *integration* as a hallmark of postmodern thinking:

> The economics of mixed-use derive from the notion that mutually supporting activities will have a synergistic effect on each other; that is, the total revenue generated will be greater than the sum of the parts. If housing and office uses are combined, for example, a market is created for shops and services which could not be

supported by either alone. This does not have to occur in one building, but the uses must be physically integrated in a way that permits pedestrian circulation between them.[8]

Environmentalists concerned with traffic, loss of open space, and the continued expansion of the urban fringe, created pressure to increase density in existing communities. From this tension emerged new zoning devices making mixed-use development possible once again. These devices included planned unit development (project approval on a case-by-case basis based on the merits of the proposal—as opposed to declaring a whole neighborhood for single family homes only) and condominium ownership (allowing housing units to be clustered at high density over commercial uses—thus maximizing land by using "air space" above buildings and parking lots.[9]) Form-based codes, an even more innovative way to allow for a mix of uses, are being adopted by cities across the country.

Combining Mixed Use with Mixed Income

Many studies have shown the virtues of higher density, but history tells us that density with too many poor people in one area does not work. Dorothy Gautreaux taught us that mixing of income levels in our neighborhoods bears many positive results. (Chapter 1 describes the Gautreaux lawsuit that forever changed our country's housing policy.) But convincing the public of this is not easy.

In an article about a proposed mixed-income beachfront development on one of the last undeveloped parcels in Los Angeles, a Brentwood real estate broker opposing the development says, "Vastly different life styles need to be separated by physical barriers and distance." The same article goes on to say that this kind of philosophy "smacks of stereotyping in the Deep South before the 1960s, not the new millennium Los Angeles."[10] Henry Cisneros, former HUD Secretary, warned in 1993, "We risk a societal collapse by the first decade of the next century if we tolerate racism and the economic isolation of millions of people."[11] Strong words—bearing resemblance to those of Old Testament prophets.

Combining *mixed-use and mixed-income models* may sound impossible. But in the narrative you are about to read, Ray and Marilyn Stranske relate how Ray courageously accomplished it. The greater up-front planning and risk, especially when seeking out different markets simultaneously—businesses, and low, moderate, and market-rate residents—is worth the effort. Ray's underlying passion for the poor of Denver brought him into relation-ship with the city's earlier players from when a mixed-used community was vibrant and alive. From these relationships an award-winning mixed-use development now stands.

But as wealth returns to our city cores, gentrification threatens to push out lower income people, making affordable housing essential if we are to have healthy God-honoring cities—where all income levels are welcome.

Ray Stranske is on the cutting edge, making this a reality in Denver, Colorado.

The Point

RAY STRANSKE WITH MARILYN STRANSKE

This year will be set apart as holy, a time to proclaim release for all who live there. It will be a jubilee year for you, when each of you returns to the lands that belonged to your ancestors. —Leviticus 25:10, NLT

At The Point, completed in 2003, stands a historical marker extolling the rich culture of the Five Points neighborhood. Behind the marker, rising four stories, is a mixed-use, mixed-income development on a corner of the five converging streets from which the area draws its name. Of the thirty-three for-sale and thirty-five rental residential units, two thirds are affordable to families making 80 percent or less of the median income. Balconies from these condos and apartments overlook the Denver skyline, with an interior landscaped courtyard. Retail and office space are on the ground floor. Some residential units have spiral staircases ascending to lofts. Others feature vaulted ceilings. Each is distinct. Residents who rent one-bedroom apartments for less than $300 per month share the elevator with residents who bought their condos for $250,000.

One day, I went down the elevator with a middle-aged couple who did not know I was the director of Hope Communities. They expressed unsolicited amazement to find a beautiful new apartment with enchanting views of the Rocky Mountains for such a low price.

As a woman toured through a model unit, she was thrilled and immediately talked of purchase. Remembering visits to her grandfather, a musician deeply involved in the Five Points made her feel she would be coming "home." A young architect now owns a unit across the hall from three college students working their way through school. On another floor a local TV news reporter is neighbor to a nonprofit executive. Many are in their first homes, thanks to a range of available purchase assistance.

Today, Miss Gladys and her daughter Birdie are delighted to rent two spacious apartments at The Point. Mother and daughter have participated in Hope Communities since 1980, when we acquired their apartments.[12] Birdie's children, now parents themselves, were some of the first involved in our summer recreation and tutoring programs. One of Birdie's daughters purchased a home nearby through our homeownership program. Reflecting on our entwined histories, I wonder how many generations will continue to be part of the community.

Next door to The Point is the famed Rossonian Hotel, a former jazz hotspot. Listening now with the ears of my imagination, I hear strains of the neighborhood's rich heritage singing a new song. The chords and complex rhythms of the past are blending with new energy and hope for the future.

Daring to Listen

Listening to History

Five Points needed a boost after decades of being maligned by the media, shunned by Denver's suburban population, redlined by lenders, and neglected by investors. The Point is our daring attempt to reignite the neighborhood's old engine.

Five Points once boasted of jazz greats such as Duke Ellington and Ella Fitzgerald. Department stores, movie houses, professional offices, barbershops, restaurants, banks, and dance halls teemed with business— run by African Americans. Churches, the YWCA, and numerous lodges made for an active community. Generations of families owned Victorian-era homes, fenced and well-maintained. Trolley cars ran from the "five points" just a few blocks to downtown. Old-timers light up reminiscing about the glory days. Of course, the downside to this thriving scene was that racism, represented in Jim Crow laws, made it difficult for the population to live anywhere else.

After fair housing legislation was passed in the 1960s, Five Points headed downhill. Most African Americans with money and influence left for neighborhoods from which they were previously excluded. Who could blame them? Yet the neighborhood exodus and urban renewal demolitions caused the population to plummet from 25,000 to 8,000 between the 1960s and the 1980s. The loss of neighbors with financial means resulted in empty buildings, failed businesses, and lost jobs.

Listening to God

"Listening" began for me in seminary in the early 1970s, hearing the quiet voice of God's desire for justice among his people. A new awareness of God's interest in the "stranger," the "poor," the "outcast" popped out from biblical passages I had read all my life. Especially fascinating was the Levitical requirement to hold a year of Jubilee every fifty years, a time when debts were forgiven and the disinherited got back their land.[13] Could God be asking us to practice a radical economic system where those who fall into poverty get a chance to start over?

The day I graduated, I intentionally moved into a low-wealth neighborhood, committing myself to my neighbors and a small urban church. Rather than seek ordination, I earned my living as an electric motor repairman. While frustrating those at the seminary placement office, I knew I was putting my degree to good use. In that urban church I met and married

Marilyn. Sharing similar commitments, we began seeking Spirit-led ways to build God's kingdom by serving our community together. We taught adult classes at church, assisted people with job and housing issues, and helped start a neighborhood association—a power base to deal with city government. We were learning to hear the economic realities of a changing neighborhood, where investors had intentionally undervalued the real estate around us.

One day we looked out our front window to see Margaret, a member of our church, with her three small children, moving by shopping cart back to the projects, a mile and one-half away. They could no longer afford the rising rents. After helping them move, Marilyn and I reflected on the inequities of a system that would allow Margaret's forced move. This experience confirmed our call to community development and to provide affordable housing. In July 1979 we quit our jobs and put our energies into a citywide coalition of pastors and church leaders that launched the work that would become Hope Communities, Inc.

Looking for faith-based models of housing production, we made visioning trips to Washington, D.C., drawing wisdom from Jubilee Housing and The Church of the Saviour (see chapter 4). Locally, with a growing group of volunteers, we researched the changing neighborhood demographics, and how it was affecting housing and displacement. After prayer, study, and discussion, we began a listening process in Five Points. Homeownership was only 22 percent, less than half of the Denver average, with the majority living below the poverty line. Almost every block was dotted with abandoned buildings; businesses ceased to attract even local residents. We started looking for our first property, knowing we had only begun to listen, only begun to learn.

Listening to the Neighborhood

Before buying the first property, we visited residents individually and in small groups. We listened as they told us of using their ovens to supplement each unit's small space heater and of putting buckets under multiple ceiling leaks. Most said they would gladly work with us to help fix things up and to serve on resident management committees.

As we contemplated Hope Communities' long-term role in the neighborhood, we needed to listen to larger numbers of residents in a more organized fashion. In 1983–84, with help from The Piton Foundation, our local councilman, and another neighborhood group, we conducted a door-to-door survey of more than 550 households, using locally trained interviewers. What we heard shaped many of our future directions. They felt rooted in Five Points and wanted to stay, and to own, but they needed help to do so. Almost everyone wanted more places to shop. Over half were willing to work with neighbors to address identified problems such as crime and trash.

Moved by the findings, Hope Communities' board and staff decided to concentrate on the Five Points neighborhood. To achieve stability, a neighborhood must have many homeowners—people investing in the area's future. So, we initiated our first-time homeowners program and educational programs that reweave the sense of community among local residents, churches, and agencies. Eventually, we expanded our housing efforts to other neighborhoods. By the end of 2003, Hope Communities had renovated or built 750 housing units, with more than 100 of these sold to neighborhood residents.

Listening to Stakeholders

Hoping to increase retail in the area in the 1990s, Denver planners placed the first segment of the city's new light rail system along Welton, Five Point's main business street. But local business people protested, fearing that the project would disrupt their businesses. And, in fact, the construction all but destroyed some of them.

In response to the problem, design professionals, city workers, RTD officials,[14] neighborhood leaders, and institutions organized planning meetings. Their conclusion: dense mixed-use developments—combining residential with commercial uses—would take advantage of the new light rail corridor. The ease of light rail transportation would invite downtown workers and students as well as current neighborhood residents to provide an economic boost to the area. The concept of mixed-use development on Welton Street was a new idea to me; but as my friend Nate, a longtime resident and business owner commented, "We've always had mixed use on Welton. When I was growing up, my parents had a shop opening onto the sidewalk, and we lived in back."

Taking the outcomes of the planning process seriously, our board and staff teamed up with Five Point Business Association. The objectives: to keep income circulating in the neighborhood by creating or expanding neighborhood businesses providing goods and services that people need and want. Second, create exciting new housing opportunities for a variety of income levels in highly visible locations close to the light rail. We envisioned people walking safely on their streets day and night, visiting with each other, frequenting user-friendly businesses, with access to the light rail. Five Points would again be a vibrant place with the pride of belonging.

It wouldn't be easy. Development of new projects can be a lightening rod for controversy. "Daring to listen" implies the willingness to become involved in the discourse and disagreement, hopefully on the way to resolution. Five Points is a complex neighborhood with competing interests. Long-term low-income residents want to maintain their web of relationships and familiar surroundings. Newer residents want to "clean up" the neighborhood and make it trendier.[15] Long-term businesses seek to maintain their fragile existence, dreaming of a return to the glory days. Cautious new businesspeople explore opportunities, considering whether to risk their savings, while attracting business loans. A committed core continues to encourage people to come together to hear each other's unique perspectives. As we got to know each other, the possibility existed that old factions could give way to a dynamic new community, richer and stronger than the sum of its parts.

Developing Partners

Beginning as a coalition of churches, from the start we have sought partners. We believe in listening to a multitude of counselors and cultures to make and implement wise decisions. We belong to local and national trade associations. We finance deals with benevolent investors: individuals, corporate, and numerous government sources. We seek to maintain good relationships with all of our partners, including elected officials.

The Five Points Business Association

In 1999, when two seasoned neighborhood organizations combined their strengths to work toward mutually beneficial goals, The Point was born. Hope Communities had twenty years of experience developing affordable housing, arranging the financing and working with the city and state. The Five Points Business Association had thirty-five years of experience representing its member businesses. We would need every ounce of skill and experience that our alliance could forge.

As an active ten-year member of the Five Points Business Association, often the only Caucasian at business meetings, I admired their decades-long struggle to make a living. At best, the wider Denver business community often ignored them. I won a place at the table as we worked on our annual Juneteenth event and other civic functions, eventually serving on the Association board as treasurer. Other Hope Communities' staff and residents participated in the Juneteenth Parade and staffed booths at street fairs.[16]

The partnership between our organizations was a natural fit—an alliance between tried and trusted people, accomplishing more than either of us could have done alone. Jamaican-born Marva Coleman, executive director of Five Points Business Association, often tells people that she and I are joined at the hip. Without trusted relationships, launching a bold project would have been both inappropriate and politically difficult. Even so, with Hope Communities' experience in the building industry, our long history in the community, and our racially diverse staff and board, some still perceived us as outsiders. Gratefully, I heard Association members admiring the construction progress, referring to it as "our building." And, indeed, it is.

Government

To attract capital to a neighborhood with a history of disinvestment, our expensive structure required beneficent partners. Since city governments have a stake in the vitality of all their neighborhoods, the city was the first place we looked. Government programs at all levels are likely to have pots of money, such as low-interest loan pools, to bridge the gap between modern-day development and construction costs and the amount that low- and middle-income citizens can afford to pay for housing. The city made loans to purchase land, which were later paid off with construction funds. The Colorado Division of Housing provided grants and low-interest deferred loans. By taking the risk position, government-backed money pools enabled the project to attract a large construction loan from a major bank.

Mission to the Americas

At first we didn't recognize the immense importance of our partnership with Mission to the Americas. When they planned a headquarters move from Wheaton, Illinois, to the Denver area, they sought my help to locate a suitable site. With their desire to own offices in a low-wealth neighborhood similar to communities they serve, we saw a connection. Their offices were integrated into our project, with an opportunity to design their own space. Their contract to purchase, along with their earnest money, gave us the additional credit needed to enhance security for our construction loan. At an energetic celebration on the plaza, Rick Miller, their executive director, addressed the crowd, dedicating the offices of Mission to the Americas to God's work.

The Neighborhood

Hope Communities and Five Points Business Association held several information-gathering sessions with neighborhood residents and community organizations to test our development plans. Was our neighborhood ready for our "product"? Were we still operating in line with established community goals? Indeed, the vision set a few years prior continued to govern plans. The Point was the fulfillment of a neighborhood vision, not a developer's opportunistic move.

Doing the Work

Acquiring the Land

As chief developer of in our partnership, I began to look for land. Our first choice was a parcel on a corner of the Five Points intersection where a tired building stood, once home to a chicken franchise, now a convenience store adjacent to a sizable parking lot. The parking lot, divided into two parcels, had two separate owners. If we built there, we would need all three parcels, which meant negotiating with three owners to assemble the combined 37,000 square feet. But none of the owners had plans to sell.

From experience, we knew that just having the backing of the neighborhood and the city does not guarantee an easy property purchase. In fact, owners often increase their perceived value of the property when others express interest. We were relieved and excited when, after long months of negotiating, we finally made a deal to purchase these parcels.

Assembling the Financing

With a $13 million budget,[17] our bottom line was not to maximize profits but to rent to low-income families earning between 30 and 80 percent of median income,[18] and selling a third of the condos to low-income families. Retailers in disinvested neighborhoods also need special breaks to start and keep businesses running. It required multiple layers of public and private sources. With the capital raised applying only to particular uses, and with incompatible funding requirements, financing a mixed-use project is especially complex.

A tax credit allocation made the rental portion affordable. To secure the credit, we had to complete the purchase of the land and have all financing commitments in place by the end of 2000. That took all our time and energy, forcing us to delay attention to project design, except for the schematic phase. Now the challenge was to make the project design fit the budget created by the financing commitments!

Hiring the Contractors

As we entered the design phase of The Point, given its size and complexity, we realized our selected small minority-owned neighborhood contractor would need help. We interviewed some of the larger minority-owned firms to assist him. Reviewing their past completed projects, none of these firms had built multifamily wood frame residential projects. Given our extremely tight budget and timeline, we feared the lack of experience on our specific building type could result in a missed deadline or budget estimate. Later, our decision for a contractor with significant experience was strongly criticized.

Property development always includes pressured moments, but The Point project was pressured throughout. Frequent project delays created constant tension as deadlines loomed.[19] Yet, in December 2002, the construction was completed, and the building placed in service. Had we finished one week later we would have lost the tax credit allocation, and with it, 15 percent of project funds.

Dealing with Realities

Confronting Disaster

On a cold Saturday in September 2001, after more than two years of planning, over one hundred people gathered for the official groundbreaking. The mayor, our councilwoman, and other dignitaries dug their shovels into the ground as television cameras recorded the event. Elated, we didn't mind the cold weather. Miss Charlene, a longtime proprietor of Charlene's House of Beauty and chaplain of the Five Points Business Association, led us in prayer. "Lord," she prayed, "Give us a strong love for one another!" Little did we realize how much we would need that love.

Three days later, September 11, 2001, brought incredible challenge to our fragile effort. Denver's already tenuous real estate market was set back in ways we would not fully appreciate for months to come. With great effort we had gathered the required number of presales to obtain construction financing, but after that tragic day we had few sales, forcing us to restructure our construction loan to allow a slower payback. Once construction was complete, sales were slow despite a full-scale marketing effort, causing nervous lenders and further difficulties in attracting prospective buyers, a cycle hard to overcome.

Of the 6,100 square feet of retail space, 2,500 had been leased. Our goal of lively shops within a few steps of new residences was slowed by the economy. Nevertheless, Blackberries, a coffee and ice cream shop, the dream of an enterprising young woman, opened in one of our three retail spaces. Residents are excited to have a sidewalk café, spilling out onto the plaza. With firms throughout the metro area going out of business, many losing jobs and moving away, retail property owners are in tight competition. Dreams, even those seeking to fulfill the Bible's vision of community, are not exempt from hard times.

Coping with Project Delays

This was hardly our first challenge. In the midst of designing The Point, our architect left his firm and moved to another office. A fight ensued between architectural firms, halting our project until a solution was negotiated. When the design was finally complete, our contractors concluded they could not build the project for the budgeted amount. The financing plan, assembled the previous year, could not be changed, unless we sought additional funds and renegotiated with all the players. It would take months, if it could be done at all. A new (to us), well-known, and experienced contracting team evaluated the project over a weekend and determined they could meet our project budget and deadline, ominously near.

Our sense of relief was premature. Minority contractors, interviewed previously, wanted another chance to bid on the project. This filled precious months with rancorous disputes as our beleaguered team put together a contractor team who could complete the project on time and on budget. We hoped minority contractors would view their partnership with an experienced builder as an opportunity to advance their own construction credentials. Yet, in one case a disgruntled local plumbing contractor—not selected—said the project would end up as nothing but a hole in the ground.

Hearing this, our selected plumbing contractor felt threatened and pulled off the job. A new contractor was found and brought up to speed.

This conflict is emblematic of a dilemma in efforts to develop communities. On the one hand, our goal is to produce housing as affordable as possible—critical when many families now pay 40 or more percent of their incomes for housing. On the other hand, while we want to give preference to local minority contractors, their costs are sometimes higher or, if the contractors are young, they may have yet to demonstrate their capacity to complete the work on time and on budget. Our pockets were not deep enough to absorb delays or cost overruns, which then have to be passed on in the final cost to renters or owners. Which is more important: affordable housing or construction work for neighborhood contractors? On The Point project we sought a difficult balance between these goals. The resulting reality was imperfect. Past societal injustices breed misunderstandings and raise old wounds for which there may be no healing in the moment.

We might have abandoned the project early on had we foreseen the challenges. For-profit developers would jump at the chance to do projects such as The Point if they were easy or readily profitable. Risks are inherent when daring to change the usual equation of who gets decent housing and who doesn't. Through tears and laughter, we are comforted by the words of our longtime mentor Gordon Cosby, founder of The Church of the Saviour in Washington, D.C. (see chapter 4), "Sometimes the more you lean into the vision, the more absurd it becomes." Jesus spoke about "counting the cost." For us that means measuring a vision of justice-made-practical by the best planning, the most innovative financing, and the most constant monitoring we can achieve. It means willingness to deal with and learn from misunderstandings, setbacks, and mistakes as we move through uncharted territory. It means making our best prayerful evaluations and moving forward if the still small voice continues to beckon.

Discovering Insights

At Hope Communities, we regularly evaluate our efforts, what is going on around us, and what we are learning from our experience. We take time to give thanks and enjoy successes. As we reflect, a few insights come into focus.

> *The power of community.* Coming from a large cross-section of neighborhood residents, leaders, city staff, public transit workers, and design professionals, the vision resulted in something larger than any one group dared dream. Together we saw beauty and justice made concrete.
>
> *The value of deepening relationships with neighbors forged by struggle over time.* The process was costly in terms of time, but rich in growing relationships among various neighborhood constituencies.

The value of deepening relationships with Denver's business community. Hope Communities' real estate committee of successful developers, brokers, and lenders advises our management and board on potential projects. The Point opened their eyes to the economic and social realities faced by such neighborhoods. The project's visibility strengthened our relationship with Denver corporate partners interested in successful urban neighborhoods.

The need to be ready when the outside world takes notice. During construction, the Fannie Mae Corporation, a buyer of tax credits for the project, used our site for a press conference. Present were the Secretary of HUD and most of the Colorado congressional delegation. Because affordable housing was a major issue in an intense citywide election, many would-be city leaders visited The Point seeking to understand mixed-use, mixed-income developments. In addition, we were nominated for a major award by the Downtown Denver Partnership. When the outside world takes notice, opportunities are gained to tell the story, challenging stereotypes and misconceptions. This leads to new visions, new projects, and new relationships.

The ability to learn from criticism rather than to be paralyzed by it. I overheard comments from a group of African American youth as they walked by The Point construction, "Yeah, this is going to be for those rich white folks." While the comment was not based in fact, it reminded me that not all observers of the same event see the same thing.

The humility to acknowledge how unexpected events force change despite our best, most determined efforts. In the early 1980s, we filled six large poster boards with photos of abandoned buildings in Five Points. Planning for The Point twenty years later, we had difficulty finding available land. Our best efforts played a role in revitalizing the area, but the hot real estate market forced prices up.

Each new project deepens our trust in God, giving us hope for community transformation and building God's kingdom. For twenty-five years Hope Communities has partnered with others to this end. We are sustained by the vision of justice, by God's obvious hand as we follow his lead, and by our many mentors. Gordon Cosby, to whom we dedicate this chapter, said,

Hope is a form of faith that tends to produce what it sees.
Despair is a form of faith that tends to produce what it sees.[20]

Thanks, Gordon, for reminding us of the important choice that is always ours to make. Isn't that "the point"?

My Friend's House

Home Rehab Company

MARY KING

Introduction to the Faith-based Housing Model

BY LISA TREVINO CUMMINS

I write this after almost fifteen years of work with the poor, mostly in community development banking in "redlined" low- and moderate income neighborhoods. Three stories have shaped my role in faith based affordable housing. The Gonzales family, renting a home in a San Antonio inner-city barrio, would soon become homeless. For more than twenty years, they had raised all their children in this small, dilapidated home. With only an outhouse, Mr. Gonzalez eventually saved enough money and built a bathroom himself. When the county judge asked me to intervene, we discovered that the landlord had not paid the taxes and, in fact, no longer owned the property. The Gonzales family was completely unaware—and the landlord continued to collect their rent. Even more heart wrenching, Mr. Gonzales had a low-wage job, but his tenure over ten years with the same company made him "bankable"—eligible to buy a home—but he never knew he had that option. Eventually I made a twenty-year mortgage loan to him with monthly payments equal his rent. If only his church, to which he was faithful, had informed him of his opportunity to own a home and build economic strength.

The second story involves my first occasion to pray a blessing over a house. I had been involved with numerous initiatives that resulted in the development of thousands of new housing units, but I had never prayed over one of them. As I prepared to pray, I realized that while the work of building homes is noble, it is not sufficient. It would not be a home unless joy and peace resided there. The new or improved home is symbolic of the work that must also happen within the inhabitants of these dwellings.

The third story occurred while I struggled with the effectiveness of community development banking. I discovered the power of congregations working in a community. My husband and I watched God's love transform one of St. Louis's poorest neighborhoods. New City Fellowship intentionally placed their church building and administrative offices in the heart of the poor neighborhood they were seeking to reach. They chose to reach this neighborhood by living out the mandate to love their neighbors as themselves.

Work teams repaired the homes of the elderly. Ex-gang members worked alongside the men of the church and earned a modest income. With so much time spent in the neighborhood, some church members moved from their suburban homes to become literal neighbors. Creating a separate nonprofit organization (a community development corporation, or CDC), they followed a God-filled strategy to purchase vacant property and boarded-up homes. They developed a business plan, listened to the stakeholders, engaged mortgage lenders and counselors, set up lines of credit, developed relationships, and more. The learning curve for these talented, energetic, fully invested people of faith was steep; but they went at it with an urgency that demonstrated results within a few years. Once the homes were built or renovated, families living in the neighborhood as renters became owners, like the Gonzalez family in San Antonio.

These stories and experiences fueled a passion for and a calling to work that connects, strengthens, and supports the work of community-serving faith-based organizations. My husband and I pursued this calling back in 2001 through the halls of the White House, where I launched the White House Faith-Based and Community Initiative and assisted HUD and the Corporation for National and Community Service in their efforts to partner with faith-based organizations.

Through my career in banking, and now through Urban Strategies, I have had the privilege of getting to know many community heroes. One such hero is Pastor Jim Ortiz of My Friend's House in Whittier, California. Mary King writes Pastor Jim's story, showing he is on the "radical side" of living out his faith. Through My Friend's House, Pastor Jim is leading efforts to transform his neighborhood through an opportunity provided by the federal government to rehab abandoned, foreclosed properties and resell them to low-income families. As you read about his work, examine the individual and corporate gifts and talents in your congregation and discover how these resources can play a role in placing God's imprint on neighborhoods and families throughout our country.

Home Rehab Company

BY MARY KING

"We must give them both a loaf of bread and the bread of life."—Pastor Jim Ortiz

This story is simple. A few Christians in Southern California simply responded to Jesus when he said to feed the hungry, satisfy the thirsty, clothe the naked, and invite in the stranger. Yet the impact of their faithfulness is profound.

Alfredo

Alfredo Valero cycled his rusty bicycle down South Norwalk Boulevard on that hot, dry fall day in 1998. A former member of the "Quiet Village Gang," he had been in and out of prison on drug charges, petty theft, and DUIs. Now thirty-five, recently out of jail, he rode his bicycle through town looking for menial jobs to support his wife and two children. Stopping at the beige adobe church building with the sign "My Friend's House," he found Pastor Jim Ortiz. Pastor Jim suggested sweeping leaves on the gravel parking lot, mowing the lawn, cleaning two classrooms. Throughout the day, they shared Pepsi and conversation…As the sun set, Alfredo received his wages and learned of a Father, ready to forgive his past. Pastor Jim Ortiz and the Youth Pastor Marcos Flores prayed with Alfredo to deliver him from drugs and alcohol through a Savior who would help him begin afresh. Overwhelmed by the presence of Jesus Christ, which came like an emotional power surge, Alfredo physically fell backward. He experienced the touch of God. Pastors Jim and Marcos helped him stand up.

Alfredo brought his wife and two children to worship services at My Friend's House, a charismatic Assembly of God Church. God gave him new life, yet he struggled with the consequences of a destructive lifestyle, Attention Deficit Disorder, a hard time reading, and difficulty finding regular work.

Alfredo applied for a job with Jerry Morgan of JM Services/Construction in Whittier, a private contractor who worked with My Friend's House under agreement that they could send him former alcoholics and felons. Alfredo learned how to paint, and other renovation skills. But he had a relapse, stopped coming to work on time, and lost his job. Jerry showed him grace, reinstating his employment when Alfredo sought forgiveness. Five years later, Alfredo continues to work for Jerry. A church willing to take a chance helped him stand.

Daring to Listen

James (Jim) Ortiz was born in 1948 in East Harlem of Puerto Rican parents. When Jim was twelve, his father passed away, and Jim's mother moved to Southern California. That same year Jim accepted the Lord; by fifteen, he knew God had called him to be a preacher. At eighteen, during the Jesus Movement (1966–1970), he attended Southern California College (now Vanguard University) and met his wife Yolanda (Yolie). Deliberating their future, Jim envisioned leading evangelical crusades in South America. Yolie's childhood friend, Andy, spoke frequently of a vision for reaching kids in East L.A. "I didn't want to go to East L.A.," Jim recounts. So instead, he became a youth pastor in Oxnard, California. This lasted six months. "I started with five kids in my ministry, and I ended with one. I decided then to be obedient…and go to East L.A."

Jim and Yolie found jobs and evangelized during off hours. In those years Whittier Boulevard was the cruising capital. "We'd tell the kids about the Lord while sitting on their car fenders…and not a soul came to Christ." Such moments proved ultimately defining, as Jim later witnessed the impact of uniting words with works. When an Assembly of God director sent fifteen Anglo kids to "the mission field of East L.A.," 160 youth accepted Christ. On July 14, 1971, following a concert in a borrowed church, Jim stood up and announced a new Bible study. Forty kids showed up. So began his congregation. One of Jim's first financial supporters was Chuck Smith, who wrote a $150 check for the first month's rent at their storefront location. "We were a bunch of street kids," Jim recounts. "I was only 22 years old. We were all very excited to see how God provided."

The group took 160 submissions for a church name. The most votes went to "My Friend's House," a name from two street kids, who explained: "When we came here, we found a friend for the first time in our lives."

Satisfaction through Action

Despite the abundance of commitments to Christ and new life, Jim felt inwardly absorbed by all the pastoral duties. "We were losing community focus and becoming church focused," Jim explained. He missed going out to the lost, the clear mission of Jesus. When John the Baptist expressed doubts, Jesus responded by framing his credibility in the evidence of his actions:

> Jesus had just then cured many people of diseases, plagues, and evil spirits, and had given sight to many who were blind. And he answered them, "Go and tell John what you have seen and heard: the blind receive their sight, the lame walk, the lepers are cleansed, the deaf hear, the dead are raised, the poor have good news brought to them." (Lk. 7:21–22)

Following Jesus' example, Jim again began to proclaim Christ, through word and loving action. "The mission of our church is to preach the gospel–the mission of Jesus in Luke 4–in such a way that people can see, hear, and touch the love of Christ," Jim said.

In 1996, in obedience to this mission, Jim helped form the "Whittier Area Evangelical Ministerial Alliance," bringing local church pastors together for prayer. Sharing their collective burden for the city, they united with a vision to serve their neighbors. Jim suggested a "Convoy of Hope Food Distribution," based on a model by Operation Blessing. The pastors cautiously agreed.

On April 19, 1997, almost 1000 volunteers from twenty-five local churches came to the Pioneer High School football stadium at 4 a.m. They handed out 110,000 pounds of free groceries, ministered to almost 7,000 people, and had about 2,300 conversions to Christ. Jim recounts, "I just broke down crying…to see the possibilities when churches come together, putting aside their doctrinal differences to focus on sharing the good news in word and deed." The excitement overflowed into the following weeks. "We need to do more of this!" local pastors responded. They discussed community needs, identifying low-income housing as one. As they explored opportunities with HUD, several pastors balked at the amount of ground-work, the risks, and the unknown. But My Friend's House signed up.

Developing Partners
HUD and David Zepeda

In the 1970s, HUD developed a program specifically aimed for non-profit organizations. The organizations were to bring the homes up to code and create viable living conditions, and then resell them to low- or medium-income families. When he began to explore HUD low-income homes in 1998, Pastor Jim had the faith and support of the My Friend's House board of elders. To acquire a property, the church put up its own church building (built in 1958, purchased in 1977) as collateral. The congregation was willing to take this risk to combat poverty. Jim's assistant, Bessie, ensured that accounting records were in tip-top shape, as they were subject to scrutiny by a new set of eyes at HUD.

David Zepeda had accepted Christ through Pastor Jim in 1975 and then spent fourteen years pastoring another local church. In 1999, David joined My Friend's House staff as Director of "Metro Impact," an umbrella label for the church's community/economic development and social services programs. The church developed food and clothing programs, a child care center, drug intervention, family counseling, a computer learning lab, an after-school tutoring center, ESL classes for parents, and now a housing program called the "Open Door Development Project." David's seven years of work as a journeyman roofer made him a perfect head of this program. "I don't understand how people can read the Sermon on the Mount and not recognize our calling to social justice," he contemplated. "It's all there."

Jerry Morgan—Construction Contractor

Jerry Morgan, founder of JM Services/Construction, a for-profit company of twenty people, proved a great partner in the home rehab effort.

Jerry shared the church's heart for the neighborhood. "From a Christian upbringing," he testifies, "God has blessed me. I feel an obligation to give back. I give money—but this is just another part of that." Jerry takes time to teach the needed skills when he could hire someone already skilled and get the job done in half the time. He promised his employees L.A. Dodgers and Angel's tickets as rewards for good work. But sometimes they have broken trust. Jerry recounts, "I have been burned a few times—one of the guys was something of a con artist, he knew what to say, and I helped him buy a car, pay rent, only to find out he was doing drugs. He ultimately disappeared with all my major power tools." Despite losing thousands of dollars in some cases, Jerry perseveres. "God, you've really tested me!" Yet, he resolves, "It's not that I won't do it again. I just do it with more caution."[1]

Realtors, Lenders, Insurance, and Legal Counsel

When My Friend's House signed up with HUD, countless real estate agents and lenders started knocking on the church doors. Several agents, due to the nature of the sale, were willing to discount their usual 6 percent agent commission to 3 to 4 percent. The church teamed with Wells Fargo and Bank of America to host seminars for potential HUD home buyers, including members of the congregation. Lenders trusted the project, since most loans come directly from HUD. The church found how essential it is for nonprofit organizations—especially churches—entering the ministry of providing homes to understand HUD's unique qualifications for a homebuyer. Fire and liability insurance are required on the homes during the reconstruction, so the church built relationships with insurance agents. Additionally, legal counsel was necessary on HUD applications, and purchase and selling documents, so the church partnered with attorneys.

FAME and Churches United for Economic Development

One day in 1998, Jim attended a luncheon lecture with Victor, a church member. They sat near the front to be close to the podium. As the event got started, the Reverend Mark Whitlock, founder of FAME (First African Methodist Episcopal) Renaissance, the country's largest African American community development corporation (CDC), sat down at the table. So did the President of Bank of America and several VPs. Looking at Victor, Jim said, "I think we are sitting at the wrong table!" and started to get up.

Mark grabbed Jim by the shoulder and insisted, "There are no reservations here. You sit next to me." Five minutes into the conversation, with a streak of boldness Jim asked Mark to stand up with him. "Can you tell me how many brown faces you see?" Jim asked as they surveyed the crowd. Mark looked at Jim surprised and responded: "We have been trying to connect with our Hispanic brethren and have not been able to; would you help me?"

So began a unique partnership. The relationship between FAME and My Friend's House helps to provide ownership training, mortgages, access to economic development expertise, encouragement, and access to joint grants. Additionally, My Friend's House was invited to join a collaboration of African American, Asian, and Hispanic congregations committed to business incubators and low-income housing. This group, "Churches United for Economic Development," was started by Reverend Mark Whitlock and Dr. Don Miller, Director of USC's Center for the Study of Religion and Civic Culture.

Doing the Work

Gaining initial certification from HUD took approximately six months. It involved reading about one hundred pages of instructions and filling out twenty separate sections of the application, while providing forty pages of photocopied financial statements and documentation. The church recertifies its eligibility with HUD every two years, taking about three months each time. The three-part process referred to as "Requisition, Rehabilitation, and Resale" takes from six to nine months.

Requisition

Requisition begins on a Tuesday morning, when the weekly list of available foreclosed and repossessed homes comes available on the HUD Web site. After sorting through fifty to sixty homes in Los Angeles, Riverside, and San Bernardino Counties, David Zepeda picks approximately ten to fifteen homes, and does "drive bys" over the course of the week, often through the most depressed areas. The following Monday, he puts in his bids. Nonprofit organizations receive a 30 percent discount from the HUD price. Two days after bidding, HUD randomly selects buyers, requiring a $2000 deposit per home. The buyers have seven days to finance the purchase, with thirty days to close escrow. The church bids on homes selling for between $75,000 and $100,000. Open Door usually puts down about $7000 to $10,000, borrowing the remainder from HUD with a six-month adjustable rate loan. The requisition part of the process generally takes a month and a half, David says.

Rehabilitation

After a successful HUD home purchase, rehabilitation begins. Jerry Morgan and his crews re-tile bathrooms, fix kitchens, put in new toilets, paint the walls, or whatever necessary. They don't know the extent of the work until they are far into the reconstruction. Some homes must be rewired; others replumbed. David would often put on his jeans and spend a week replacing the roof. The cost of the renovation usually totals $25,000 to $40,000, taking around three months.

Resale

When renovation is complete, a real estate agent shows the newly renovated home to low- and medium-income families. The agent finds qualified buyers according to zip codes. Extended deadlines, nonqualified buyers, and difficult credit histories can hinder a quick sale. The sale cycle generally takes three months.

The church cannot sell a HUD home for a profit of more than 10 percent. For example, if a home cost $75,000 to acquire and $25,000 to rehab, resulting in $100,000 of total cost, My Friend's House cannot sell it for more than $110,000. With unanticipated reconstruction costs, the goal of providing housing that is truly affordable is a challenge. In the end, My Friend's House generally completes the entire process with approximately $4000 to $7000 in profit–amounting to less than minimum wage for the time investment of David and other church staff. "We clearly don't do this for the money," Pastor Jim jokes.

Dealing with Realities

Pastor Jim notes that dealing with the bureaucracy at HUD is the most difficult challenge. Lost paperwork, long hold times for phone calls, and deferrals of needed answers are hurdles he cites.

Recertification

Two years after the initial certification process in 1998, My Friend's House submitted paperwork for their recertification. But in 2000, this HUD program had come under great scrutiny because of scandal and fraud. Hundreds of firefighters and teachers coast to coast were allowed to purchase HUD homes in depressed areas at a 50 percent discount, but many violated agreements to live in the home for at least three years. Realtors also abused HUD regulations, filing as fictitious nonprofit organizations. "I remember sixty-five realtors in L.A. being indicted by the FBI," Pastor Jim recalls.

As a result, HUD went through a major housecleaning in 2000, denying all requests for recertification, requiring nonprofit organizations to start over with the six-month certification. After striving to meet all of HUD's requests with meticulous detail and the highest standard of ethics, Pastor Jim was incensed. He wrote a letter expressing his frustration to Father Joseph Hacala, Director of HUD's Nonprofit Program under Andrew Cuomo, Clinton's HUD Secretary. Later that fall, both Father Hacala and Pastor Jim attended a HUD Conference in Los Angeles. Pastor Jim, with great passion and gentle zeal, cornered Father Hacala in the hallway and asked if he received his letter.

"Yes, Reverend Ortiz, I did," the priest replied.

"Well, what did you think?" Jim asked. My Friend's House received its full two-year recertification letter in the mail two weeks later.

Unrealistic Capacity

Initially, Open Door Development Project claimed five houses without realizing their capacity to only do two. Because of the $2000 upfront deposits on each home and additional incurred costs, the church lost $10,000. The learning curve was steep.

A Wait and See Approach

The hot demand for real estate in Southern California has greatly hindered the Open Door Development Project. "Affordable housing is an oxymoron in L.A.," David notes, explaining why they have not invested in HUD homes since 2001. "Homes that historically cost less than $100,000 are now all priced over $400,000. Real estate investors are bidding $20,000 to $30,000 above the asking price on HUD homes." To obtain a HUD home in this increasing demand market, the high upfront cost could not be covered while maintaining affordability. The church's "wait and see" approach is wise. If the current real estate market is as highly overvalued as many believe, David notes, "in time we will see a huge wave of foreclosures flood HUD. This would be very unfortunate. But we will be trying to salvage and redeem that housing."

Discovering Insights

With passion and perseverance, My Friend's House refurbished eleven HUD homes. At an average price of $100,000, this small church in East Los Angeles has turned around almost $1 million in low-income housing. Eleven families have celebrated Christmas, sang happy birthday, hosted fiestas, and cooed while watching a child cross the floor in their own homes. The faithfulness of My Friend's House has had an impact that reaches far beyond these eleven families.

HUD asked My Friend's House to contribute literature and advice to assist churches across the country to form partnerships with HUD. The church created a list of "Top 10 Reasons Churches Should Team with HUD," thus inspiring church communities seeking to provide low-income housing.

GATEWAY, a South Whittier Redevelopment Organization that partners with the L.A. Design Center, a nonprofit organization well known for beautiful affordable housing, contracted with David Zepeda to complete eighty low-income residential units.

A vice president in the University of California system invited My Friend's House to participate in a "University Community Partnership Program" to tutor children. Pastor Jim says this never would have happened without the church maintaining their focus on caring for the wider community through Open Door Development Project and other Metro Impact programs.

By serving low-income families outside the four walls of the church, My Friend's House witnessed a flood of blessings pour into their own congregation. For example, Jerry Morgan salvaged twelve used modular portables from the City of L.A. Sewage Treatment Department. My Friend's House now uses them for summer/after-school programs.

Also, by actively engaging in economic development, the church has brought valuable financial lessons to their members. For example, when purchasing a home, rules for HUD home buyers dictate that one should not take on a debt load that absorbs over 30 percent of one's annual income. While Christians with little guidance from their churches are throwing such time-tested investment principles out the window, My Friend's House is helping members achieve these goals. David Zepeda is especially sensitive to stewardship principles, and hosts Crown Financial Seminars and other debt/investment workshops. He notes: "As a pastor, I'm a student of culture. Excesses are apparent in the housing market, which is symptomatic of the consumer culture to which we are all susceptible. When consumerism increases, tithing diminishes."

The key insights Pastor Jim stumbled upon through this entire process are the church's untapped potential and the church establishment's failure of imagination. He says: "There are far more capacities for engaging in community development projects than churches realize. They have so many resources to leverage! And yet, I see a lot of unwillingness to try something new...only doing what is easy and comfortable. But we must take risks!" To follow Jesus requires risk, to stand up and obey Christ's mission, resulting in multiplied joy and blessing.

Raising Lazarus from the Dead

RICHARD TOWNSELL

Introduction to Indigenous Property Management
BY DON MINER WITH JILL SHOOK

You are about to read Richard Townsell's story of raising "Lazarus"–a burned-out building. But resurrection wasn't enough–it also needed proper management. Churches and nonprofit organizations historically don't tend make the best landlords, but Townsell figured out how.

Before you read Townsell's experience, let me share how I figured out how to manage buildings–managing my first building at seventeen. My parents moved to Seattle, Washington, while I stayed behind in Spokane to graduate from high school. I also became the manager of our family's apartments. My high school Spanish teacher wondered why I was so tired in class. After showing her the building, she remarked to our class, "Don has the responsibility of a grown man!"

Since that day, I have managed over two thousand properties (representing countless units) in Los Angeles County as a Trust Real Estate Property Manager for Bank of America.

Developing Respect and Pride

In a building behind the Ambassador Hotel, the trustor/owner collected rent by bringing a box of cash to the building. He cashed the tenant's employment checks, kept the rent amount, and gave them the difference. I would not disrespect the tenants in this way. When I told him I had my own management style, he predicted: "You will never get the rent!" But I made it clear that it's not my responsibility to collect rent; it's the tenant's responsibility to pay. I set up an account at the local Bank of America where tenants could cash their checks and deposit their rent. I never asked anyone for his or her rent and never had any problem with late pay.

139

As I made my rounds, I discovered all the units were furnished with tired old furniture the tenants didn't like. By letter, I awarded the tenants ownership of the furniture and requested that any discarded furniture be placed behind the building for weekly pick-ups—amounting to loads of furniture! One day, the trustor observed furniture being delivered to the building. Assuming I was purchasing it, he objected. He was quite surprised when I explained that the tenants were not only paying their rent, but also getting their own furniture. A sense of pride was developing among the residents.

On-site Indigenous Leaders

One tenant showed such pride from the beginning. "I'd love to clean this place up!" she said one day. She became my resident manager. I called her my "champion." She had mattresses in every room of her unit. If she could handle that many people, she could handle the whole building. Her job to be my eyes and my ears helped me do my job as the property manager. Her broad smile and daily sweeping of the corridors turned this building around. She received a well-deserved rent deduction, and I received immense satisfaction and increased value on our bank's asset.

I found it beneficial to have an on-site indigenous leader to manage my buildings—my "champions." The story you are about to read is about the importance of indigenous leadership. Richard quickly learned that to instill pride in the community, they had to employ from the community. They also learned that professional management is not synonymous with good management. Without good management, Lazarus could again become a blight on the area.

Wayne Gordon, pastor and founder of the Lawndale Community Church in the Chicago area, mentored Richard Townsell. The church followed principles of indigenous leadership and good "property management"—taking on "management" of the community. To understand Richard's story, you must know the church's beginnings.

The Lawndale Experience

Wayne Gordon says that when he moved to Lawndale, he "increased the white population by 100 percent." As a coach at the local high school, well aware of the school's limited athletic equipment, he opened a weight room in the front of his apartment and began a Bible study. As these kids came to Christ, Wayne encouraged them to find a good church, but they insisted that *he* be their pastor. As the only white man in Lawndale, he thought this preposterous—until the girls attending his wife's Bible study kept saying the same thing. Through these kids, God confirmed Wayne's call. With no formal pastoral training, he saw the next logical step was for the church to find out what the neighborhood needed and to meet those needs. So he sent his church into the neighborhood.

Beginning with Projects

They returned with a list. A place to wash clothes was on the list. On their knees they prayed; that weekend someone from the suburbs called to see if they could use a washing machine. With bolstered faith, their decided on their next project, purchasing a burned out building across the street and building a gymnasium. They dug it out by hand, until someone with a tractor opened part of the brick building to finish the job.

Indigenous Leaders and Clear Boundries

From the beginning, the church has looked inside the community, knowing that African American leadership was essential.[1] As the church was electing leaders and taking shape, Wayne was relieved to have his friends and college students from the suburbs come to help. But it was clear to the young church leaders that these well-meaning outsiders were reshaping the church culture, changing the music, choosing the discussion topics, etc. So, they adopted a motion that set the future direction of the church for decades to come. Their ruling by unanimous vote declared: Only residents of the Lawndale neighborhood could belong to the church.

Outsiders who wanted to become part of this now vibrant church could attend; but if they wanted to join, they must move into the neighborhood. A few did. As the impact of the church grew, more followed—neighbors with resources and connections. A doctor moved in and started a health clinic in the church. Another soon joined him. Someone moved in to help establish a community development corporation and begin fixing up the hundreds of vacant homes that blighted the neighborhood. With this narrow geographical range, the church has spawned an amazing array of ministries and businesses serving as a catalyst for neighborhood revitalization, creating leadership and career opportunities for youth indigenous to Lawndale.[2]

Today, nearly thirty years after their memorable membership edict, Lawndale Community Church, through their 1,000 members, has a Christian health center that provides for over 100,000 patient visits a year, and since 1990 has invested millions of dollars into creating affordable homeownership and rental properties throughout their community. They have helped over one hundred families to own their own homes, including single-family homes, condominiums, and two-flats. Few would deny that the Lawndale Community Church sparked and fueled the dramatic rebirth that is now reclaiming every street and alley in the neighborhood.

At the church, Pastor Wayne Gordon has a map on the wall detailing the boundaries of Lawndale's "parish" —the property and people God has given them to "manage" with love and vision. On another wall are pictures of church members together with their purchased homes—those who never believed they could have a stake in the American dream. Like Gordon, Townsell responded to God's call, at first by leading the raising of Lazarus, and then by "raising" many other properties. The process itself is about resurrecting a people to the glory of God. Here is Townsell's story.

Raising Lazarus from the Dead

RICHARD TOWNSELL

Your children will rebuild the deserted ruins of your cities. Then you will be known as the people who rebuild their walls and cities.—Isaiah 58:12, NLT

One day when Pastor Gordon was coaching football at Farragut High School in North Lawndale, his star quarterback failed to show up for a championship game. The quarterback's apartment had caught fire the night before. Everyone had to move out. Fire damaged the roof on the east side. Through the years the buildings suffered further decay from rain, snow, and significant vandalism. The buildings were off the tax record for years, with squatters as the only residents. Finally, in 1992 Lawndale Christian Development Corporation purchased the buildings for back taxes through a Cook County program. They found them full of trash and occupied by mostly white squatters. For all practical purposes, these two buildings were as dead as Lazarus.

Today the Lazarus Apartments are home to 150 people in 48 units. The building was totally renovated in 1994. The Lazarus Apartments comprise two buildings, each four stories high, with solid brick exterior walls and exposed brick interiors. Its "green" countertops, windows, decorative wall sconces, and other elements helped win architectural awards. In the process those who helped to renovate it and those it houses were also revitalized. God has resurrected "Lazarus" from the grave–physically, spiritually, and economically. Today, Lazarus is a testament to God's faithfulness and a community's refusal to let the yolk of injustice continue.

Daring to Listen

I was born in North Lawndale in a basement apartment in a single-parent household. After the riots in North Lawndale and the assassination

According to 2000 data, the Chicago community of North Lawndale, with a median income of $18,342, has a 45 percent poverty rate and an unemployment rate of 27 percent. Between 1970 and 2000, Lawndale experienced a dramatic decrease in affordable housing units. The remaining housing is in poor condition, leaving families burdened with a high rate of violent crime, drug and gang activity, underperforming schools, and a frightening incidence of lead poisoning in children.

of Dr. Martin Luther King Jr. in 1968, my family moved to a public housing project on the southwest side of Chicago. To my mother, public housing in the Le Claire Courts seemed like a much better choice for raising our family. However, that changed in the late 1970s. The gang problem we left in North Lawndale began to emerge in Le Claire Courts.

My mother worked long hours hauling mail for the U.S. Postal Service. One day, when I was in seventh grade, she suffered a stroke and was paralyzed the rest of her life. Money was scarce. My sole focus was to bring my family out of poverty–and out of the neighborhood. Before my mother was paralyzed, I was an average student; this reversal pushed me to become an outstanding student.

As an honor student and valedictorian of my eighth grade class, I wanted to attend a school with a great reputation. When we crossed into the white community to go to Dunbar High School, violence was perpetrated against blacks. While wrestling as a freshman, I met Rev. Wayne "Coach" Gordon. As a sophomore, Ozzie Porter and I qualified for the state wrestling tournament. Off-season, we began a weight-training program at Lawndale Community Church and attended a Bible study Rev. Gordon led. I had already made a commitment to Jesus Christ at a local Baptist church, but saw the great opportunity to be discipled by Pastor Gordon.

Listening to God's Teaching

The summer of 1984, we took an intensive course from Pastor Gordon on the three principles of Christian Community Development: relocation, reconciliation, and redistribution.

First, we learned how God left his comfortable home in heaven and relocated among us. And he was usually found among those most in need. Therefore, as Christians we must be willing to follow Christ's example to be found among those in need.

Second, the cross is the ultimate symbol of reconciliation. The vertical bar represents our reconciliation to God, and the horizontal bar symbolizes our reconciliation to each other. Christ bore on the cross all of the barriers that divide us: race, class, legal status, gender, geography, and culture.

Mission: The Lawndale Christian Development Corporation (LCDC) was established by the Lawndale Community Church in 1987 to bring holistic revitalization to the lives and environments of North Lawndale residents through economic empowerment, housing improvement, educational enrichment, and community advocacy. It is also affiliated with the Lawndale Christian Health Center, the Carole Robertson Center for Learning, and the regional coalition United Power for Action and Justice. LCDC has three components: development, community organizing, and education.

Third, Gordon taught us the principle of redistribution. God did not desire anyone to be permanently in need or in a dependent relationship. The book of Nehemiah is a powerful example of God's desire for everyone to be a part of the rebuilding process, using their gifts and talents for the community good.

Listening to God's Call

These three "R's"—relocation, reconciliation, and redistribution—made sense to me, except relocation. I had an issue with moving back to the neighborhood of my birth—North Lawndale. As far as I could tell, the only people who stayed had no other options. It was fine for missionaries to do that work, but not for me. I felt that I could make a difference without moving back to Lawndale, and that was my intention.

When Pastor Gordon and the board of Lawndale Christian Development Corporation (LCDC) offered me a job as the executive director of LCDC in 1991, I turned it down—not wanting to move back to Lawndale with my new wife, Stephanie, who was raised in a nice Kansas City neighborhood. She became an engineer for Amoco, located in a more upscale part of downtown Chicago where we were considering a home purchase. While she was on a six-month Amoco assignment in Decatur, Alabama, I went to visit her. We toured the Martin Luther King Center in Atlanta. Stepping off the train, we couldn't help but notice the neighborhood near the King Center—it looked like Lawndale! The center that bore the name of one of America's greatest prophets was in one of the most devastated parts of Atlanta. It made me think of my high school, on King Drive—a tough area. I thought about every city where I knew of a King Drive, King Street, King Avenue...they all seemed to be in disinvested areas. I was greatly troubled. Every speech I'd heard or every book I read about King's life became very concrete.

Seeing his sacrifice and courage for the sake of the gospel made me ponder, "What was I willing to give my life for?" That night, I couldn't sleep. I could no longer ignore my calling. God wanted my wife and I to move into North Lawndale and take this job. I said no to Pastor Gordon. I couldn't say no to God. When Stephanie got back to Chicago, working on a design for a chemical plant in Indonesia, she began to feel distant from where her heart was—North Lawndale. I called Pastor Gordon...the job was still available.

Listening to God's Relocation Plan

I was hired in March 1992 as the first full-time executive director of Lawndale Christian Development Corporation. Our very capable development director, David Doig, who later would become the CEO of the Chicago Park District, was the brains behind the purchase and initial strategy for what would become Lazarus Apartments. We had never done a project of this magnitude. It was a time when other church-based community development corporations were beautifully rehabbing many older buildings, but having trouble with the management. Pastor Gordon worried that this project could bring down our whole ministry.

I knew that God had called me to this work, that this was a miracle that God would bring to pass. I came up with the name "Lazarus Apartments" to symbolize the work that Christ had done with Lazarus and what he was going to do in us and the lives of families who desperately needed affordable housing. This step of faith caused fear, but we knew we were on the right track.

Listening to Past Failures of Poor Design Features

Growing up in public housing, I had firsthand experience with how well-intentioned, but often clueless, bureaucracies tend to strip the dignity of people in low-income communities. The design and amenities of the housing that I grew up in caused my family many problems. Cinder block construction offered no insulation. In the summer, we lived in a brick oven. Outside our apartment, play equipment was installed on concrete. Today, there would be a rubber surface or wood chips. My younger brother William, pushed from the "monkey bars," was knocked unconscious and in a coma for a day. I still remember crying myself to sleep, praying that he would live.

Playing football one day, my knee hit a low concrete divider that separated most yards. You could see all the way to the bone. They rushed me to the County Hospital for stitches. The scar on my knee remains a daily reminder of that poor design. At the time, no one had aroused the public conscience to make affordable housing with features and amenities that anyone would love. Naively, even some nonprofit organizations helped produce affordable housing that was just "good enough" for the poor. Then, and even now, a public mentality assumes poor folks should appreciate anything "we do for them."

Many conversations over the years have led me to believe that too often, systems are built on assumptions that "protect" poor people from themselves. I hear, "What training do you give your tenants so that they won't tear up the property?" and respond to these well-meaning, but uninformed, questions saying, "People everywhere want a beautiful place to live. When something is designed to look like a museum, people of all economic backgrounds appreciate the beauty and want to keep it up." I see poor design, low quality, bland colors, and very few amenities as the antithesis of what we're trying to do. In my experience it seems that these decisions are often based on low expectations for people in poverty.

Listening to Past Management Failures

As our team met for our weekly staff meetings–Kim Jackson, Bernard Harris, William Little, and myself–we decided to learn from others' successes and failures...Especially since this was our first major project.

One of our mentors, Glen Kehrein of Circle Urban Ministries in Chicago, told us that nonprofit developers didn't always make good landlords. They were naively too mission-oriented and not sufficiently business-minded. They didn't always demand accountability by collecting rent and evicting tenants. Sometimes a church's mission to help the poor competed with their bottom line to keep the apartments in top financial shape. We decided to be tough, but fair, demanding people pay rent on time, evicting those who abused the system. We would have zero tolerance for drug sales or domestic violence. We would consistently enforce a resident handbook that spelled out expectations for our organization and our residents.

Glen also suggested that no more than 10 percent of our renters have Section 8 housing vouchers. Research proving the viability of a mixed-income community strengthened our resolve. Some developers took advantage of Section 8 voucher subsidies by jacking up rents, making a lot of money off their 100 percent Section 8 apartment complexes, while providing very little in terms of good management and services. But those few who abused Section 8 hurt millions of Americans who truly need the assistance. We didn't abandon Section 8 renters; we just avoided management pitfalls. That meant striving for a healthy mix of incomes in Lazarus. Our challenge was to figure out how to make it work economically.

Developing Partners

As I considered my own history and the deep pain among my people, I realized very tough and unpopular decisions needed to be made. We needed to create a new way of doing business that would go one step further in giving greater honor and respect for the poor in our community. We needed to stop practices that unintentionally cut people of color out of the decision-making process. We sought to apply healthy partnership principles by hiring local minorities, trusting our instincts, learning from others' management and design mistakes, and dreaming big. In our case, it was appropriate to hire as many competent people of color as we could find: contractors, insurance companies, surveyors, appraisers, architects. We even chose to work with loan officers of color.

Pam Hallett—a Great Consultant

We hired Pam Hallett as our consultant—a social activist turned real estate developer. She walked us through the details and helped legitimize this project at City Hall. Her name on applications gave us instant credibility. She taught us how to do the first deal so that we could do the second one ourselves. We did not set up a dependent relationship; her role was to help build our team's capacity. She worked on the financials, trained our staff on construction management, and helped us to hold the general contractor accountable for performance. She was a tremendous blessing and mentor.

Smith & Smith Associates

We hired an African American architectural firm. While North Lawndale is 99 percent African American, LCDC had no relationships with black vendors at any level. LCDC had a board member—a white architect, a good man and a solid Christian—who worked for virtually little to no cost. I decided he would have to bid on the work competitively. He chose not to bid. We brought in a top-notch architectural team, Smith & Smith Associates, to design this rehab of Lazarus. Charles and Eben Smith, this father-and-son team, pushed for design elements that would make this building look like a downtown Chicago apartment building.

Local Contractors and Construction Crews

People of color are cut out of much of the private market development in major cities. We even had to push with our own Latino general contractor to hire local residents, despite his commitment to our process before we hired him. We hired black subcontractors from the neighborhood and created a neighborhood job-training program for unemployed men. They did demolition, painting, dry wall, and other laborer's work and were paid a living wage. A recent college graduate and lifetime Lawndale Community Church member, William Little Jr., headed up the local construction team. Today, William is a supervisor in the City of Chicago Department of Transportation, overseeing multimillion dollar projects.

While the city of Chicago has an ordinance requiring developers of city-funded projects to award 25 percent of the jobs to qualified minority contractors and 5 percent to women-owned firms, still most black contractors are cut out of the loop. In the construction field, the practice is to cap the number of minority contracts at only 25 percent. The 25 percent quota was to help minorities, but in a neighborhood like Lawndale, with 99 percent African American residents, this quota is used against us. Minorities—African Americans, Latinos, Asians, and people of Arabic descent—together receive no more than 25 percent of the jobs. In fact, contractors often do not meet the 25 percent goal. Sometimes they choose to pay fines, saying they can't find anyone "qualified." We are tempted to feel defeated before we try for jobs, especially since nonminorities have access to 75 percent of the public work and almost 100 percent of the private work. No wonder so much pent-up anger exists in our neighborhood.

Through Lazarus, we found a way to do something about our anger; we could stop some of this injustice by our hiring practices. We were resurrecting and rebuilding our community, not just two dilapidated buildings. From these beginnings we later found other ways to use our pent-up passions to bring about more justice through our community organizing efforts.

The insurance company, surveyor, and engineering firm were also black. Community development is not just about getting the project done but maximizing opportunities for local actors to participate profitably in the project. When a ministry desires to do real estate development and says they want be about community rebuilding, yet does not hire local contractors or other professionals, then they sidestep an essential aspect of what it really means to rebuild the community.

Chicago Rehab Network

During the Lazarus development, I took training courses in nonprofit real estate development offered by the Chicago Rehab Network (CRN)–a coalition of all nonprofit housing developers in the city. They do policy work, advocacy, and training for the nonprofit development world. They helped to demystify the world of tax credit syndications and finance. Their Urban Developer's Program and Human Development Training Initiatives are the best in the country to help grass-roots groups stick to the mission of development without displacement.

LaSalle National Bank

LaSalle National Bank was our primary lender. Kristen Faust and Pam Daniels-Halisi, a new breed of "activist banker," crafted a financial package that was sustainable in the long run and pragmatic in the short run. They made sure that this project was affordable, but would have positive cash flow throughout its life span.

City of Chicago

The biggest player was the city of Chicago. They gave us the tax credits and secondary financing. I can say, with few exceptions, I am proud to work with the City of Chicago's Department of Housing. They have some very bright, caring, pragmatic, and creative people in city government at all levels.

Local Initiatives Support Corporation

Another key piece of the puzzle, the Local Initiatives Support Corporation (LISC), provides loans, grants, and technical assistance to community development corporations (CDCs) across the country. They are responsible for billions of dollars of redevelopment in neighborhoods like ours and through their affiliate, the National Equity Fund (NEF). They provided the equity for our deal through their syndication of the tax credits.

Doing the Work

William Little Jr. worked with our architects and Pam Hallett to ensure completion in just over a year, on time and on budget the ultimate baptism by fire! William, a very skilled carpenter with an eye for detail beyond his years, had many difficult conversations with tradespeople trying to cut corners to meet deadlines. William stood firm, and Lazarus is holding up well because of his tenacity.

We kept the exposed brick walls and included great color schemes throughout the exterior and interior. Decorative wall sconces and quality lighting and plumbing fixtures didn't cost us any more—we just had to know where to look. Since quality and affordability were our stated priorities, we found they could work hand in hand. God honored our commitment to excellence to the extent that we won the Chicago Association of Realtor's Award and the Fannie Mae Maxwell Award for Excellence—Honorable mention.

Three months before construction ended, we began our marketing efforts. Our resident screening process would be four-fold:

- Credit checks of all applicants
- Proof of income and employment
- Previous landlord reference
- Perhaps most important, the home visit.

To see if they were a fit for us, we needed to get in the homes of potential residents and see their housekeeping. We were often heartbroken to see their living conditions. With such a high need for decent, safe, and affordable housing in Chicago, we were getting hundreds of applications for only forty-eight apartments. Our screening criteria, combined with a tenant selection committee who interviewed the final candidates, resulted in a great mix in our initial pool of residents. God has helped up us maintain this balance—with many others on waiting lists for our future projects.

Creating a rent affordable for the local market, yet sustainable for long-term maintenance of the building, was our number one driver. We decided on a two-tiered rental criterion, making it a truly mixed-income development. People who made at or below 30 percent of the median income for the Chicago metropolitan area paid $175 for a one-bedroom apartment, $218 for a two-bedroom, and $238 for a three-bedroom. People who made at or below 60 percent of the median income paid $375 for a one-bedroom, $425 for a two-bedroom, and $500 for a three-bedroom apartment. Our rents have increased only about 3 percent annually.

Dealing with Realities

Untrustworthy Management Firm

Pressure from our lenders and other financial backers led us to believe that we could not effectively be property managers for Lazarus. Also influenced by some high-profile failures in Chicago, we didn't want to be added to that list. So we hired a for-profit firm. However, the for-profit firm, with all of its capacity and resources, could not get us accurate financial statements and rent ledgers. We were paying them a nice sum and couldn't get basic information. After three months we fired them and took over the management. We joked, saying, "We could do as good a job mismanaging it." We had what we needed, capable leaders dedicated to the success of this venture—and not motivated only from a business rationale. It was, indeed, something that God brought together.

Unexpected Taxes

We wondered how much the new bill would be on property officially off the tax rolls for years. To our surprise, it exceeded our projections by 100 percent—we figured about $40,000; it was $85,000! We quickly learned the world of tax appeals. God sent a lawyer our way. We had to pay the $85,000 while disputing the validity of the valuation. LaSalle Bank stayed with us while we depleted our reserves, won the case, and then funded the reserves again over a three-year period.[3]

Discovering Insights

Lazarus revitalized those who helped to renovate it. Bernard Harris and Floyd Towner, both unemployed men from the neighborhood, rekindled their faith because of their work on Lazarus. Floyd and Bernard enrolled in Lawndale Christian Development Corporation's Imani program under the leadership of Thomas Worthy, who developed a biblical curriculum to help unemployed and underemployed residents obtain essential skills to find employment and increased income. Thomas, using his business savvy, pushed these men to pursue excellence. They quit smoking, rededicated their lives to Christ, became key employees of Lawndale Christian Development Corporation, and helped us to grow. Bernard became my right-hand man as the director of Real Estate Development, building many of our projects over the next decade. As a key maintenance staff person, Floyd fixed things, saving us much money. As community watchdog, he makes sure any potential drug problems in our buildings are dealt with. Today, both men serve as deacons, and Floyd became a homeowner through our homeownership program.

The insights have been transformative. We've learned to trust our own instincts and capacity—in deciding to hire within our community and to manage our own units. By trusting our instincts we found that God was there at work in us, helping us discover our strengths, our own capacity, and our skills, while also strengthening our resolve. God was rebuilding more than the burned-out building; God was resurrecting a people. We have discovered the importance of people of color in the building trades and within the staff of city government agencies—and the value of a simple thanks. The city staff is extremely receptive to invitations to see our work. Each year we give them a plaque thanking them for our partnership. When Mayor Daley came to our groundbreaking ceremony, we prayed for him and the success of Lazarus. This public witness lifted the spirits of all involved and helped keep us focused on our mission and why we do this.

Another discovery: to invite our property management team into the design phase. Based on their experience, they know everything from what kind of materials wear well over time to where the laundry room should be.

Our prophetic voice is sharpened as we rub shoulders with nonbelieving experts and residents—invaluable partners that have kept us on track and sharp due to their insight and excellent questions. It a joy to be a bit of the flavoring in the world, some of that salt that Jesus refers to in Matthew 5:13: "You are the salt of the earth." The redevelopment of Lazarus has helped us to stay salty!

Finally, when things get difficult (and they certainly do), we stop and pray. Our team is discovering how not to react out of fear or the urgent. We are learning to trust, knowing God is sovereign. God gives what we need to build the kingdom.

God allowed us to go through growing pains as we resurrected Lazarus, preparing us for a greater work. I stand amazed at the opportunities to grow, not just in the amount of housing we have been able to do, but also in the growth of our own faith as a people and an organization. Lazarus was a springboard for us, a chance to prove to ourselves that we could do it by God's grace and strength.

Scope of Lawndale's Housing Ministries

LCDC has developed single-family homes and condos for low-income families, rehabilitated over 130 rental units, and created a $3.1 million child care facility serving 220 children and employing approximately 50 people. LCDC received the SNAPP award from the city of Chicago, generating over $3 million in reinvestment in the community for infrastructure improvements, parks, and business retention programs.

The housing ministry of the Lawndale Community Church and LCDC includes: Samaritan House—transitional housing for homeless families; Hope House—transitional housing for men who have been released from prison and/or have serious drug/alcohol addictions; Nehemiah House—apartments for men successfully completing a nine-month stay in Hope House; Harambee Homes—nine owner-built town homes using a mutual self-help model similar to Habitat for Humanity; Lazarus Apartments; and Tabernacle Apartments—twenty-six units identical to Lazarus' rental structure. LCDC has acquired sixty vacant and tax-delinquent single-family homes and condominiums from the city, renovated them, and sold them to community residents—often using a lease-to-purchase model, allowing families to fix credit and down payment issues over an eighteen–month to two-year process before they assume the mortgage. (See more at www.lcdc.net.)

Mustard Tree Co-op

An Urban Search for Community

REVEREND CANON RONALD SPANN

Introduction to the Co-op Movement and Housing Cooperatives
BY JILL SHOOK

My mother set up an informal babysitting co-op with her friends. On their day to watch us, her friends transformed their home into a mini-preschool. Mom was free to go about other aspects of life on her days "off." "Every day in America, and throughout the world, people...form co-ops to meet their common needs. Through co-operation, they...maintain their independence while benefiting from the combined power of a group. They strengthen their bargaining power and reduce costs."[1]

A wide variety of businesses are owned and run cooperatively by the people they serve.[2] Household names such as Cabot, Sunkist, Ocean Spray, Land O'Lakes, and Blue Diamond are all cooperatives. One of the most successful co-ops today is in Spain: Mondragon Corporacion Co-operativa begun in 1956 by Father Jose Maria Arizmediarrieta.[3]

Today's cooperative movement traces its origins to England's Industrial Revolution. Mill workers labored long hours under dangerous working conditions for low pay, forced to buy food on credit from merchants who charged high prices for poor quality goods. Cooperative initiatives offered the promise of economic opportunity and democratic control. But none were successful until the founding of the Rochdale Equitable Pioneers Society in 1844. Learning from earlier failures, they developed operating principles to ensure success. Today, these basic principles still guide cooperatives worldwide:

- open and voluntary membership;
- democratic control, one vote for one share of ownership;

- economic participation, equitable contribution, and democratic control of capital;
- autonomy and independence;
- education, training, and information;
- cooperation with other cooperatives; and
- concern for their surrounding communities.[4]

Ron Spann, author of the Mustard Tree narrative, says that the directness of these principles is "deceptively simple." He explains how the co-op members of the Mustard Tree Co-op Apartments caught on after an unrelenting calendar of meetings—the hours given proved worth the effort, as you will see.

Shared Ownership Housing Cooperatives

The idea of shared ownership housing dates back to 434 B.C.E. in Babylonia, where condominium-type deeds are recorded on ancient papyrus. The scriptures allude to a strong theme of hospitality, with examples of shared housing and pooling of resources. Elijah received a room in the Shunammite's home (2 Kings 4:8–10), and Mary, the mother of Jesus, was taken into John's home (Jn. 19:27).

In a housing co-op, a group owns and controls the building(s), the land, and common area in which they live, unlike condos, in which ownership is limited to a person's single unit. The group members form a corporation, and agree to follow the cooperative principles and pay a share of the operating costs (usually consisting of mortgage payments, property taxes, management, maintenance, insurance, utilities, and reserve funds).

In 1876 "Home Clubs" in New York provided luxury housing. Later, Finnish artisans in Brooklyn began the first "true" cooperatives—100 percent owned by the residents. By 1962, the Metropolitan Mutual Housing Association had built Chatham Towers in Manhattan, a 21-story co-op with 420 units, known for its many architectural awards. New York paved the co-op housing path for our nation by initiating tax deductions for middle- and low-income co-ops. Later, 213 New York co-op presidents launched cooperative mortgage insurance. Today, HUD's Section 213 funds and establishes co-ops nationwide. Co-ops are prolific in New York; Washington, D.C.; Chicago; Miami; Minneapolis; Detroit; Atlanta; and San Francisco. A Silent Cooperative in Illinois is designed for the hearing-impaired. Manufactured housing communities are forming co-ops, enabling them to own their mobile homes and the ground under them and to take charge of the park's management. Some colleges promote cooperative student housing. Artists in gentrified areas ensure permanently affordable housing and studios through co-ops.

Cooperatives can be built from the ground up, as new housing, or converted from rental housing (or a lease). Fannie Mae, Freddie Mac, and the National Co-operative Bank have streamlined loan-making for such ventures. When a group decides to become a housing co-op, they determine their desired equity model: market rate, limited, or zero equity. For some, accruing equity is a high priority, so a market-rate model enables them to sell their shares for whatever the market will bear. Other groups wanting to keep the housing permanently affordable choose a zero equity or limited equity option, which limits the share's resale value.[5] In the Mustard Tree narrative that follows, Ron Spann features a limited equity model.

Mustard Tree Co-op

BY RONALD SPANN

These trials are only to test your faith, to show that it is strong and pure. It is being tested as fire tests and purifies gold, and your faith is far more precious to God than mere gold. So if your faith remains strong after being tried by fiery trials, it will bring you much praise and glory and honor on the day when Jesus Christ is revealed to the whole world. —1 Peter 1:7, NLT

Amid media coverage, with a visitor from the city council we celebrated the culmination of a six-year journey for Mustard Tree Apartments to incorporate as the Mustard Tree Co-op Apartments. This four-story "walk-up," whose twenty-four units ranged from one to three-bedroom apartments, was finally an autonomous cooperative, owned and managed by low- to moderate-income residents. To our knowledge, that had never happened in Detroit. In April 2004, Mustard Tree celebrated its twentieth anniversary as a housing cooperative. It has blossomed into a stabilizing presence, embracing families with children, couples, retired adults, and younger singles.

The seed of this vision was born in the hearts of Church of the Messiah members, then grew to transform their collective faith and sense of mission. Church of the Messiah Housing Corporation (CMHC) was established in 1978 as the legal and administrative means of taking ownership of the

"Moving into the Mustard Tree was one of the best things I've ever done. I lived there for fifteen years. My son grew up there. It was a great place to raise kids affordably. The kids always had other kids to play with. All the parents knew each other. We could be a family for those who had none. It was like our own little utopia. Everything wrong with the world, we could make right."—Gwen McNeal

building. It went on to become a veteran player in the ranks of faith-based development groups. CMHC rehabilitated eight more multiple-unit buildings, salvaging 160 dwellings in the neighborhood, including a seventy-two–unit historic building.

The visibility of CMHC's efforts rose dramatically while constructing new town houses on a several block stretch of abandoned parcels. What had lain fallow, reverting to unkempt prairie land with its own robust population of pheasants and rabbits, began to stand out as an oasis of affordable rental housing on an urban greenway. This attracted developers to build a pricier set of condominiums, thus diversifying the community's socioeconomic make-up.

When Detroit's City Council launched a program redirecting some of its federal block grants for home repair, it stipulated partnership with a nonprofit organization. The opportunity was timely. It opened the way for CMHC to repair over four hundred homes in its own neighborhood, and hundreds more in other parts of Detroit.

It all started with Mustard Tree Apartments during my tenure as rector of Church of the Messiah. At the end of October 1996, I resigned after twenty-five years of service, four of those years living at the Mustard Tree Co-op. This chapter is my grateful reflection on Messiah's baptism into housing ministry and the beginnings of Mustard Tree Co-op.

Daring to Listen

Sometime during the late summer months of 1976 fire broke out in a turn-of-the-twentieth–century building opposite Church of the Messiah—a congregation of the Episcopal Diocese of Michigan. I was in my sixth year as pastor of Messiah and not immune to anxiety over what was unfolding across the street: fear for lives at risk, and damage to nearby property, including our church. We ran to the streets. Would it be another major property loss?

Our neighborhood no longer formed the posh, eastern edge of Detroit. The building's original occupants had no doubt been a "better-heeled" clientele. Yet this stately, brick-facade structure was spared at this time from becoming another burnt-out shell open to what seemed like an inescapable pattern of dereliction, arson, and destruction. The fire, a tragic

"It's the best place for me to be. We are a close-knit family. We have the same mission and have say over the next rent increase and who we rent to. We have no manager over us; we are the managers. We feel secure and safe here. I left for several years, but came back realizing how much I missed being part of the community."
—Rev. Barry Randolph, a member of Church of the Messiah's Pastoral Team and President of Mustard Tree Co-op

disruption in the lives of the tenants, proved a beacon of new beginnings. The destinies of the apartment dwellers and Messiah members would intertwine in their common search for life-giving community. Tenants forced from their apartments spoke to our compassion. We opened the church's kitchen and fellowship hall, offering meals. For those of us living in the vicinity, it seemed natural to make the bold offer of temporary lodging in our homes—only one couple accepted. Initially, the fire simply beckoned us to help people in need. At the time, we were just learning to integrate the outward call to justice as a local church. We were more confident with inward-directed congregational concerns.

By the late 1970s, almost two hundred congregants had relocated to our Islandview Village neighborhood, committing to live by a common purse. This "Common Life Group" challenged each other: to become neighbors—and not strangers—to one another; to break distinctions of social status; to live on intentionally modest incomes; share decision-making power; care for one another's children; practice hospitality; avoid gossip; forgive trespasses; seek inner healing; and more. This intensive pastoral and administrative experiment demanded an enormous amount of energy, for which there were no textbook guides. We were attempting something akin to the life of a monastic community. In fact, for several years we had a Benedictine abbot serve as a kind of circuit-riding consultant. We were apprenticed in how to build a visible, common life in Christ. Investing so much attention to these pastoral disciplines irritated my own prophetic sensibilities as one strongly predisposed to the biblical vision of justice. Later this investment brought a huge payoff with the Mustard Tree.

The year following the fire, the building kept surfacing in conversations. Art Potter won our support for a fact-finding visit to Reba Place Fellowship, a Mennonite church that had anchored itself in inner-city Evanston, Illinois. Reba Place members had redeveloped a sizable apartment building to house their own members, as well as nonmember neighbors. Art and company returned with a wealth of insights, challenging us, as Joshua and Caleb did, to take on the giants of a promised land, firing us up to undertake the renovation of the apartment building across the street.

Our openness to the challenge came from another, more fundamental reason. We stayed in touch with residents' vivid chronicles of their frustration. The fire mirrored outwardly an anger smoldering within them: the lack of security, the neglected furnace system that led to the fire, the overall deterioration of the building, and the landlord's indifference to the history of complaints. One man even documented the landlord's negligence with a terrarium teeming with mice caught in his apartment! "The Lord hears the cry of the poor," and we were being tutored to do the same. We could not remain indifferent.

A series of congregational meetings elicited support to discern our next step. In the end, our entire membership owned the vision. We believed

God was promising us the building; we were to go about laying claim to it. We were so fired up that we sent a team to the owners (whose grandfather had built the apartments) not to bargain, but to inform them that we believed God was asking them to give us the building. Apparently, the somewhat startled family hadn't received this same message from God, but they did offer to sell us the twenty-four–unit building for $75,000–almost like giving it to us. After several church meetings, we accepted the offer. Widows, singles, and families with children looked into whatever cookie jars they had to raise the 10 percent down payment. In the end, the building was ours.

Developing Partners

Perhaps a blend of naiveté and ambition (on top of our tunnel vision for the redemption of a single building) motivated us to forge ahead without developing an extensive partnership base. Even so, this project caught the attention of a small circle of outside encouragers–friends who stayed current with the work and witness of our young ministry. One of them immediately zeroed in on our equity-poor financing as a land contract.[6] Using his own resources, he refinanced the agreement as a mortgage; within two years, and with one more generous initiative on his part, the $75,000 was paid off!

It took a good dose of pro bono legal help to set up a nonprofit corporation. Individual and organizational donors contributed $250,000 toward the building renovations. Their encouragement and generosity motivated us.

For technical assistance, we turned to nonprofit organizations specializing in co-op training and organizational development. Availing ourselves of the best resources meant securing a consultant from a secular organization–proving to neutralize any perception that the church's interest in the tenants cloaked an agenda to make Episcopalians of them all! However, philosophical differences with the co-op trainers led to tensions.

Doing the Work

Messiah graduated from onlooker to proprietor within a year after the fire. Owning this dilapidated building meant carrying out a staggering responsibility, demanding skills we had not yet acquired. Every turn led us to a first-time experience.

First, we clarified our leadership resources. Richard Cannon, a twenty-two-year-old college graduate, became our administrator. He demonstrated

> "My brother lives across the hall. He decorated the walls with antique paintings and restored the hardwood floors. There's a fireplace in every unit. This is a beautiful place to live."—Rev. Barry Randolph

precocious administrative skills that his towering six-foot-nine frame only dramatized. He went on to serve an eighteen-year term that secured his place as a faith-based development leader of national stature.

As the weight of ownership settled on our shoulders, we juggled our roles of landlord and neighbor. Our co-op solution to management addressed both. Drawing on six years of experience with our Islandview Common Life Group, we mobilized eight volunteers to move into Mustard Tree. To accommodate them, we combined two of the three available three-bedroom apartments by cutting through the floor between the units and installing a spiral staircase to form a bi-level apartment. Once moved in, they joined the rotation of parish volunteers handling rent-collection and much-needed repairs. Fresh exterior paint, touched-up landscaping, and regularly cleaned hallways improved its shabby appearance. Fitting the entry door with new plate glass and replacing a useless door-buzzer system addressed a security gap. Anyone could step through the glassless door and roam the building. Tragically, just after our purchase, a single male resident was bludgeoned to death behind the building in one of its garage bays. These, too, were then newly secured. The ministry of giving life had literally come to mean keeping death at bay.

The need for a name came up persistently. "Mustard Tree Apartments" was a metaphor of the faith that seeded our enterprise and of the kingdom of God, which we aspired to demonstrate. Like the ample shrub growing from a miniscule seed giving shelter to a variety of life forms, our building gave roost to its own assortment of "critters"—ourselves included!

The reaction of the tenants to the new owners was mixed. Moving eight mostly unrelated adults and children into one enlarged unit increased their wariness. Apartment walls proved thin, giving both populations plenty to talk about behind closed doors. Getting them to open to one another became a goal. In contrast to our bumbling business-building skills, we showed better instincts for relationship-building, as the eight patiently sought to promote an "open-door policy."

The best catalyst for relationship-building was our decision to organize the building as a cooperative. A similar development at Church of the Saviour in Washington, D.C., had inspired our vision. A cooperative offered several advantages:

- ownership would shift to the residents
- the building would come off the speculative market
- its equity value would accrue to the members
- it would call out skills in relationship-building and leadership

A co-op would introduce values of mutuality and community instead of individualism and mere self-interest—a compelling vision from our point of view as a church. From the tenants' point of view, the vision was simply alien. Richard Cannon's first round of organizing was simply to get the tenants together. Now he was introducing a co-op, a hard sell that required endless meetings. Co-op principles came with a steep learning curve. Messiah introduced incentives: lower rental rates for tenants who opted to attend meetings, to join the tenants' group, to take turns with maintenance, and attend workdays. Nevertheless, it became clear that the tenants were not in the market for a new kind of ownership experience. The long-accustomed conventions of living by lease felt more comfortable and far less intrusive.

Our efforts seemed to lead to all the wrong results. Our alien approach was so suspect that tenants caucused, setting up an alternative group that did some reconnoitering, sending a delegation to a tenants' rights service. After explaining their puzzlement over Messiah's offer to turn the building over to them as a co-op, the rights service responded by encouraging them to take up the offer as "the real thing," to the tenants' utter astonishment.

That was a watershed moment. They returned with the surprise feed-back, which suddenly gave Messiah legitimacy and respect we had not yet enjoyed in their sight. Thereafter, this enlightened tenants group agreed to work for co-op status. The leadership gradually shifted onto their shoulders as they underwent a kind of management training. They arranged hallway maintenance, groundskeeping, and other hands-on jobs. This built a kind of "sweat equity"—a public expression of their intention as future co-op members.

Not surprisingly, some residents balked at going co-op, unconvinced of its advantages. Frankly, their skepticism was not unfounded. It seemed that the only benefits for these co-op pioneers were discounted rent and the dubious privilege of filling their evenings with a flood of meetings seeking to clarify the famed seven cooperative principles that defied easy mastery. Before long, two contrasting points of view became apparent between tenants who identified with the co-op movement and those who did not. The former viewpoint, by its very existence, was an unspoken challenge to everyone else to "go co-op." Later, this translated into a spoken boldness, directly asking tenants' intentions. For those who made the commitment, a steep learning curve lay ahead on basic leadership skills, identity development, and the co-op principles and practices.

Technical assistance from our nonreligious groups introduced a shrewd, overtly political edge to the process. The tenants' increased self-confidence

"I was on the initial rental committee that set up the guidelines for incoming residents. We interviewed many before we found the right fit. We were mostly interested in knowing if people wanted to learn and grow and were willing to put in the sweat equity on workdays. It was truly a great project. I left because my needs were changing. My children were grown, and I wanted to use my time for other things." —Gwen McNeal

to deal with the authority of the church and Messiah Housing Corporation came at our expense. I grudgingly admired their adversarial way of showing the tenants how to hold the Housing Corporation accountable. We were not above being answerable to those whom we wished to serve. Depictions of us and of our motives rocked our idealized self-image. It felt at times as if we were being cast as Goliath to the co-op's David, when our desire was to be friends and advocates.

Maxine Piaseczny, an elderly widow, brought David *and* Goliath together with her hospitality. Her apartment became a "foyer" after church. Visitors followed this Franciscan-minded hostess across the street as she opened her door to parishioners, co-op members, children, the curious, and the hungry to an unchanging menu of pasta with meat sauce, salad, and cake. Some co-op members later became part of the church, and church members eventually joined the co-op.

My own family was ready for a change and moved into the Mustard Tree in 1982. Living on-site, we became aware of the gaps in the Housing Corporation's response to repair requests. As an African American family, we enhanced the credibility of the church to the African American tenants. They counted on Jackie and me to corroborate to the church things like the temperamental heating system, intercom complications, roaches, and the uneven compliance with admitting visitors to the building.

Our family, now part of the struggle to "go co-op," entered the inevitable dynamics of a new group coming into its identity. I ensured broad participation on workdays and moderated during tangled meetings. While undoubtedly I had their respect as a clergy person (and perhaps not a few suspicions as well!), I could not presume on an unearned trust. Father Ron from across the street had to simply be Ron from Mustard Tree. I had no pastoral trump cards to play!

Dealing with Realities

In 1980, two years into this ownership venture, the marriage of the two elders who headed up our eight-person household at Mustard Tree collapsed. Soon we disbanded the household. A couple from the church needing more room for their expanding family moved in. Our congregation diverted our attention to our own pain and confusion as this episode exposed our church's vulnerabilities. This launched us into a rigorous apprenticeship on closely related external realities we could not escape: race, power, and wealth.

A predominantly white and middle-class congregation, all but one of the eight-member household had been white. The other co-op residents, predominantly working-class African Americans, held a legacy of distrust, suspicion, and bad faith in regards to the white race. The injustice of American racial history dogged our every effort at communication and organization. As a black leader, I understood instinctively what lay behind the misgivings regarding our director, Richard Cannon, who was young, white, and many years shy of the skills and wisdom that would later characterize him. He found his own kind of rapport with the residents. No panaceas appeared to resolve the tangled dynamics. They could be dealt with only by a constant commitment to relationships of trust. Living on both sides of the arrangement—allied to the congregation and ultimately to Richard as his boss, as well as to the tenants as a fellow resident—I found myself stretched.

The church naively tried to be both an advocate and a landlord. We were authorized to demand rent payments and petition for evictions, but we had not reckoned on the pain of confronting, on a business basis, those we were getting to know on a personal basis. More than one family left as a result of repeated failures to pay rent or for noncompliance with the lease. Such partings were a loss…although some occasioned a sigh of relief! As the co-op matured toward autonomy, it left us on the Messiah side more than a little unnerved. We struggled with the temptation to control the process when it appeared the residents were headed toward choices disagreeable to us. We defended rent levels, explained schedules for repair, maintenance, and so on. The co-op's growth in autonomy forced the church to reframe its ambitions as an advocate—which amounted to a power struggle. For this venture to work, the co-op members had to own their choices.

The economic profile of the Mustard Tree membership was skimpy at best, with no family fortunes to draw on, no friends with deep pockets, and no banks offering financing. Settling on a selling price of $250,000 took time—this amount roughly corresponding to the funds for improvements to the building. The down payment was set at ten percent, with a forty-year land contract of $650 monthly payments. Income from washing or parking cars, barbecue or bake sales, did not reach the goal. When the closing took place in April 1984, the $25,000 was lowered to $5,000.

Discovering Insights
Business Insights

Cooperative housing is not an obvious choice, nor an easy goal. CMHC was unable to replicate this success with the redevelopment of two other multi-unit buildings. In fact, Mustard Tree Co-op sent representatives to consult with them and co-op–minded single adults and couples from the church even moved in. Co-ops were planted, but later foundered. Co-op housing attracted us for its ideals of putting ownership and unprecedented control in residents' hands. Such control, however, was not a priority of the urban public we served. Co-ops are labor intensive; again, not what conventional tenants want. Access to equity, integral to the co-op vision, was beyond the reach of a low-income population when start-up costs took capital they did not have.

Important questions must be answered. As a co-op becomes successful, the value of a share should go up as the property and enterprise appreciates in value, making the cost of membership at a later stage grow out of reach for a low-income aspirant. Therefore, co-ops must impose a limit on equity earned. For equity to build there must be an adequate income from the monthly carrying charge, beyond operational costs and reserves. Carrying charges, the co-op term used for "rent," are paid to the co-op itself, not to a landlord. With sufficient carrying costs, after an allowed time, a co-op member could leave, taking an agreed-on percentage of the equity. The question of higher carrying charges, however, was not one that CMHC felt free to push, nor apparently did the Mustard Tree Co-op once it was on its own. For better or for worse, they decided on a fixed equity model, keeping a monthly carrying charge as low as possible. A fixed equity model can render the co-op barely distinguishable from a conventional rental experience.

Despite the amateurish economics of the Mustard Tree Co-op venture, it proved invaluable to Messiah's schooling in housing ministry and vitality as a church. Throughout his lengthy, wise career, community development mentor John Perkins has stressed that a local church stays healthy by being responsible for something outside of its own life. A struggling church may very well find the seeds of its own renewal by daring to reach out with compassion for the struggles of its neighbors.

Affirming integrity of the co-op's autonomous identity was to affirm our own as a church. Partnering with trainers from secular organizations shifted a load off of the Housing Corporation, freeing it to be about the business of being a landlord, albeit a "redeemed" landlord.

Biblical Insights

Both the co-op and the church faced the constant task of forging a common life out of separate identities by finding unity in diversity. Each group had to find a just way to share power with one another, making themselves mutually vulnerable to financial, legal, and other decisions with implications for each member's welfare. In religious terms, "Be subject to one another..." (Eph. 5:21).

Sharing power raised up leaders who embodied and extended each group's identity, whether co-op or church. Just as Richard Cannon epitomized the development of grass-roots leadership within the church, Mustard Tree had a high-profile counterpart, Gwen McNeal. Gwen, a single mother who had already beat some sinister urban odds, served an extended

"When member's parents are ill, I share scripture and pray with them. I feel totally comfortable here, saying, 'Let's pray.'"—Rev. Barry Randolph

term as co-op president, heading up negotiations with the Church of the Messiah Housing Corporation. Gwen's co-op experience boosted her confidence. She was elected to CHMC's board and found work that more authentically corresponded to her giftedness. In religious terms, her efforts reflect the biblical call to "be transformed by the renewing of your minds...We have gifts that differ according to the grace given to us..." (Rom. 12:2b, 6a).

We equipped ourselves with communication skills to deal with conflict and to learn the things that make for peace—such as managing gossip and rumor. We learned to be ruthlessly honest about our flagrant failures and come up with just policies—rules of engagement that create order in our shared life and work and foster life-giving relationships at a sustained level. We are reminded by Paul that, while "speaking the truth in love" (Eph. 4:15a), to "[l]ive in peace with each other" (1 Thess. 5:13b, NIV).

We became stewards of a considerable economic arrangement, finding ways to redistribute goods and commonly own them: "All who believed were together and had all things in common" (Acts 2:44).

We became involved with co-op members' human sufferings such as illness, death, and grief; and they attended funeral services for church members. The Bible calls us to "[b]ear one another's burdens..." (Gal. 6:2), and reminds us, "Blessed are those who mourn, for they will be comforted" (Mt. 5:4).

Mustard Tree members sowed the seeds of community from the start. "Co-op" meant fund raising projects like parking cars when the hydroplane races took place at nearby Belle Isle. It meant throwing parties at the slightest excuse: birthdays, anniversaries, holidays, while often inviting the Messiah congregation to join in. Co-op meant creating a gardening commons, mutual child care at the playscape, spur of the moment visits, leaving keys with neighbors. Dropping rivalries and becoming friends is now commonplace— each proving the transforming power of the co-op journey.

The meaning of this all came together for me when Larry Wells, a resident who first disputed the idea of a co-op, said, "You know what? We have our own version here at Mustard Tree of what you all are doing over there at the church." His words sent a thrill through me. I thought to myself, "Friend, flesh and blood did not reveal that to you!"

By challenging the Mustard Tree residents to turn themselves into a cooperative, we effectively asked them to form a community—the very strategy we used to renew our congregation. We were both living out our dreams for community by sharing power, identifying gifts and leadership, learning to build relationships and communicate well, sharing a common economic base, working and playing together, showing mercy and care. These building blocks of community—religious and secular—yield fruits like joy, peace, and love. In other words, the inner workings of the human search for community are inescapably spiritual.

Temescal Commons

Seeds of Hope

J. R. BERGDOLL JR.

Introduction to the Co-housing Model BY THOMAS AND CHRISTINE SINE

Two Housing Trends

We are facing two housing trends in North America–the first, an explosion of expensive palatial mansions. These trophy homes, often in gated communities, insulate residents from the real world. A surprising number of wealthy Christians are among those opting for this super-sized lifestyle…seemingly unaware of the values these extravagant communities reflect or the stewardship issues they raise. In the early 1980s, New York's high-end houses averaged 3,500 to 5,500 square feet; today that range is 6,500 to 10,000 square feet.

A second trend also is escalating: The American poor cannot afford to live indoors or must squeeze multiple families into dwellings. Middle-income families are priced out of the American dream. Few from my generation paid more than 20 percent of their income–even my family's single income at a Christian college, equivalent to welfare–on housing costs. As I travel today, I meet an astonishing number of young couples spending over 50 percent.

A Harvard Law professor, Elizabeth Warren, reports that over the last twenty-five years, family bankruptcies have risen a shocking 400 percent. She projects that one family in seven, many headed by college-educated professionals, will file for bankruptcy by 2010. When families invest such a huge amount of their working hours over thirty years to pay off a mortgage, it undermines their economic viability, closing off a broad range of life options. Churches *could* establish no-interest revolving loan programs for young Christians using their lives to make a difference–thereby paying mortgages in only seven to ten years. We must imagine and create new housing and lifestyle alternatives. One option is cohousing.

Invented in Denmark in the 1970s, co-housing began as a cluster of small private dwellings, each with a small kitchen, complemented by an extensive shared "common house." For both social and practical reasons, the layout emphasizes pedestrian access and open space, all designed and developed by those choosing this shared living experience. A balance of privacy and community provides a safe and supportive environment, particularly for children and elders.

Co-housing isn't inherently affordable unless planned and financed as such. Jim Bergdoll owns a two-bedroom affordable unit at Temescal Commons, subsidized in exchange for resale restrictions that keep it affordable to future low-income owners. Others save on shared operating costs: fewer yards to mow, fences to mend, and appliances to own. Bergdoll shares with you the Temescal Commons story. This was the first Christian co housing in North America. A second, the Bartimaeus Community, in Washington, is now completed. Other co-housing communities with affordable options include the Southside Park Co-housing in Sacramento, partially funded by the local Redevelopment Agency, with five of its twenty-five units set aside as affordable for low-income families, and six for moderate-income. Of the forty units in Higher Ground Co-housing in Bend, Oregon, two are Habitat homes. Wild Sage Co-housing in Boulder, Colorado, has four Habitat homes of its thirty-four total.[1]

As you read Bergdoll's narrative, imagine how co-housing could flesh out the Christian values of mutuality, service, and celebration, as opposed to individualism, privacy, privilege, and conspicuous consumerism. By reducing the amount of floor space and housing expenditure, time and money is freed up to serve others.

Temescal Commons

J. R. BERGDOLL JR.

"I tell you the truth, unless a kernel of wheat falls to the ground and dies, it remains only a single seed. But if it dies, it produces many seeds."
—John 12:24, NIV

Kids run laughingly through interconnected yards. Mary lovingly tends the flower gardens and enjoys some rare solitude. Years of monthly workdays—including the teenage boys and four-year olds—have produced bountiful vegetable beds, flowers, trees, handsome fences, benches, and a basketball hoop. Neighbors share in our community life with Cub Scout meetings, first aid training, and celebrations like Fourth of July barbecues. Twice a week, twenty-five to thirty neighborhood kids and adults gather in the common dining room, hold hands, and give thanks for the meal. This specially crafted cluster of homes, people, and activities—intentionally near a more challenged edge of Temescal Neighborhood—forms our attempt at a new type of Christian co-housing community…and our commitment to build the kingdom of God.

A broad range of nine households live at Temescal Commons, birthed out of the local Rockridge United Methodist Church. We share a vision of creating a different future for our children and neighborhood. Tom and Cheryl Garlick, with four children, bring hospitality to neighborhood kids. Gene, loyal to Saturday workdays, rented the same studio unit for thirty-plus years. Helen initiated neighborhood movie nights. Tom and Mary Prince have three teenage sons. Tom, a local schoolteacher, constantly propels us to live out our gospel values in new ways, while his wife keeps us grounded with her remarkable gardening. Deborah Quay is an enthusiastic, young, single artist. Kate Madden Yee and Randy Yee bring organization to our chaotic lives while caring for two young boys. I enjoy tending the ancient rose bushes and planning the workdays. Other renters add their spice, including two households that live nearby.

With my family across the continent, I appreciate being part of a community—especially for holiday meals. Initially, I feared little respite from the children, but I have all the privacy I need, and kids to play with anytime I want. With families and singles usually living separately in our culture, *this* particular arrangement provides role models for the children and is a welcome relief from everyone's normal routine.

Our community consists of older remodeled homes (including a Victorian) along with newly constructed homes. In all, there are three four-bedroom units, one three-bedroom, three two-bedroom flats, and two studios. Each new home was designed with smaller kitchens, dining areas, and living space, knowing we would have a common house. The common house—with a large kitchen, dining, laundry, and TV area—is near the center of our housing cluster. It adjoins an old barn with a dusty ground floor for bicycles and supplies, while the hayloft is a well-used recreation room with a ping-pong table and weights.

Six units and the common space are set up as a condominium association. All residents pay monthly dues for maintenance, utilities for the common area, and a long-term reserve fund for replacement of roofs, equipment, and such.

Co-housing projects are known for environmental sustainability. But we push the envelope: solar electric (photo-voltaic) cells are integrated into the metal roofs, producing most of the electricity we need. Solar cells above one home charge a rebuilt electric car, used for short trips in the area. Tankless water heaters supply heat to radiant heating coils and faucets, saving significantly on power bills; linoleum floors and wool carpets reduce toxic offgassing and landfill—due to their longer life. We used environmentally sensitive materials and methods in the wood framing and insulation. Initially, for some of us the cost seemed too high, but now we are thankful. The planning and execution were not without pain and conflict, however.

The fruit of our work has come slowly, after cold bleak times when we questioned what God was doing. We began with beautiful visions crafted in our late night meetings, whose seeds had to die, dry up, and lie buried in the ground before they could be reborn and produce fruit. Jesus' parable of the seed dying before it could be born was not a conscious theme, but emerged after reflecting back.

Daring to Listen

The origins of this vision had various beginnings. Two founding families had been involved in co-ownership of multifamily buildings; others had lived in Christian communities. My friend John, an aspiring architect, and I, a planner/developer in training, sketched our dream on a napkin in the early 1990s. At that time, our dreamed-up plan included the houses and low-income elderly apartments that adjoined our church. We envisioned removed fences and added play areas to create an intergenerational community. But the cost of land was prohibitive. The years passed by.

Listening to God

In a Bible study Mark Lau Branson led, the words of Nehemiah challenged us to do more than just preach and pray for the problems in our corner of Oakland. Dysfunctional public schools, weak social networks after decades of flight to the suburbs, rapid demographic changes, feeble crime prevention, abandoned properties, and trash dumping plagued the area. Nehemiah described his city, "'[T]he walls of Jerusalem...had been broken down and its gates...had been destroyed by fire" (Neh. 2:13b). But he didn't stop there; he moved to Jerusalem and organized the people to do something about their plight. God was also calling us to do something.

Our church had developed a decentralized way to foster discipleship and outreach with "mission covenant groups." John and I formed a Community Builders Mission Covenant Group to conduct housing and community development projects. We desired decent housing for the poor, but also realized our own living situations did not always reflect our gospel values. We slowly concluded that to make a significant neighborhood impact we must heed Nehemiah's example and relocate in the community for the long haul.

At the same time, a few of us were also crafting the "Essentials"—the church's defining identities and priorities. As a result, our housing and a neighborhood plan became an integral part of the church's vision.[2] We had dedicated tutors at Emerson Elementary, but no one had children attending the school. Conversations mentioned integrating our work, home, and worship lives, sharing child care and other responsibilities to reduce the stress on individuals and families. A critical mass of Rockridge members were moving to Temescal. The time was ripe to try living cooperatively.

Crafting Our Vision

As we initial co-housing pioneers committed ourselves to each other and the flurry of activity surrounding the project, we set aside time to craft our vision. Our vision statement begins: "We live in God's creation. We are to love God, each other, our neighbors, and to care for the creation." From there emerged three goals: to create community, be good neighbors, and care for God's creation.

For us, creating community meant simplifying our lifestyles, minimizing our expenses by sharing meals, cars, and major appliances, and raising children within an "extended family." We wanted freed up time and money to invest in our families, schools, and the neighborhood. This meant making our homes affordable to prevent the multiple jobs or long hours necessary to pay higher mortgages. It meant sharing yard work, prayer, and recreation.

To be good neighbors meant hospitality, Christian neighborliness, justice, and service. The neighbors hungered for relationships, so we envisioned hosting community meals. Emerson Elementary, near the bottom of the city's rankings, needed our skills. Because of Rockridge's tutoring program at Emerson, two members became teachers there. Our church's involvement with a nearby transitional home opened our eyes to those residents' challenge to find decent affordable housing in good neighborhoods upon completing their program. So we agreed to incorporate an apartment for formerly homeless families. We longed for the collective energy that co-housing would provide to help address Oakland's crying needs.

Caring for God's creation meant something different for each of us—from pruning orchids to looking at the stars through a telescope. We desired space for our varied passions, to enjoy the beauty and fruit of our gardens. We wanted every aspect of our sustainable building designs, construction, and operation to demonstrate our care for creation.

Developing Partners

With our having germinated in the Rockridge United Methodist Church, the congregation was our primary partner. Early on, we formed a legal entity, the Temescal Co-Housing Group, to facilitate the design, financing, and construction—enabling us to enter contracts with the architect, contractor, and lenders. Published materials and experienced friends provided support to a process that was very new to most of us.

Architect and Co-housing Consultant

We hired The Co-Housing Company of Kathryn McCamant and her husband and partner Chuck Durrett. Since we were our own developer, their architecture and project management experience fit well with our goals. In facilitating meetings to build consensus around the design, McCamant proved a good translator of our vision into the site and building plans—even though she came from a different spiritual tradition and was in her first faith-based co-housing community. Her observations are telling:

> There were fun meetings and difficult meetings. As someone who finds her spiritual center in nature, it took me a little getting used to their frequent biblical references. When they hit a particularly difficult issue, they would sometimes decide to hold the issue to the end of the meeting and then pray on it. Having worked with many different groups on difficult decisions, I could not help but to think "Why not?" It worked for them, and it seemed to be as good a method as any I've seen. Throughout the project, I saw the group benefit from the larger support network of their extended church community.[3]

Nehemiah Project/Oakland

To facilitate the "affordable housing" portion of our housing, we needed to raise money; to do that we needed a nonprofit partner. Of the proposed two "affordable" units, one would be owner-occupied and sold at a discount with resale restrictions, and the other owned and managed by a separate nonprofit—an unusual arrangement, but appropriate for our project. Every nonprofit housing developer we approached declined to participate for various reasons, so we looked to our church as the nonprofit partner. Concerned with liability and fund-raising limitations, we created a separate nonreligious legal entity, Nehemiah Project/Oakland, for this and other future church projects.

Mustard Seed Neighborhood Development Corporation

I worked part-time with Mustard Seed, a faith based construction and development enterprise some members of our church had recently formed. Mustard Seed would be the contractor for two of the six units and for the rehab of the two-story Victorian.

Doing the Work

Developing partners was not easy or quick, but the real challenges lay in executing the plan. We felt overwhelmed, but that caused us to lean on God. Like Nehemiah in Jerusalem, we received unexpected help from unusual allies. "And because the gracious hand of my God was upon me, the king granted my requests. So I went to the governors of Trans-Euphrates and gave them the king's letters" (Neh. 2:8b–9a, NIV).

Property Acquisition

Mark Lau Branson, his wife, Nina, and their sons, Noah and Nathan, lived in a house adjoining two underdeveloped lots–an ideal location for our community. Six-year-old Noah daily peered out his window at an abandoned-looking barn and vegetable garden on the vacant lot. Mark and Nina prayed with him each night for these properties. One day Mark saw a real estate agent on the site and learned it was difficult for the owner to let go of the land, having been in the family since the 1870s. By the time the lot was officially on the market a thick file of interested buyers stood in line. Interviews with five prospective buyers were set. We enlisted the church's prayers before, during, and after our interview. We offered above the asking price, and we were still outbid by $30,000. But the owner, excited about our plans to save the old house, with abundant vegetable gardens, wanted us to have the property! She offered to sell if we increased our bid by $15,000, which we gratefully did! She gave us eyes to see the importance of this piece of history. When the agent brought the keys, Noah knew those keys were an answer to his prayers.

Variance Approvals

After months of refining plans, the hurdle now was city approval of our code variances. Although little opposition existed, we requested sensitive things: a density variance to make the project financially viable, and smaller rear-yard setbacks–to create a shared middle yard as opposed to separate yards in the rear of each house. Due to the presence and work of our church, the neighborhood was supportive, yet immediate neighbors, the local neighborhood association, and planning commissioners had to be won over. Knocking on every door within a block, we obtained over one hundred signatures of support and held a town hall meeting. To address the concerns of the neighborhood association design review board, we presented our plans, listened to their input, and revised our plans.

At the planning commission meeting, we faced strong but civil opposition from one commissioner. He challenged all three of our variance requests, representing a popular sentiment that resists anything unlike a single-family detached development. Our research, however, showed how we were consistent with adjacent properties and the intent of city policies. Armed with prepared data and intercessory prayer, we saw God come though! Church members were supportive, but most surprising were the number of neighbors who came to the evening hearings and spoke on our behalf in the face of opposition. After the two-month campaign, the planning commission approved our proposed variances by a thin margin of three to two!

Celebration

At our groundbreaking ceremony in the spring of 1999, contractors, designers, neighbors, pastors, friends, and relatives joined the celebration, eager to build after almost two years of planning. The "St. Art" mission covenant group created temporary fantastic sculptures with salvaged iron, wood, and wire from the barn and demolished garage as part of the event. Celebration—one of our defining identities—was at its height with our public worship that day!

Dealing with Realities

Our co-housing group began inspired and enthusiastic, but our innovative ambitions were bound for challenges. Similar to the people in Nehemiah's time, our strength would be tested: "Meanwhile, the people in Judah said, 'The strength of the laborers is giving out, and there is so much rubble that we cannot rebuild the wall" (Neh. 4:10, NIV).

Financial Realities

We worked hard to make all the homes affordable. With funding from the Nehemiah Project/Oakland, we were to offer lower-cost ownership for those who were below 80 percent of the area median income. As the only buyer who qualified, I was willing to deal with fund-raising and restrictions. I wrote for the *Co-housing Journal,* telling part of my own journey during this time:

> We thought naively that doing this together at a high enough density, the houses would be fairly inexpensive. Therefore, with limited incomes we should have no problem, right? Wrong. Construction and other development costs forced us to face the reality that some of us wouldn't be able to afford this—even with a simple, bare-bones design and doing some of the construction ourselves. Our architect, Kathryn McCamant, loved the vision but cautioned that we probably couldn't build as cheaply as we wanted. Her husband and fellow architect Chuck bet her that we could get our design built for under $80 per square foot. Fortunately, he won the bet. We did get the cost down, but even so, my two-bedroom 840–square-foot flat would cost approximately $175,000. My home was left unpainted and unfinished so I could put in "sweat-equity." With over three hundred fifty hours of my labor, I still wasn't sure it would be affordable. After generous donations, much effort at a volunteer workday, and a yard sale, we made it half-way to the $60,000 deficit on my unit. Thankfully, Oakland offers no-interest "second" loans to low-income first-time homebuyers. Plus, the officials liked the project. We had made it![4]

My faith in God was greatly strengthened with this accomplishment after working so long with so much uncertainty.

Tom Prince and Mark Lau Branson were especially passionate about sustainable construction, renewable energy, and raising food; yet, it seemed impossible considering the up-front expense. Their desire to contribute beyond the standard costs might have remained a dream if not for an unexpected inheritance and employee stock options. They created a restricted account to fund major ecological features.[5]

Landscaping Squabbles

With construction almost complete, we were derailed by a major disagreement. Most co-housing projects face intractable conflict at some point, according to McCamant and other mentors. Ours was over the seemingly innocuous issue of landscaping. In the one camp, the sustainability advocates wanted almost everything edible. The other camp wanted landscaped beauty, cautious of the time involved in harvesting and maintaining edible plants and trees. Both were valid, yet we couldn't come to consensus after months of research, talking, and frustration. We wanted to walk away and do nothing until we happened upon an alternative: *Discerning God's Will Together*, by Danny Morris and Charles Olsen.[6] Following each suggested step to discernment led us to the solution. We let go of our individual desires—in some ways, we "died" a little for the good of the group. We laugh now over the controversy, thrilled with our landscape—where every corner of the common yard, garden, and walkway give us food *or* beauty.

Construction Woes

The construction started beautifully. Our primary contractor was enthusiastic and seemingly the best fit. We had interviewed and carefully checked references. However, by the time we realized he was in trouble, the damage was done: sloppy, defective work and serious delays. The initial optimistic five or six month construction window stretched to almost a year, while we waited anxiously, living out of boxes. Eventually, the relationship broke down. We terminated their contract and hired Mustard Seed and three new subcontractors.

As the owner's representative, I was disappointed and stressed. I had committed to start another full-time job and had gone a couple of years without a significant vacation. Thankfully, Mark, our "jack-of-all-trades," coordinated the subcontractors in the midst of his already packed schedule. And Cheryl coordinated some repairs. We spent $35,000 more than planned, not including indirect costs of the delays. After these six extra months, our group was exhausted.

Loss and Limits

In addition to maintaining the intensive schedule for co-housing meetings, we also maintained our demanding regular church commitments.

This kept us from fully enjoying what was unfolding before us. We were being formed into a community, yet with no time to relax and strengthen friendships. Births and birthdays were celebrated at meetings.

After we moved in, two founding families reluctantly heard and followed God's call to leave our community. In such a small co-housing cluster, the impact of their loss was painful. At the same time, our church experienced difficult times. We lost key members, including our pastor, friend, and leader of over fifteen years. Leadership and support structures for covenant discipleship groups and Bible study slowly disappeared. The church "Essentials" were suddenly up for grabs. Lack of leadership capacity forced us to put the transitional unit on hold. We had to let aspects of the original vision die, not knowing if they would rise again.

The commitment and inspiration of the new renters and owners have filled the holes. Deborah lifts our spirits in the way she plays with the children and colorfully painted our common house. Mike and Nathan, as Young Life workers, add to the lives of our youth. Lynn Elizabeth, a new owner, has become another champion of community life. My own spirit has improved dramatically with marriage to Jill Ildefonso, who has transformed our small home with her decorative gifts and hospitality. Building community is an evolving creation.

Discovering Insights

God had different plans for both the church and the co-housing development, with each gradually less dependent on each other. We are still healing from the pain of the losses. We have taken encouragement from Jesus' words, "I tell you the truth, unless a kernel of wheat falls to the ground and dies, it remains only a single seed. But if it dies, it produces many seeds (Jn. 12:24, NIV). Tom Prince, our resident who aptly articulates what some of us have a hard time putting into words, said this:

> Perhaps it is not a bad thing, though it certainly is not a pleasant thing, to feel like we are rotting on the ground like a fallen kernel of wheat. Some of our dreams and hopes have been dashed, but I suppose that it does not follow that we are not right in the middle of God's work among us. How long did the original harmony in the Garden of Eden last? Did Moses the deliverer enter the Promised Land? God does not seem nearly as worried as we are if things don't work out just so. He seems much more interested in our souls and He seems to do much of this soul work in brokenness. He does not avoid humiliation, weakness, or even death, in the midst of his otherworldly work among us; and He calls us to follow and promises his presence. This we seek.[7]

Here are other major insights discovered by our co-housing group:

- *Create a clear vision statement.* This kept us on track.

- *Have sufficient participants.* A co-housing project is best with a minimum of a dozen households with responsible adults to share the burdens.
- *Be realistic about the time and energy needed to accomplish the task.* Taking on a major project requires giving up other things, but it's worth it.
- *Make sure the church structures are supportive and flexible.* More fully recognizing the process of building our own homes as part of helping create the Kingdom in the city would have minimized meetings and complexity, and added to our goal of simplifying life.
- *Find the right partners. Trust, honesty, communication, and a shared vision must be priorities.* Partners with experience and a commitment are essential (especially contractors and architects). This may take time—but pays off.
- *Plan time to play, pray, and just be with one another.* Keep realistic expectations of relationships and closeness. Friendships grow and fade; people move. Success should not be overly dependent on specific people. We are called to fulfill God's plan and not do more than we can handle ourselves, so we can watch God work. Setting aside time for serious prayerful discernment releases individual desires in order to allow us to be molded into what God wants—not what we individually want.

Somewhat humbled, with our hearts more open to God's will, we give God thanks for seeds that had to die and those that have produced the abundance we enjoy. The co-housing "movement" has given us a form and a language for ideas we were already pursuing, opening us to a new way of living out our faith, participating in building the kingdom of God.

Vista Hermosa

Fruit that Lasts

ROGER BAIRSTOW

Introduction to the Workforce Housing Model BY JILL SHOOK

Companies' providing housing for workers have a long history in the United States. In 1848, William Greg set the precedent in this country, building cottages for his textile mill workers in Granville, South Carolina.[1] Other employers built whole towns; coal mining, copper mining, and lumber mill towns were common. Their goal: to keep workers content, productive, and nearby.

The idea of company towns was borrowed from Europe. In the 1800s, George Cadbury constructed a planned village around his chocolate factory with unheard of benefits at that time. He conducted morning Bible studies, gave half-day Saturdays off so families could be together, provided free healthcare, established schools for the children, and enabled his workers to purchase their own homes and businesses. One hundred and fifty years later, Cadbury Chocolates still places a high value on its workers; the area remains a model of prosperity.

Inspired by Cadbury, George Pullman designed his own town for workers on his luxury railcars. However, instead of investing in the workers, he was driven by profits alone, and the town failed miserably.[2]

The lack of housing for company workers is "taking an economic toll across the country."[3] Bobby Rayburn, of the National Homebuilders Association, says,

> Many teachers, police officers, fire fighters, and other moderate-income workers–representing the heartbeat of any community–are

working two and three jobs to meet their monthly housing expenses or are looking at housing 50 miles away or more from their jobs.[4]

Today, employers are finding it difficult to recruit and retain good workers and pay sufficient salaries to meet housing costs. One report found that janitors could rent a one-bedroom apartment for no more than 30 percent of their income in only six of the sixty largest metropolitan areas across the country.[5] "People may not realize that preventing the development of housing, over time, will eventually destroy the community's ability to accommodate economic growth."[6] It is estimated that the lack of workforce housing in the Twin Cities area of Minnesota is causing businesses to lose an estimated $137 million in profit annually.[7]

The marriage of labor and housing ebbs and flows. In 1982 the New York City Housing Partnership was formed when businesses could not hire good workers because of lack of housing.[8] So far the program has provided 20,000 new houses.[9] Police officers, required to live in the city, are given preference. In fact, half the homes are for workers living in the city. A Realtor® zeroing in on this market admits that her associates who are selling expensive homes make much more than she. However, as an ex–school teacher, she knows what it is like not to be able to afford a home. She enjoys her steady and grateful clientele.[10]

Some employers give direct financial assistance to their workers to purchase homes. Others, such as some employers in San Jose, have organized advocacy groups to attend public meetings that support housing. Some universities and hospitals provide homeownership for employees on their land, using a ground lease similar to the land trust model. (See chapter 14.)

Surprisingly, workforce housing suffers the same stigma as housing for lower-income citizens. "Housing for our Heroes" and other catchy phrases seek the approval of NIMBYs. A billboard with an attractive woman with a clipboard and stethoscope reads: "She can save your life, but she can't be your neighbor." This chapter will expose an even stronger resistance against the Latino migrant population.

Roger Bairstow's narrative below emphasizes that the Broetjes' success is measured not by profits, but in the success and well-being of their employees—and of all workers. For them, that includes the 94 percent of the world outside of the United States—three billion of which exists on 5 percent of the total resources available.[11] Cheryl Broetje says, "For us, it was impossible to separate business goals from spiritual values."[12]

Vista Hermosa

ROGER BAIRSTOW

*And now, Israel, what does the L*ORD *your God require of you?...He gives justice to orphans and widows. He shows love to the foreigners living among you and gives them food and clothing. You, too, must show love to foreigners, for you yourselves were once foreigners in the land of Egypt.*
—Deuteronomy 10:12a, 18–19, NLT

In rural Eastern Washington State lies a place many have referred to as a piece of the kingdom of God on earth. Despite a desert landscape, it is lush with apple trees as far as the eye can see. Many rural communities have experienced their population fleeing to the city, but here lives a vibrant and growing Latino community of approximately 600 people. The residents named the community *Vista Hermosa*–meaning "Beautiful View." Indeed, the view and the quiet work of God in this place are beautiful.

Vista Hermosa and Broetje Orchards appear as a surprising oasis after an eastward drive from Pasco, Washington. Stucco buildings with red-tile roofs are artfully placed on manicured lawns comprising 133 single-family homes and garden apartments, a chapel, preschool, post office, laundry facilities, market, gymnasium, soccer field, playground, and garden plots. Vista Hermosa is designed as a type of intermediary housing, where workers coming from a migrant lifestyle have the opportunity to live in a safe, nurturing community and gain additional skills. The average three- and four-bedroom homes of 1,200 square feet include a family room, kitchen, two bathrooms, and an attached garage. These rent at 60 percent of comparable housing. Our rents do not exceed 30 percent of a family's income. A long waiting list is not uncommon. With lower rents and affordable child care, families save enough to own homes in the Tri-Cities area thirty minutes to the west.

Broetje Orchards, one of the largest privately owned apple orchards in the world, manages over 5,300 acres of Fuji, Gala, Braeburn, Granny Smith, Red, and Golden Delicious apples, and 115 acres of cherries. Because of a new packing line installed in 2004, workers only have day shift hours, allowing all family members time together in the evening. While many other family-owned businesses are fighting to survive, Ralph and Cheryl Broetje use proceeds to invest in their workers. The Broetjes' business-as-ministry model involves more than 900 people, primarily Latinos, working year-round in the orchard and warehouse.

Daring to Listen

I first met Ralph and Cheryl Broetje after a long, cross-country trip. I was in love with their daughter Suzanne. She and I met in 1997 at Michigan

State University. With a mutual passion for international development and social justice, we were heading to Kenya to conduct research. Expecting only what Suzanne modestly called "their orchard," I was astounded. I saw a place bringing a long-needed return to Adam Smith's original conception of capitalism practiced within a code of morality–a foreign concept to some and a rare example for me. The Broetjes had a faith in people and in God that I had never before witnessed.

As a youth, Ralph Broetje dreamed of owning an apple orchard and using the proceeds to help needy children in India. Five years later, he met his wife, Cheryl, who dreamed of "building community" to nurture the potential and personal call of others. Their dreams would eventually dovetail, but here's how it all started:

> In 1980, after farming successes and failures, the Broetjes settled on the banks of the Snake River. Ralph was one of the early pioneers who realized that the dams then being built on the Lower Snake River would create opportunities for new businesses by furnishing inexpensive electrical energy and an ample supply of water…He dared to dream on a large scale…The desert soil, which had never suffered the leaching action of persistent rains, produced prodigiously once irrigated.[13]

As the Broetjes pursued their dreams with the mission to be a quality fruit company bearing "fruit that will last" (Jn. 15:16), God blessed them with a fruitful harvest. Recognizing the Christian mandate to serve the common good, especially the "least of these" (Mt. 25:45), they believed that faith and business could thrive together.

Listening to the Plight of Migrants

When they began farming in 1967, practically all the farmworkers were Caucasian. By the end of the 1970s, however, workers were by and large exclusively Latino immigrants. Most spoke no English, had only a few years of schooling, and often worked without legal papers. They lived isolated and marginalized within a U.S. culture that generally distained them.

Cheryl Broetje often describes the Bible as a book of migrations: "God uses migrants to move history, while calling people of faith to action." Cheryl and Ralph felt called to understand their employees' plight. So in 1983, on a "trip of perspective," as Cheryl likes to call it, they saw firsthand what their workers had left in Mexico: families living on barren land alongside mosquito-infested riverbanks, with homes in garbage dumps and cardboard boxes the size of clothes dryers. By the end of their trip, the Broetjes' perspective had changed: They came to see their workers as economic refugees. Even in the U.S. they often live without access to healthcare, education, adequate housing, or a place of social belonging. A migrant cycle of employment brings them through California to Washington and back again. In 1989, unauthorized workers comprised only 8 percent of the farm labor force, compared to 51.5 percent in 1998.[14]

Listening to the Employees

In 1987, the Broetjes established the "First Fruits" warehouse and packing line, giving them additional opportunities to listen:

> "Once you have more than 150 women working on the same line, you start hearing stories that we didn't hear from the men [working in the fields]," Cheryl says…"They would keep older kids out of school to baby sit," contributing to the high dropout rate among Latino students.[15]

The families knew this was not a good situation. But they had to work, and Cheryl says, "We had to do something!" So the Broetjes built the New Horizon Preschool to provide for their employees' children during the day.[16] "We started with their felt needs…child-care facilities that would prepare their children to start kindergarten in the U.S. and be on par with Anglo children in language."[17]

Ralph and Cheryl continued to listen. They heard stories of inadequate housing—children bitten by rats at night, leaky and broken plumbing and roofing, and outrageous rents. Transportation for the thirty-minute drive from Pasco, where most of their workers lived, was also a problem— exacerbated by the sad history of car crashes and resulting deaths caused by drunk divers on the route, and stops by immigration officials. These major hardships and disruptions led the Broetjes to develop a safe community with decent affordable housing.

Developing Partners

Neither Ralph nor Cheryl considered themselves experts in housing. However, they felt called to move forward. They initially considered low-income housing tax credits. But the majority of the orchard's farm-working families earned above 60 percent of the area median income—the threshold to qualify for tax credits.[18] Many workers are trapped in that category of "near poor"—too poor to afford adequate housing or child care, but not poor enough to qualify for assistance. The Broetjes ultimately approached their workers and family members as partners in developing Vista Hermosa.

As farmers, the Broetjes often were alone in their mission to serve the migrant population. As recently as 2001, the city of Pasco, which is 60 percent Latino and home to approximately 50 percent of Broetje Orchards employees, attempted to ban services for the poor in their downtown corridor.[19] "Thanks to one courageous person," Cheryl recalls, "the city council was reminded of a federal law against prohibiting churches from offering support for the poor."

Doing the Work

Financing the construction of Vista Hermosa was done primarily with the economic muscle of the orchard business. The Broetjes knew that the land, an abundant harvest, and prosperity were gifts of God, given to be shared with those in need. Using their business for equity, a loan of $5.5 million was the sum total of loans and profit that the Broetjes used to build the community. Snake River Housing Incorporated became its legal for-profit owner and manager.

The real work began once the buildings were up. The larger, more challenging, task was that of building a community—an environment that would nurture individual growth and generational change. Of the original families who moved in, in 1991, approximately one-third of their children had prior gang involvement. It was a conscious choice to offer housing to these families, but as Ralph and Cheryl explain, "We felt that we had no right to develop housing for these families without providing assistance to address the problems that first led to youth gang involvement." Thus, the orchard business became a catalyst for a myriad of educational programs: English and GED classes; youth enrichment programming in the arts, sciences, and drama; college preparatory programs; women's support groups; physical education activities; cultural events; and more.

Nonprofit organizations emerged to extend these programs: The Vista Hermosa Foundation (1991),[20] which operates an on-site K-6 elementary school; the Center for Sharing (1986);[21] Jubilee Boys Ranch (1996);[22] and Mano à Mano (2003).[23] The Vista Hermosa Foundation partners with communities in Mexico, India, and around the world. After the Broetjes' adoption of six children from India, their ministry had a more global focus.

To staff positions created by these emerging entities, Cheryl Broetje recalls:

> We looked around for who was ready to grow. They have become our pre-school staff, housing managers, and social service workers in addition to becoming agribusiness managers on a world-class level. Along the way, we have implemented continuing-education goals for these people according to their stated needs. Over the years, we have become a training ground for emerging Hispanic leaders, many of whom go on to become first time home owners, and eventually take their place of leadership.[24]

After years of beginning programs to meet the needs of their residents, today the Broetjes have partners from public, private, and religious sectors who are helping dramatically: the YWCA, the county health department, private counseling, legal services, advocacy and awareness programs, local community colleges, universities, farmworker's clinics, and more. The college prep and elementary programs have expanded with two federal grants (one under President Bush's faith-based initiative).

Developing Snake River's Management System

At age seven Eva Madrigal began a life as a migrant laborer. She intermittently attended various schools along the migrant route her family followed. She finished her "formal" education at the age of twelve and began working in the fields to contribute to her family's income. Eventually, Eva married and found herself employed at Broetje Orchards, beginning in the Broetjes' tree nursery and then seasonally harvesting the orchard's cherries. Since then, she has completed her GED and college classes. Now, as Director of Snake River Housing, she serves the very community that once served her. She is the mother of three children, all in college, with one in a graduate degree program. Her youngest received a full college scholarship from the Vista Hermosa Foundation.

With capable leaders like Eva, the first residents decided on a list of basic rules under which they agreed to live—rules of common decency and mutual respect. For example, alcoholic beverages are restricted to inside the home. Only those listed on the lease agreement may reside in the community. Slower speeds must be maintained in or around housing. Minors not allowed to drive. In the first few years there were violations and evictions due to noncompliance. Over time, the rules' benefits were internalized, and now residents place these expectations on one another. For example, neighbors quickly notice drug and alcohol abuse, domestic violence, or a lack of basic necessities among resident families. With self-monitoring, Snake River Housing staff simply acts as a catalyst to resolve issues through family interventions and community meetings. There is a delicate balance between respecting a family's right to privacy and enforcing rules. We err on the side of grace—a good policy—giving families every chance to comply. We have evicted only five families over ten years.

Investing in the Workers

Early in its creation, Snake River Housing needed assistance from Broetje Orchards to overcome cash flow problems, management oversights, and facilities maintenance. Today, Snake River Housing, whose board I chair, is a self-reliant organization. Our partnership with Broetje Orchards enables us to have flexible rent payment schedules. With year-round workers, hours ebb and flow due to bad weather and market conditions. During the winter months, when there is generally less work, Snake River Housing maintains flexibility for families unable to pay the full amount of rent due until incomes increase in the spring. The orchard business monitors who has the ability to pay, making a flexible payment system possible.

Snake River's profits are measurable, but small. The 2003 net profit margin was approximately 3 percent. Each year roughly 13 percent of total expenditures is used to support educational programs. The initial $5.5 million investment to build Vista Hermosa was never intended to be repaid by rental income. The Broetjes' return on their initial investment is expressed by the success and growth of youth and adults in the community, the high employee retention rates, and employees' dedication to quality work.

Dealing with Realities

In their goal to create community, Ralph and Cheryl optimistically believed that everyone would quickly come together living in harmony. However, initial attempts to unify became divisive. Spirituality, education, and the business-as-ministry model are continuing challenges.

Challenges to Spirituality

Every spiritual community has a culture embedded in the soul of its parishioners. The Broetjes have learned this culture must be honored to create an environment for spiritual growth—a key ingredient to create a safe, nurturing community. Ralph and Cheryl's initial dream for Vista Hermosa was one interdenominational service. They hired a passionate lay pastor. For the first two years, ecumenical services, often with a standing-room-only crowd, live music, and personal testimonies of God's blessings poured out from the chapel. Faith grew, giving people the strength to seek healing, to stop abusive behavior. "As they were touched by God's renewing spirit," Cheryl says, "many people...began to develop their own sense of what seemed right in terms of religious expression. More and more, they began to have questions and to exert their freedom to speak." The pastor and others became defensive and increasingly opposed to congregating as one group. Some misinterpreted service attendance as an obligation to keep their jobs with the orchard. Eventually, the interdenominational concept dissolved. The pastor was dismissed, and people began to repair the divides. "The best thing to do was to allow various groups to continue meeting in their own established or emerging traditions," says Cheryl. Through grass-roots initiatives, denominational services rose up. Five weekday mornings, two evenings, and on holidays, services fill the chapel with the activities originally envisioned.

Challenges to Education

A culture of poverty and survival creates barriers to educational opportunities and advancement. Because many families came as "economic refugees," their primary focus is enough money to pay for food, rent, and transportation. Thus an ongoing task is showing children their options, how to be their own agents of change, and that they are ultimately responsible for their learning, personal development, and achievement. But a young person's undocumented status poses particular challenges. It leaves youth with a sense of hopelessness, curtailing educational dreams and a sense of control over their lives. Legislation such as the Latino/a Educational Achievement Project (EHB 1079), passed by the Washington

State legislature and signed by the governor in 2003, is a great start to ameliorating such issues. This allows undocumented students graduating from a Washington high school to pay in-state rates for state colleges and universities.

Challenges of a Business-as-Ministry Model

Ralph and Cheryl have worked hard to promote and encourage other wealthy farmers and families to engage in similar work. To their dismay, their efforts yielded few results and often strained their relationships with those in the business world. In addition, some people, coming from a *workers'* perspective, only wish to see business as a problem that contributes to the detriment of employees and the environment, as opposed to a solution toward the greater good of the community. Over the years the Broetjes have noticed these attitudes decreasing, but they still surface at times.

Discovering Insights

The road to Vista Hermosa has been an incredible journey—one that strikes awe and humility in those who visit and those of us who see it anew through a stranger's eyes. Today, a new chapter in the story of creating a community is being written. Ralph and Cheryl responded to the needs at hand as they listened and responded to God's lead. There was little if any time to contemplate theory, develop models, or create organizational charts. Now, the staff has this luxury. In this next phase of development, in my role with Snake River, we are building stronger leaders and organizational structures, allowing the community to have more control over the programs and issues affecting them. Citizen participation is the bedrock of this concept, recognizing that children and families are the primary stakeholders in their own lives.

The following story illustrates many insights the Broetjes have discovered as God has tutored them to take ever-increasing steps of faith. In this story, the job of fruit packer is elevated to one of benefactor and decision-maker, allowing immigrants to improve their own hometowns in Mexico and elsewhere. This story encapsulates principles of leadership development and God's quiet and powerful work taking place at Broetje Orchards.

The Cherry Crop

In 1996, Ralph announced he would cut down fifty acres of cherries, as they had never made a profit. Cheryl and Ralph retreated from this decision, reflecting on the parable about the fig grower who decided to give the tree one more year:

> "A man planted a fig tree in his garden and came again and again to see if there was any fruit on it, but he was always disappointed. Finally, he said to his gardener, `I've waited three years, and there hasn't been a single fig! Cut it down. It's taking up space we can

use for something else.' "The gardener answered, `Give it one more chance. Leave it another year, and Ill give it special attention and plenty of fertilizer. If we get figs next year, fine. If not, you can cut it down.'" (Lk. 13:6–9, NLT)

The Broetjes decided that if the trees produced a profit that year, they would give all the profits to God. Later that year, they were at Pimpollo Children's Home, an orphanage in Oaxaca, Mexico. It desperately needed funding to renovate and enlarge their facilities. Quickly seeing a link, Ralph and Cheryl agreed to give Pimpollo the cherry profits for that year. They left the children with one request: to pray for an abundant harvest.

For the first time ever, the Broetjes had a bumper crop, enabling them to send Pimpollo a check for $350,000. Each subsequent year, Ralph and Cheryl kept their promise to God and the cherries have enjoyed remarkable success. Decreasing their role as benefactors, Ralph and Cheryl now divide the profits among committees of workers, who themselves determine what charitable causes to support.

In 2003, over $700,000 was donated through three cherry crop committees, representing all employees in the field warehouse and non-profit work. They chose to support five projects in Mexico: Pimpollo Children's Home in Juchitan; Niños de la Calle, a World Vision outreach ministry for street children in Mexico City; a flood relief/housing project for fifteen communities in Central Mexico; DESMI, a micro-lending organization working with indigenous Mexicans in Chiapas; and the rebuilding of a church in Oaxaca, Mexico.

Since 1996, the Pimpollo children have sent photos and hand-written thank-you letters to the employees at Broetje Orchards. The first of these mailings warmed the hearts of workers, resulting in twenty-four men signing up the next week for weekly payroll deductions to donate to the orphanage—joining fifteen workers who were already donating between ten and seventy-five cents each week. The next week, another fifteen signed up, and the next week ten more.

God heard the prayers of Mexican children for a bountiful harvest. Now the God of heaven is multiplying the generous spirit among workers at Broetje Orchards—a spirit that says there is enough for everyone if we all give and trust in God. The culture of poverty is breaking. God is committed to the redemption of an obscure orphanage in Southern Mexico, of cherry trees and people seeking economic refuge at Broetje Orchards. Ralph and Cheryl's childhood dreams have come true. God is transforming lives, building community, instilling hope and faith in this oasis in the desert. While I introduced the community as a piece of the kingdom of God on earth, experience reveals Vista Hermosa to be a continual work in progress. It is our greatest prayer that, from God's vantage point, it truly is a "vista hermosa"—a beautiful view, with fruit that lasts.

14

HOME

Catholic Land Trust Communities

JILL SHOOK

Introduction to Community Land Trusts BY JILL SHOOK

I traveled to Maine and toured through three of the six land trust communities of Homeworkers Organized for More Employment (HOME). I was deeply impressed by this unique underused model and the charm of the shingle-sided, storybook Cape Cod and Saltbox style homes. This chapter gives us a bird's eye view of this viable, little-known model of permanent affordability—and a peek into rural poverty.

Recently I heard a brilliant presentation on Community Land Trusts (CLTs) by Rick Jacobus with the Local Initiatives Support Network in San Francisco.[1] I was impressed again! Cities far and wide are inviting Rick to present CLTs as a workable solution to preserve and grow their affordable housing stock. In the United States and Canada, more than 120 active CLTs exist, and a growing number are developing—from Cleveland, Ohio, to Portland, Oregon; in university communities from State College, Pennsylvania, to Boulder, Colorado; and in expensive resort communities from the Florida Keys to the San Juan Islands off Washington State.

A community land trust is a democratically controlled nonprofit that owns real estate in order to preserve affordability.[2] A land trust can be on contiguous land or on sites scattered throughout a community, and can lease to any variety of uses—ownership, cooperatives, rental, offices, and so on—but is primarily for homeownership[3] When a CLT sells homes, it leases the underlying land through a long-term renewable lease (usually for ninety nine years). When homeowners decide to move, the land lease requires the home be sold back to the CLT or to another low-income household. To give homeowners a fair return for their investment, each CLT designs a resale formula that keeps the price affordable for future low-income households, thus preserving the subsidy in perpetuity without repeating a subsidy each time a home is sold.[4]

CLTs improve divested areas and fight absentee ownership and gentrification. The earnings of absentee landlords are not usually spent in local stores and often is not used to improve the property. A CLT removes land from the speculative market, requiring owners to live in their homes.

Like Habitat for Humanity, Community Land Trusts can trace part of their beginnings to the early 1960s with Clarence Jordan, founder of the Koinonia Farm outside of Americus, Georgia. Jordan, a Baptist minister with a doctoral degree in theology and a masters degree in agriculture, was "as much at home on the seat of a tractor as he was in the pulpit."[5] In Koinonia's efforts to racially integrate the Deep South, it suffered dozens of violent attacks and boycotts against its farm's products. Despite and perhaps even because of the racial prejudice, the business grew. There was a market for people wanting to invest in a socially responsible way, even in housing. Koinonia's founders and supporters envisioned a racially mixed community with homes built by volunteers and the future residents. This experiment launched both Habitat and a seed in the imagination of Robert Swann, who researched alternative approaches to housing in India and Israel. To settle village violence after Gandhi's death, Vinoba Bhave discovered the problem. "One villager stood up and said simply, 'we need land.' Pointing to the man who had just spoke, Vinoba said, 'My brother here is without land. Who can give me some land for him?' To his amazement, one man stood up and said he had some land he could give. Then another stood up and another until there was enough land for...two or three landless families."[6] But land was not enough. Families didn't have the credit or the means to buy tools, fertilizer, or seeds, and they ended up back on the streets of Calcutta. To remedy this, the land was given to the village as a whole, which acted as the land's trustee.

Meanwhile, back in the United States, Martin Luther King Jr.'s cousins Slater and C. B. King went with Robert Swann to Israel to study the *kibbutzim* (cooperatives), and *moshaviem* (villages), emerging as successful models to prevent land speculation. When they returned, they began our county's first Community Land Trust.[7]

———

In the following narrative you will read: "Poor people...think it's their fault that their lives have gone off the rails"—a conclusion poor people often make about themselves, and that society often makes about poor people. Sometimes this conclusion is true, but often it is not. The assumption can produce undue depression, guilt, and hopelessness. Groups such as

HOME build community among the poor, ridding them of a destructive isolation that makes them feel that everything is their fault. But often state, national, and global dynamics contribute to their plight. Today, for example, the waters off Maine are overfished, logging mills are shutting down, and jobs and industries are exported overseas, as in many areas of the country.

Sister Lucy Ann Poulin, who began HOME, brought CLTs to Maine. HOME's mission builds upon the God-given hope and desire of poor people to help themselves. One way HOME does this is to offer the American Dream of homeownership—something many never dared believe possible.

HOME

JILL SHOOK

"'The land must not be sold permanently, because the land is mine and you are but aliens and my tenants." —Leviticus 25:23, NIV

After a long bus ride to this charming rural community of Maine, I sat in the kitchen and began my interview. I asked about changed lives. I wrote as fast as I could as I listened to the amazing story of the Carter family. They chose to love each other against their parents' wishes; therefore, neither set of parents had anything to do with them. This young family lived in a tent prior to HOME's taking them in. They moved to this rural part of Maine because of Portland's soaring rents. Dwayne worked backbreaking minimum wage jobs raking blueberries in the summer heat and migrating to northern Maine in the fall to pick potatoes. Meanwhile, Janet and their two children, Matthew and Chuck, made do in the tent.

HOME, an intentional faith-based community, "serves first those who suffer most." Dwayne and Janet Carter first heard about HOME years ago, when they used the HOME food bank. At the end of 1998, the Carters came again. It was getting cold; they stopped to look for space in one of HOME's shelters to provide the children with a roof, real beds, and indoor plumbing.

As part of routine intake procedures, housing options are discussed—shelter, transitional housing, and permanently affordable homes. As it happened, a home was available on one of HOME's land trust tracts. But the Carters had never established credit—a huge obstacle! A bank was willing to finance as long as the family had a co-signer and down payment. Because of HOME's affiliation with Equity Trust, they agreed to co-sign and provide the down payment. Closing day came. When the Carters saw their new home, their eyes were wide with wonderment and gratitude. Ten Sedgwick Land Trust families prepared a turkey dinner with all the fixings to celebrate the Carters' arrival.

With the stability of a home, Dwayne developed a stronger sense of self-confidence, resulting in better-paying jobs and helping him believe he could do more with his life. Via Interactive Television (ITV) he received his AA, which qualified him for the university system. Thanks to scholarships and grants, today Dwayne is a teacher contemplating graduate school. His wife gained the confidence to attend a local high school and obtain a GED. Their children are well adjusted, intelligent, and self-motivated. When eight-year-old Matthew set up a lemonade stand, he used a computer program to keep track of his costs, sales, and profits. After school their home is open to children in the land trust—there are no latchkey kids in Sedgwick!

The Carters needed a boost. With HOME's broadened vision to include the development of community land trusts, families like the Carters can purchase permanently affordable homes and find the long-term stability needed to thrive.

HOME's 300-acre Covenant Community Land Trust (CCLT) is made up of six communities: Hayes/Reid with three families, Patten Pond with six, Midvale with five, Soper Lot with three, Sedgwick with twelve, and Bucksmills with three. HOME is presently building the Dedham and the Facteau land trust communities. HOME also built two non-land trust affordable homes for families in other areas—one energy efficient—making a total of thirty-four affordable homes.

Daring to Listen

HOME

HOME began in 1970 when some low-income local people were looking for a way to augment their meager earnings. It started with the kind of entrepreneurial spirit demonstrated by little Matthew with his lemonade stand. When a woman lost her job in a shoe factory, because of the more globalized economy, she asked a nun, "If I make quilts, can you sell them for me?" Upon hearing this, the seed of a craft co-op store dropped into the heart of HOME's founder—Lucy Ann Poulin, an ex-Carmelite nun. Sister Lucy grew up poor on a Maine farm. She vividly recalls the difference between the way she was treated when she worked at a plant plucking chickens and the respect she now enjoys as a nun. "I was the same person," Lucy says. She explains how "the way to judge a society is by how it treats the weakest people in it."[8]

Listening and responding to needs did not stop with the crafters' building a store.[9] Some craftspeople couldn't read, so HOME opened an Adult Education Learning Center and the first alternative high school in the district—the only one in Maine with childcare.[10] Today, HOME's educational programs include literacy and GED tutoring, college-level programs, job training, and workshops in pottery, leather, wood, and weaving. Then a food pantry, a produce cooperative, and a soup kitchen opened. They started vegetable gardens, greenhouses, an orchard, and community gardens, leading to a farmers' market, a revolving loan fund, and education on how to farm using free or low-cost natural resources. Then Heifer Project International came to Maine—providing business planning and livestock—where recipients agreed to share the offspring of their livestock with others in need, making them partners with Heifer in the fight to end hunger and poverty. Discovering that people could not pay for doctor visits and often put off going until it was too late, HOME organized a free health clinic and later a dental clinic.

Confronted with an acute problem of homelessness, HOME kept opening shelters. With five shelters and two transitional housing complexes, permanent housing solutions were needed. So Sister Lucy wrote legislation to begin Community Land Trusts in Maine. She traveled to Augusta, Maine, several times between 1974 and 1976 to sell the idea. They ran a weekend seminar bussing people from shelters to attend public hearings. The legislation passed! Community Land Trusts began to spread in Maine—a movement responsible for a steady development of housing affordable in perpetuity for the poorest people in the State.

Everyone on HOME's land trusts come from substandard conditions—some have lived in cars, buses, and tents, like the Carters. Working with the poor never involves just one solution. They cannot pay for homes without adequate work, which leads to programs to address education and skill development. But perhaps hardest of all is developing hope and self-respect. "Poor people are probably clinically depressed to some degree. They think it's their fault that their lives have gone off the rails."[11]

Molly Ivins, veteran columnist and former *New York Times* bureau chief, was impressed enough with HOME to feature its work in a recent article:

> Perhaps the most impressive thing about the whole operation is that it is not terribly impressive...There is no posh administration building, no fancy anything anywhere...Almost everything around HOME is made of waste or scrap or is recycled. This is the logical obverse of a consumer society in which planned obsolescence is the foundation of the economy. And as our society seems to regard more and more people as disposable, the need for another way becomes clearer and clearer.[12]

HOME works without fanfare and expectation of recognition, preferring to put money into helping families in need rather than in fancy buildings. When a family such as the Carters is able to achieve home-ownership, HOME celebrates the family. The Carters needed a boost, but they also needed to know that they accomplished most of their success on their own. The HOME community walks quietly in the shadows, just as

Christ did when he was unrecognized by his disciples on the road to Emmaus. There is nothing easy about making housing happen. It can feel as if we are walking alone, but Jesus is there even when we don't recognize him.

Developing Partners

Housing is a key quality-of-life factor, but even more important is the stability owning a home provides. By offering opportunities for economic development, HOME helps to create a more stable environment. HOME expands its expertise and finds reinforcement on a national and international level through Emmaus International, Rural Coalition, OXFAM America, volunteer work groups, Saint Francis Intentional Community, and financial institutions.

Emmaus International

The founder of Emmaus, Abbe Pierre, organized rag pickers in Paris, France, to find, mend, and fix discarded clothes and household goods in exchange for meeting their basic needs. From these experiences came the International Bill of Human Rights and the four principles of Emmaus. These principles reinforce HOME's work to do the following:

1. Help those in need.
2. Help people to help themselves.
3. Help communities, not just individuals.
4. Overcome oppression.

With Emmaus, HOME is part of an international network striving to achieve these four principles through conferences, education, and training. Emmaus is a relief for rural programs, which often tend to feel isolated. Today, with little commonality between the haves and have-nots, Emmaus is a reminder of how everyone is connected to one another and therefore equally obligated to be stewards of our planet. When HOME's elected representative recently attended the Emmaus Salon in France, a common thread emerged. In France they are buying farmhouses and making them into transitional housing. In India, where the "Land Gift" movement

In 1948 Abbe Pierre worked with the United Nations to write the Universal Declaration of Human Rights, which states in part: "Everyone has the right to a standard of living adequate for the health and well-being of himself [or herself] and of his [or her] family, including food, clothing, housing and medical care, and necessary social services, and the right to security in the event of unemployment, sickness, disability, widowhood, old age, or other lack of livelihood in circumstances beyond his [or her] control" (full declaration at www.un.org/Overview/rights.html

initiated early thinking about CLTs, the idea persists that we are not here as owners, but stewards of the land, and to respect its equitable use.

Rural Coalition

Rural Coalition works to change society through policy and advocacy for rural artisans and farmers of all races, creeds, and economic backgrounds. They work on issues such as environmental justice, workers' rights, immigration, and farmers rights. Rural Coalition acts as a watchdog to make sure families like the Carters are able to qualify for needed services such as food stamps and WIC[13] vouchers. Families who own HOME's Land Trust homes are determined to keep their homes by keeping their credit good and their payments current, but they sometimes rely on this assistance to make that possible.

OXFAM America

Oxfam America, which is part of Oxfam International, started in Oxford, England. They provide financial and technical support and evaluation. For example, HOME originally asked land trust families to put in 250 hours of sweat equity. Thanks to Oxfam's evaluation tools, HOME determined that 250 was too many hours to expect of struggling families.

Volunteer Work Groups

Volunteers, some who have never picked up a hammer before helping HOME, complete about 50 percent of the construction. Old Greenwich Church in Connecticut, for example, has come twice a year for twenty-five years. They believe in instilling the life of the gospel in their young people by giving their time, talent, and money to serve the poorest of the poor in rural Maine. HOME also visits the Old Greenwich Church craft fair in November to receive food donations from their Harvest Sunday service.

This team helped to save a land trust home. In April 2004, a single mother living in Sedgwick was not making payments. The bank had foreclosed. The Old Greenwich team fixed the broken pipes, frozen because her gas bill wasn't paid. They did sufficient work to enable the owner to take out a home equity loan and get financially caught up. In the meantime Pam Spencer, head of HOME's Housing, worked night and day for several months to come up with the $5,700.02 needed to save her home. Sister Lucy used her credit card for the last $800, and Pam said she would put in the two cents! A credit manager worked with the owner to set up a budget, and now she has a full-time job.[14]

Saint Francis Intentional Community

Without the help of Saint Francis, much of HOME's land trust work would not happen. Saint Francis Community started soon after HOME began. The Sisters purchased a rocky piece of property to farm as their place of residence. They raise small Norwegian fjord workhorses, a perfect breed for harsh winter climates. Selling one per year covers the Mandala Farm's property taxes. A local farmer, needing to leave town, dropped off forty Cashmere goats, so now they also raise goats. They grow organic vegetables and raise chickens for eggs, both for their own consumption and to be sold at farmers markets. These small businesses help sustain the Sisters, who are dedicated to helping the homeless become active members of society.

The Mandala farm was mortgaged and used as collateral to purchase land and finance several land trust projects. Additionally, wood harvesting at Saint Francis enables HOME to significantly cut the cost of materials on each home built.

Long- and short-term volunteers live at the community on the 350-acre farm, five miles from HOME. This community shares in work, shelter, food, and worship. During the week, they volunteer their time and labor at HOME, and on Saturdays they work at the farm. Sunday is a day of rest.

Financial Institutions

Finding financial institutions to offer mortgages for this unique model—owning the home, but not the land—is a challenge! In the past, a local bank helped us. They said they would give up to $200,000 in mortgages, but they have exceeded that figure by half a million! They work with the Federal Home Loan Bank of Boston; Washington, D.C. based groups such as HUD; and several foundations. The Housing Assistance Council (HAC) and the Institute for Community Economics (ICE) provide funds and technical assistance. ICE is the premiere U.S. technical assistance and capacity building group for CLTs. To build to their capacity HOME is setting up a revolving loan fund. Yet few banks are interested in smaller-scale affordable housing.

Doing the Work

Land trust homeowners are encouraged to use the land in an environmentally and socially responsible manner. Because of the holistic nature of HOME, many services and supplies are provided internally. HOME harvests trees from land trust land, processes the lumber in its own mills, and produces furniture, doors, and cabinets in its own woodworking shop. In this way, money is kept in the community and many people are employed.[15] HOME has construction crews that cut the community's own lumber for framing and building and produce white cedar shingles for siding. The woodworking shop manufactures all the finish and trim lumber,

Carlos lives on the Hayes/Reid Trust. His wife Yvette is a weaver and spinner in our craft cooperative and Carlos works in woodworking making Christian Doors.

and also produces cabinetry, including kitchen cupboards and solid "Christian doors"—named "Christian" because of the cross created by the four panels. HOME is blessed to have a state-licensed master plumber, saving between $5,000 to $7,000 per house.

Sister Sharon Yount, Order of Preaching, Dominican Sister of Hope, came to HOME after teaching in New York and New Jersey. She runs electrical wiring throughout each land trust home under the direct supervision of a state-licensed master electrician. "I never thought I would leave the halls of academia to work long hours running heavy electrical wire through tiny holes," she says.

An architect donated two professionally drawn sets of blueprints, one for a Cape Cod style house and one for a Saltbox. Repeated use of the blueprints saves in additional design costs. The homes are built in such a way that families can add on, making their home more uniquely theirs.

When HOME qualifies the families according to low-income guidelines, they begin pre-purchase counseling, and the search to finance a mortgage for the prospective homeowner begins. The family attends home-ownership workshops, entitling them to receive lower interest rates. They can opt for sweat equity in the final painting, cleaning, and landscaping, which saves them and HOME money. Carpets and flooring are then installed.

On move-in day the family receives the keys to their new home, and post-purchase counseling dates are set. The pre- and post-purchase counseling are required if HUD funding is used. But without HUD funding, it is still essential to ensure that families know how to maintain their homes. To date, though some have been close, no family has lost their home to the banks!

Dealing with Realities

Paul was blinded and was struck dumb on the road to Damascus, until he was willing to receive the light, compassion, and love of Christ. Many politicians are like Paul before his conversion—they need eyes to see and ears to hear. For example, the planning board can discuss building permits with blindness to issues of homelessness and poverty. They can easily look only at the negative, including some of HOME's past mistakes:

In 1998, HOME helped a couple seeking shelter. They seemed to fit in, with their daily life and work ethics, helping out in various areas. But on the Saturday before Father's Day the television program *America's Most Wanted* ran a segment about a man who, along with his wife, had run away from the sentencing phase of his trial. After a series of unwelcome events and much questioning, we found out that the couple HOME was helping had been wanted in Massachusetts on several counts. We had not checked the couple's references, because they came to us seeking help and shelter. Much publicity was given to this, but not the kind of publicity HOME needed! In fact, volunteer groups called to see if it was safe for them to bring young people.

This incident initiated many internal changes in HOME's policy manual and practices, to protect both HOME and the town. The whole community was devastated. It resulted in HOME's being vilified by the planning board, making it almost impossible to get building permits. HOME gave land to the town for a new fire station, and the town sends HOME many of the people in need who apply for general assistance. Town officials often refer people to HOME first, before they consider how the town might be of service, but when you are blinded like Paul, it's hard to see.

Taxes

Property taxes are paid by the trust—not the homeowners. Owners only pay taxes on their home. While nonprofits are protected from paying taxes on funds they raise, many towns do not like to exempt nonprofits from property taxes. Sister Lucy insists that HOME pay because the land trust families use the school systems and other services. "It is only fair," she says.

Discovering Insights

God is changing lives though HOME. My own exposure to HOME has changed me. I see this model as closely aligned with biblical concepts of land and ownership. In fact, I am so convinced of the viability of this model that I am seeking how to reconfigure my traditional homeownership arrangement so that it will be part of a community land trust. I see land trusts as the model of the future. By taking land out of the equation and off the speculative market, a permanent source of affordable homeownership can be created, thus retaining a healthy income mix in our gentrifying cities.

For the people of HOME, creating the Covenant Community Land Trust has been a learning experience at every step. They have discovered the value of good partnerships that have a global focus and that keep their work in perspective, grounded and focused. They have discovered the value of keeping the land trust communities small, with no more than twelve homes per community. They have discovered the value of a commitment to policies that protect them and those they serve; the value of a good name in the community, and good character to back the name up, which

Jason, who supervises our sawmill, shingle mill, and garages, fell in love and married Erin. They bought a house in Milvale land trust. It was the first time Erin had lived without extended family and felt secure enough to do what she wanted; decorating her daughter's room with large cutout ladybugs demonstrated her newfound freedom.

entails practicing what they preach about forgiveness toward those who seem to be against their efforts. They know the value of being grounded in God, especially in the trying times. They have also discovered the value of controlling a significant portion of the operation, not only to keep the homes affordable, but also to instill pride, skills, and employment opportunities that come with involving homeowners in aspects of the construction.

I left this small rural community keenly aware of God's grace and love for the poor. Despite HOME's past instance of oversight on volunteer screening, and some financing woes, they know God has called them to this work. Today hundreds of Maine's poorest have the joy of home-ownership, like the Carters, for whom homeownership on a land trust community has made all the difference. The HOME "family" embraced them, unlike their own. The day the Carters walked into their land trust home, their son Matthew exclaimed, "Now Santa will know where to bring my presents." Such moments put all the efforts into perspective.

The Nehemiah Strategy

South Bronx Churches

LEE STUART WITH JOHN HEINEMEIER

Introduction to the Community Organizing Trust Model
BY DR. ROBERT C. LINTHICUM

The remarkable story Lee Stuart is about to tell you reshaped Brooklyn, then South Bronx. Stuart shows how "relational institutions"[1] came together to address commonly perceived needs–congregations, unions, school associations (like PTAs), and civic associations. Relationships are the basis of community organizing.

The genius of community organizing was made clear to me when twenty elderly women in my Chicago church shared their fear of becoming victims of neighborhood crime. Not knowing what to do, I took them to meet with the professional organizer our community's churches had recently hired. He listened sympathetically as the ladies shared their fear.

Vivian, the group's spokeswoman, challenged the organizer, "Sir, what are you going to do about the crime in our neighborhood?" He replied, "I'm not going to do anything about crime! You are! It's not my problem. It's your problem. What are you going to do about it?"

"What are we going to do about it?" Vivian indignantly answered. "What can we do about it? We're nothing but little old ladies!"

The organizer shot back, "You may be little old ladies. But you are not 'nothing but little old ladies.' You are very powerful little old ladies. And if you want to learn how to use the power you already have to stop crime in this community, you can!"

"But we don't know what to do," Vivian wailed.

"Of course you don't know what to do," the organizer responded, "because if you knew what to do, you would have already done it and there wouldn't be any problem of crime. But that's my job as an organizer–to teach you how to use the power you already have at your disposal and to help you organize to use it. My point is, however, that if you want crime to disappear from this neighborhood, you have to make it stop yourself!"

The ladies looked at each other. And then Vivian answered for them all. She replied, "We need to stop it. We want to stop it. Our faith as Christians demands us to stop it!"

"Okay," responded the organizer. "Then let's get to work!"

And to work they got! Trained by that organizer how to recognize, accept, and use the power at their disposal, those "little old ladies" organized all the little old ladies and all the little old men of that community—hundreds upon hundreds of them—to confront the precinct captain and eventually negotiate directly with the police chief. Through their efforts the Chicago Police Department increased the number of police patrols, "Neighborhood Watches" were organized, and cops walked beats for the first time in thirty-seven years. Not all the hundreds of people they organized were Christians or even people of faith. But the little old ladies were! And they were putting their faith into action! Crime plummeted, and those women won back their community and safety once again!

From this I learned the iron rule of organizing: "Never do for others what they can do for themselves." These ladies didn't have wealth, privilege, or political power at their service. What they did have were powerful relationships. Using those relationships, they built a base of people and organized those relationships into an "action" that would get the chief of police to react. They developed a powerful organization of the churches that built a strong, viable future for that community.

These little old ladies learned how to exercise power. Power is the capacity, ability, and willingness to act. Capacity is having the resources at your disposal to act—those elderly men and women of that community. But they didn't recognize that those relationships could be organized to beat crime. So they perceived themselves as powerless.

But power is also the ability to act—having the skill, aptitude, and competence to act. The organizer taught these women how to use the capacity they already had to negotiate acceptable agreements with the Chicago Police Department.

Finally, power is also the willingness to act. As long as these ladies didn't believe they had the ability and didn't perceive the capacity that was already there, they were unwilling to stop crime. Once trained, they became willing to act; and that neighborhood was transformed.

These ladies addressed crime and safety. In other communities, it might be education, immigration, or healthcare. When I directed a work in India with World Vision International using this same process with the Dalits or "Untouchables" needing housing, they won 6,000 government-constructed homes for purchase! In East Brooklyn and South Bronx, home ownership was also one of the needs. This was democracy in action! They organized their relational power among churches to provide the money, the land, and even the homeowners. They organized the social, public, and private sectors of society and by so doing "formed a rising tide" and literally transformed these communities.[2] This is the miracle of people-power at work!

Before I left World Vision in 1995, I was privileged to be asked by the Untouchables to visit them and their "new city" (as they called it). There I toured that former slum and met with the leadership and asked them how they felt now in their new housing. I will never forget what one woman said. "When I lived on the streets, my soul was very unhappy; it was restless, it had no place to sleep. But now that I live here, in my very own home, my soul is quiet within me because it has now found a home where it can be with God."[3]

Whether in a developing country, or in the United States, whether in a rural or urban setting, whether with professional organizers[4] or not, the power to transform that lies at the heart of broad-based community organizing rebuilds both communities and their people...as you will see in Stuart's story that follows!

The Nehemiah Strategy

LEE STUART with **JOHN HEINEMEIER**

"You see the bad situation we are in, that Jerusalem is desolate and its gates burned by fire. Come, let us rebuild the wall of Jerusalem so that we will no longer be a reproach."—Nehemiah 2:17, NASB

At about 4 p.m. Christmas Eve, 2002, while visiting friends in Alaska, I (LS) received a phone call from the South Bronx Churches (SBC) attorney, Karen Sherman, who was supervising the last SBC Nehemiah Home closing of 2002. A woman who had been a teenager when her mother purchased one of the first South Bronx Nehemiah Homes in 1993 was now twenty-six and was purchasing one of her own. The second generation of Nehemiah homeowners in the Bronx had come of age, and they just wanted me to know!

This chapter's focus is how over ten years SBC used the principles of organizing to produce nearly 1,000 units of affordable housing using the Nehemiah Strategy.[5] In contrast to the will of outside developers, SBC's Nehemiah housing originated from the will of the people. *They themselves became the carefully trained, astute organization that created the political will to carry out the Nehemiah Strategy.* The Nehemiah purchasers were all first-time homeowners. Many moved from public housing, thus freeing up desperately needed low-rent apartments. The Nehemiah homeowners, and continued organizing lifted entire neighborhoods, as public services such as sanitation, police, and public education were revitalized, and commercial activity expanded. SBC remains a powerful citizen's organization that continues to reweave the social fabric of a once physically devastated community.[6]

Police Officer Eddie Ramirez of the 40th Precinct described what he observed in a letter to South Bronx Churches:

> I have been a police officer in the Mott Haven community for 13 years. I am writing this letter to commend you on the revitalization of Mott Haven, through the SBC and Foresite Construction partnership for urban renewal. Since the homes have been built crime has decreased dramatically. Garbage that filled empty lots has disappeared. Abandoned buildings once occupied by drug gangs have been replaced with beautiful homes occupied by hard working citizens. It is no coincidence that the crime rate has dropped significantly as a result of the construction of these new homes. This community has definitely changed for the better.

The Birth of the Nehemiah Housing Strategy

Simply put, the Nehemiah Housing Strategy is a way to organize money, land, relationships, and power for the purpose of creating large-scale housing developments. The large scale is essential to take advantage of economies of scale during construction and thus allow for increased affordability. Scale is also important after construction to create a critical mass of homeowners to lead the ongoing transformation of the neighborhood.

The first Nehemiah Strategy was developed by the Industrial Areas Foundation affiliate East Brooklyn Congregations (EBC). EBC leader Rev. Johnny Ray Youngblood named the strategy after the biblical leader Nehemiah. Just as the first Nehemiah rebuilt the walls of Jerusalem, EBC (and later SBC) would rebuild the walls of their Jerusalem: New York City. Among the critical building blocks for the Nehemiah Strategy were the following:

- a construction financing pool of several million dollars, loaned at no interest from denominational judicatories
- a visionary builder
- enough land to build at least 1,000 homes
- sufficient power and knowledge within the leadership of the EBC and SBC to carry the initiative through the intricacies and intransigencies of New York City government

An article in *The Washington Post*[7] captured the excitement of one of the early EBC homeowners, Sandra McCollum: "I knew I could never afford a home. That was like wanting the impossible." And then having heard about the program from her church, she began to save money by every means possible.

> There were times I said, "I can't," but then every day after work, I'd walk over to the empty lots where they were going to build. There was garbage and abandoned cars. I'd try to envision what it would look like. I'd claim it for myself. Nehemiah was a dream and my dream was to be part of Nehemiah.

Then there was the great day that she moved in. "I got my keys. I ran to the house and I shouted, 'It's mine! It's finally mine!'" Between the work of EBC and SBC, this story has literally been repeated 5,000 times.

In 1990, SBC adapted EBC's Nehemiah model as the ownership arm of its housing agenda. Other efforts focused on organizing tenants in public housing and renovating buildings for rental occupancy. SBC's Nehemiah program (968 units) was built in two phases. From 1992 to 1996, SBC built 512 homes (224 single-family homes and 288 condominiums) primarily on contiguous lots. In the second phase, which was largely in-fill housing and ran from late 1998 through 2003, SBC built 205 two-family homes and 44 single-family homes for a total of 454 dwelling units.

SBC financed the Nehemiah construction by borrowing $3.5 million at no interest from the Evangelical Lutheran Church in America, St. James Episcopal Church, Trinity Episcopal Church, and several Roman Catholic religious orders long active in the South Bronx. Using a highly disciplined approach to construction and sales, SBC created more than $85 million in housing (now appraised at over $145 million), repaid the religious lenders ahead of time, and left itself with approximately a $1 million endowment from unspent contingencies and savings.

The "Nehemiah Equation" is staggering. In the South Bronx, Nehemiah homeowners invested a cumulative $4.5 million of their own equity in the form of down payments. The city invested $14.6 million in public subsidies and another $2 million for land acquisition and demolition. Neighborhood banks provided over $68 million in mortgages. *All of this was possible on the basis of a revolving seed loan of $3.5 million from religious institutions, which has since been repaid.* The Nehemiah mortgages are approximately one-half the current rental market in the South Bronx. Thus the Nehemiah homeowners and their tenants save over $5 million a year in housing costs. The Nehemiah Strategy is an economic engine; it works at the level of the family, the neighborhood, the community, and the city.

Daring to Listen

Listening to the History of South Bronx

In the mid-1980s the South Bronx had become infamous in the national imagination as the epitome of urban poverty with ample help from films

such as *Fort Apache, The Bronx* (1981), and books such as Tom Wolfe's *The Bonfire of the Vanities* (1988). But the South Bronx did not become what it was by accident, nor because of any particular action or inaction on the part of its people. Instead, the creation of the South Bronx's problems was a consequence of a series of government policies spanning thirty years. In the early 1940s, the South Bronx neighborhoods were solidly working-class Irish, Italian, and German people. A major population shift occurred in the Bronx after World War II as housing programs for returning veterans sparked a mass migration of whites to the suburbs. By the mid-1950s, the South Bronx had become primarily African American and Puerto Rican. African Americans moved into the area from Manhattan, some by choice seeking the larger apartments available in the Bronx, and others displaced by "urban renewal." The African American population also increased as part of the post-war migration from the rural south to northern cities. The Puerto Rican immigration was part of the displacement that occurred as the island's economy shifted from agriculture to industry.[8] In addition, in the mid-50s, the Cross Bronx Expressway (one of Robert Moses's great public works projects), split the Bronx in half, destroying entire neighborhoods and displacing upwards of 50,000 people.[9]

The South Bronx experienced its own "urban renewal" in the 1960s when block after block of buildings were razed without the funding to build them back. By the 1970s, New York City was in a fiscal crisis, facing bankruptcy, and the South Bronx became the target of another devastating policy: "planned shrinkage." As part of the effort to save its core financial industries, New York City reduced city services–that is, closed hospitals, schools, fire stations, and police precincts in the South Bronx. With the reduction in police presence, crime inevitably increased. Buildings were abandoned when rising maintenance costs could not be met by limited rents. Arson was rampant as a way to recover insurance claims. Nearly half the people living in the South Bronx left. Those who remained had no place to go, or too few resources to leave; others had a faith and determination that allowed them to persevere against all odds. The private sector essentially closed shop. Over half the people who remained received some sort of government assistance, and half the active payroll was devoted to social service. Of all the churches, the only ones with resident clergy were Roman Catholic and Lutheran. It was in the face of this devastation that South Bronx Churches (SBC) was born.

Listening to the People: Reverend John Heinemeier

Every good story has its humble hero and visionary genius, and for SBC and Nehemiah, his name was Rev. John Heinemeier. Rev. Heinemeier, a Lutheran pastor who served first in Brooklyn found a willing audience for organizing in the South Bronx. He first rebuilt his congregation by applying organizing principles. He met individually with members in their homes. He also met with seventy-five or so fellow clergy, asking each one whom else he should talk to. This network grew geometrically as congregations became the building blocks for South Bronx Churches. Rev. Heinemeier summarizes what he found in both boroughs:

> The clergy were motivated to organize a new form of ministry, one with the power to have serious social impact. Most had spent years in inner-city ministry, going from one crisis intervention to another, and it was clear that this form of ministry was insufficient for the task at hand. The social problems they faced needed something more than amelioration; they needed transformation. For them, the new ministry had to be ecumenical, harnessing a number of faith groups to provide sufficient critical mass. It would have to be geared toward public transformation, not service (though service would not be abandoned). And, it would have to engage professional organizers to help articulate and implement their goals. These insights were challenging, and required listening to their own hearts, recognizing that what they had done so far was simply not sufficient, and listening the One who called Nehemiah to rebuild Jerusalem.[10]

South Bronx Churches Is Born

When Pastor Heinemeier had generated a critical mass of interested congregations, the Industrial Areas Foundation (IAF), the oldest community-organizing network in the country, assigned one of their top organizers, Jim Drake, to the South Bronx. One key element of community organizing is one-on-one meetings designed to build the basis for a public relationship through mutual sharing of vision, anger, story and imagination. From 1985 through 1987, Drake spearheaded thousands of one-on-one meetings among the clergy and lay leaders of the South Bronx. The one-on-one campaign was followed by hundreds of house meetings, small meetings in living rooms and church basements where people shared their stories and priorities for a revitalized South Bronx.

When thousands of people had told their stories, and when relationships were sufficiently forged among the leaders of the thirty-five churches engaged in the effort, an initial agenda of primary interests was identified. The founding convention of SBC was in February 1987, and even though housing was a high priority, SBC was not organized in order to build houses. *The intention of SBC was to lay a foundation for a highly organized community so it could rebuild itself on multiple fronts. Housing alone is never enough.* Between 1987 and 1990 SBC successfully built its strength and relational network in numerous ways. Hundreds of South Bronx residents learned the skills of direct action and made sweeping changes in their neighborhoods. SBC leaders successfully fought for improvements in school safety, subway maintenance, supermarkets, and community policing. They forced the demolition of unsafe buildings, the fencing of vacant lots, and the creation of neighborhood parks. SBC leaders took part in NYC Charter Revision sessions, and in voter registration and mobilization. Through these five years of direct action SBC gained the confidence to take on the even bigger issue of housing. By 1990 SBC began to formulate its Nehemiah Strategy, knowing that this vision would take years to realize.

Developing Partners

The Social Sector

The first allies SBC approached to generate construction financing were the judicatories of their member congregations.[11] Each denomination in SBC began a series of meetings seeking moral and financial support from national bodies, dioceses, synods, and presbyteries.[12] The Roman Catholic funding for SBC Nehemiah came from private individuals and three religious orders, each having served for over 100 years in the South Bronx: the Redemptorist Fathers and Brothers, the Sisters of Charity of New York, and the Holy Cross Fathers. The Evangelical Lutheran Church in America loaned $500,000 to the effort, based on its previous participation in EBC's Nehemiah. The Episcopalian participation came in the form of million-dollar loans from two of the endowed parishes of New York City: St. James Church on Madison Avenue and The Parish of Trinity Church (Wall Street).

Organizing Model for Social Justice

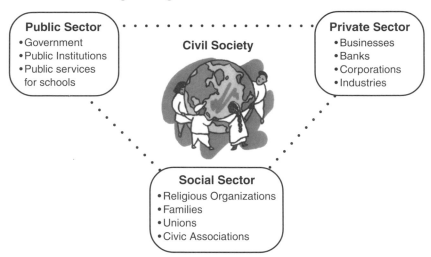

Public Sector
- Government
- Public Institutions
- Public services
  for schools

Civil Society

Private Sector
- Businesses
- Banks
- Corporations
- Industries

Social Sector
- Religious Organizations
- Families
- Unions
- Civic Associations

When civil society is operating properly, the public, private, and social sectors are mutually connected and the social sector has sufficient power to advance and protect its interests in the public arena.

Each major lender named a trustee and the trustees jointly served as the finance committee for the project. The trustees, particularly Peter Gevalt from Trinity Church and George Fowlkes from St. James, provided years of dedicated service to SBC Nehemiah. Both realized they were participating in ministry, not merely development, and both admitted being transformed in the process. Gevalt and Fowlkes, highly successful businessmen in private life, realized that working with SBC to build Nehemiah Homes required a faith dimension beyond that required in their regular transactions. In the process, both men gained new insight into how their gifts could be used by God. They noted the joy in being asked by their church to do something requiring all their talents and strength.

The Public Sector

In the public sector, SBC, as EBC did before and in spite of initial resistance, developed relationships with elected officials at all levels and with a myriad of government agencies involved in development. SBC's Housing Task Force—after being trained by the IAF—initiated a series of meetings with New York City's Department of Housing Preservation and Development, the City Planning Commission and the Departments of Buildings, Finance and Taxation, Transportation, Sewer and Water, and Sanitation. SBC did not hire consultants, but *the leaders themselves learned how to navigate this complex territory with many barricades to affordable housing.*

Like Nehemiah, SBC needed wisdom, discernment, and perseverance to be granted permission from the king and official letters of approval.

> Then I said to the king, "If it pleases the king, let letters be given me to the governors of the province Beyond the River, that they may grant me passage until I arrive in Judah; and a letter to Asaph, the keeper of the king's forest, directing him to give me timber to make beams for the gates of the temple fortress, and for the wall of the city, and for the house that I shall occupy." And the king granted me what I asked, for the gracious hand of my God was upon me. (Neh. 2:7–8)

Affiliates of the IAF rely on "relational power" when trying to get something done.[13] Relational power is the idea of building power "with" others rather than "over" them. Building relational power requires pragmatism, theological maturity, and faith.

What this meant in practice was that SBC had to be true to its theological ideals while facing incredible resistance from bureaucracies, elected and appointed officials, and others who did not support the effort. As Nehemiah did, SBC had to be willing to use direct confrontation to get the attention of the authorities (as in Neh. 5). Eventually bureaucrats and politicians got the message: SBC meant business.

The Private Sector

The same approach to developing relationships in the public sector applied to the development of relationships in the private sector. Primary among the private sector were those relationships with construction professionals. I. D. Robbins was the builder for the first phase of EBC Nehemiah (2,000 homes) and SBC Nehemiah (512 units). Upon Robbins's death, his team dispersed rather than continue with the second phase. Building on a long term relationship the Redemptorists had with a local developer, SBC hired Joseph Denn to manage the construction of the 454 units in the second phase of the South Bronx Nehemiah program.

Doing the Work

The united power of the SBC worshiping congregations provided the political will and the financing for construction to occur in a place where nothing had been built for thirty years.

Acquiring the Land

The 1980s tax maps of the South Bronx showed a preponderance of land held *in rem*–land taken by the city in tax forfeiture. SBC leaders studied the maps, and identified nearly twenty acres of this land, nearly thirty-five city blocks. One night, at the beginning of the Nehemiah campaign, armed with hammers and flashlights, SBC leaders fanned out throughout the neighborhood. The next dawn saw signs declaring that affordable Nehemiah Homes would be built on these sites "if the City Council approves."

By noon they had been taken down. The next night, SBC leaders staked out their claims again. Again they were taken down…and again and again.

The centerpiece of the land struggle was a four-acre site known as "Site 404." SBC wanted Site 404 to be the anchor of the entire Nehemiah campaign. But Bronx political leaders preferred higher density housing to Nehemiah's single-family homes. A series of meetings failed to deliver a compromise. SBC decided that direct action demonstrating massive public support for its proposal was required. So SBC organized 5,000 residents to challenge the city to provide the land needed to accomplish their dreams.

The "Site 404 Assembly" was a highly organized effort to turn out specific numbers of people from each of SBC's member churches. My own parish, St. Augustine's Catholic Church, had an average Sunday Mass attendance of 350 and a turnout quota of 200 for the Site 404 Assembly. Each Sunday after every Mass, our designated turnout captains would sign up people to come to Site 404. Each SBC member organization was doing the same thing. When I rounded the corner adjacent to the site; I had to stop in my tracks. Tears came to my eyes. There really were 5,000 people there! (Some reported as many as 8,000.) It was a brilliant April day. A stage had been constructed at one end of the site. People were dressed for church and were singing.

I remember Rev. Heinemeier's speech that day. In simple terms he stated the case for Site 404 and beyond. He testified how SBC had its own money, the $3.5 million from the churches. He exalted our builder, who was willing to leave his profit on the table in order to make Nehemiah Homes more affordable than the city's alternative proposal for Site 404. He chastised those who might want to rebuild the Bronx by bringing "a better class of people" through more expensive housing (the word "gentrification" was not yet a commonly used term). He confirmed that Nehemiah Homes would be affordable for the very people who were standing before him, those who lived, worked, and worshipped in the South Bronx. He blessed the people who had borne the brunt of the South Bronx's abandonment and promised that they would reap the rewards of its rebirth. He made us feel as if the Bronx really was Jerusalem and that God had called us, as God had called Nehemiah before us, to rebuild the walls of our city. We each picked up a stone from the ground as a symbol of our rebuilding. To this day, some of these stones are still enshrined as keepsakes by those who own a Nehemiah Home.

In the end, SBC lost Site 404. It was designated to the Partnership, a consortium of banks and major NYC corporations, working with private developers to promote development in "difficult" neighborhoods.[14] David Dinkins was elected mayor and, despite his absence at the Site 404 gathering, his administration's housing commissioner, Felice Michetti, immediately began to identify land for SBC Nehemiah. It was hard for SBC to remember that while Site 404 had been our hoped-for centerpiece, it was not the whole project. Despite the Site 404 loss, the neighborhood had lots of room to work. Soon, SBC and the Department of Housing Preservation and Development had negotiated a phased development plan for the Melrose and Mott Haven neighborhoods.

December 20, 1990–eight years after Rev. Heinemeier had started his one-on-one meetings with Bronx clergy, five years after Jim Drake had been assigned by the IAF as lead organizer to SBC, three years after SBC's founding convention, and a year and a half after the Site 404 defeat–150 SBC leaders went to City Hall to witness the passage of Resolution 696. The opening paragraph of the resolution said it all: "Resolution approving an urban development action area project for the Bronx Nehemiah Project." We leaped to our feet with applause and cheering. Finally the words of Nehemiah that had inspired us from the beginning could be fulfilled:

> I told them how the hand of my God had been favorable to me and also about the king's words which he had spoken to me. Then they said, "Let us arise and build." So they put their hands to the good work. (Neh. 2:18, NASB)

This resolution was the first of ten that the New York City Council passed over the next decade designating land for SBC Nehemiah. The first resolutions covered land that the city owned through tax forfeiture. Subsequent resolutions covered vacant land parcels that the city took through eminent domain, thus investing over a million dollars in land acquisition costs to support SBC Nehemiah. Further resolutions involved land, either city owned or privately held, that had demolition or environmental problems. The city did the environmental testing and initially tried to fix the environmental problems and do the demolition, but eventually, it paid SBC contractors under grant agreements to do the work. They learned that under SBC control the projects could be done faster, better, and ultimately at lower cost. The grant agreements eventually totaled nearly two million dollars.

Innovative Financing

In addition to providing a $15,000 per unit subsidy, delivered as part of a reduced mortgage to the buyer, New York City made a further investment in affordable housing that is extremely rare. First time homeowners in Nehemiah are given twenty-year tax abatements. For the first ten years, the homeowners pay real estate taxes only on the land. Taxes on the homes start in the eleventh year, with taxes phased in by 10 percent increments until full taxes are paid in year twenty. What this means is that instead of paying about \$250–\$300 a month in real estate taxes, Nehemiah and Partnership homeowners pay only \$25–\$30, and even this can be reduced to approximately \$10 a month through a state tax exemption for owner-occupied homes. These lower monthly payments are hugely important to create true affordability.[15]

By creating a mechanism for self-financing, in the form of the no-interest loans from religious bodies, Nehemiah Homes minimized transaction and related costs regularly incurred when a project requires multiple funding agencies. Self-financing also allowed prompt payment of all bills, which reduced construction costs. By not relying on government sources to fill a substantial gap (only the \$15,000 per unit subsidy), SBC Nehemiah was able to avoid the complicated accounting and reporting requirements that often accompany government subsidies and tend to increase costs. By organizing construction on a large scale, we obtained better prices from contractors and took advantage of economies of scale in both the labor and materials markets.

Benefits of Organized Buyers

In addition to organizing the financing and construction, a key element of the Nehemiah Strategy was to organize the sales process. Teams of volunteers gave presentations in SBC member congregations during the marketing phase of Nehemiah. Interested applicants outnumbered available homes by more than five to one. Applicants were screened by Nehemiah staff and supported throughout the mortgage process. Through relational power, SBC was able to encourage the mortgage banks involved to take a wholesale approach to Nehemiah, looking at the entire project (hundreds of mortgages a year) instead of considering them as a series of individual mortgage applicants. With banks taking advantage of economies of scale, they could offer better products relative to smaller, more labor-intensive projects.

"An Economic Miracle—Milagro Económico"

The result of combining the demand for the houses (organized buyers), the supply of the houses (organized construction), and the means of production (organized money for construction and end loan financing) was to virtually eliminate the risk from SBC Nehemiah and therefore eliminate another costly part of development—protection against project risk.

With every part of the project well organized, what the Spanish language newspaper *Siempre* called a "milagro económico" (economic miracle)[16] was then possible. Society was re-knit with substantial participation from the three sectors of society. The impact of the constant attention to costs equates to real opportunity for the families who purchased the homes. James Francis, a South Bronx Nehemiah homeowner explains:

This South Bronx Nehemiah phenomenon was a dream come true for people like me. My wife and I will never forget that warm summer evening in late August 1992. We were slowly approaching our new home, after picking up our two children from John F. Kennedy Airport. They had just returned from spending the summer with their grandparents who still lived in the Caribbean. Two and a half months before, when they left for Antigua, we lived in an apartment complex where drug dealing, drug usage, and assaults were common. When we stopped in front of our driveway and announced to James Jr. and Nicole that 670 East 158th Street was their new home, their faces lit up. It was such a beautiful experience to see the broad smiles on their faces. The stories they were sharing about their vacation immediately changed to unbelievable excitement; we were all so happy. After settling in their new rooms, they were now ready to explore the rest of their new home. To the basement they ran. It did not take long for them to discover there was also a backyard with newly laid beds of grass. Despite the late hour, they wanted to play in their very own backyard. All along, tears of joy filled my eyes.

Dealing with Realities

Adapt the Design to the Context while Embracing the Universals

In the Bronx, the Nehemiah project included single-family homes, condominiums, and two-family homes, some built on contiguous lots, some as in-fill housing. The flexibility in design was driven initially by external political demands for increased density and then by a change in mortgage financing that made two-family homes more affordable. The universal requirement was that we had enough scale in each model to achieve efficiencies and cost-savings in construction. Also we were able to standardize our interiors and finishes for similar efficiencies and cost-savings.

Demanding Accountability

Housing is at times a dirty business in New York City, and elsewhere. There were many interests seriously challenged by SBC's entering the housing arena. SBC Nehemiah did not tolerate kickbacks (a too-common practice in which contractors "buy" labor peace, prevent site vandalism, get inspectors to blink at violations, or any number of things often obtained with payoffs). Our policy required workers to be on the job and working. We refused to bow to intimidation. We rejected shakedowns (pressuring for payoffs or extortion of any form). We expected city agencies to do their regulatory work professionally and on a schedule. We also maintained impeccable standards when it came to screening potential buyers. All of these commitments flew in the face of business-as-usual. We demanded accountability for ourselves and we demanded it from others. We gained comfort from the fact that Nehemiah himself had the same problem with his detractors Sanballat, Tobiah, Geshem the Arab, the Ammonites and the Ashdodites, and even internally from his own followers (Nehemiah 4–6). And eventually we gained a level of true partnership with the city's Department of Housing Preservation and Development.

Organizational and Time Constraints

The Nehemiah project consumed tremendous amounts of organizational time and leadership. A separate development arm was eventually created so that the core work of organizing could continue without being swamped by the day-to-day demands over years of large-scale development. SBC created a small professional development staff of usually one to three people. We made sure we were not seen as self-serving—creating employment for ourselves. We paid as much attention to control of soft costs, particularly our own administrative costs, as we did to hard costs.

Quality and Care Cannot Be Sacrificed

SBC had to deal with some work done in the first phase that had not been up to standard. Consequently, the construction oversight, warranty, and follow-up procedures in the second phase far surpassed that of the first phase. While the overall goal of affordability is important, quality and care in construction cannot be sacrificed. It was critically important to have rigorous oversight on both the construction *and* the administrative sides of Nehemiah Homes.

Finding the right partners—Complete Transparency

SBC in particular benefited from full partnership with their second-phase construction manager, Joseph Denn, the principal of Foresite Construction. He brought a degree of professionalism to the SBC effort that was highly unusual. Before working with SBC, he built luxury homes in wealthy Westchester County. As part of the premier luxury development company in the area, Denn at first seemed an unlikely choice for SBC. But as he said, "I grew up in Catholic schools. The nuns always told me I had a higher purpose in life, but I never knew how to do it in construction until I met SBC." Thus inspired, Denn was able to bring the full force of his construction knowledge and fiscal control to SBC. He realized that affordable housing construction needed to follow the same rules as his luxury development had. Both had the same goal during construction: to build the best, highest quality home possible with the funds available. The difference came in the sales philosophy: the sales goal in luxury housing is to sell at the highest possible price the market will bear in order to maximize profit. The sales goal in affordable housing is to sell as close as possible above true cost, providing only for a prudent reserve. Oddly, both luxury and affordable construction have the same philosophy toward savings, but again with different ends. Savings in luxury development add to profit, while savings in affordable construction increase affordability.

Although Denn technically served as construction manager in the second phase, and was paid a flat fee for this service, he essentially acted as a general contractor working on behalf of SBC's interests. This allowed for complete transparency of budgets, an elimination of change orders (changes in scope of work or design that occur after contract documents have been approved and contracts signed), and the ability to pass savings back to SBC in the form of increased affordability. This type of relationship is rare to nonexistent for most nonprofit developers. They rarely have the construction knowledge on their side of the table, and this lack of knowledge acts to their detriment. Affordable housing projects structured with a typical, bonded, general contractor automatically add 10 to 20 percent to the hard costs of the job simply because of the structure of the business relationship. If all the risk is on the builders, they will have to charge more. The bonding requirements are simply a transfer of subsidy to insurance companies and add an unnecessary cost to housing. Only with a reputable builder as a partner can this be done. The idea that there is excess risk in affordable housing production is really a scandal. Nonprofits can manage the risk by completing sales before construction, directly purchasing materials, and facilitating the political process.

Discovering Insights

As work on the Nehemiah project has evolved over the past twenty years in Brooklyn and ten years in the Bronx, certain things have become easier while others have become more difficult. Fortunately the city remains committed to an aggressive policy of creating affordable housing, even in the face of diminishing land. Banks and other financial institutions have created innovative mechanisms for both construction and end-loan financing. But the growing gap between housing demand and supply, and the requirements of government regulators to hang multiple social goals (e.g. job creation) on affordable housing production while requiring high priced development consultants to augment the staff of the nonprofit developers has created a *trend in many communities that is causing affordable housing at times to be more expensive to build than market rate housing in the same community.*

As projects become more expensive, and as subsidies are layered on, the financing package for development becomes more complex. Attorneys multiply, and with them, the transaction costs associated with the financing. Subsidies from the federal government are often tied to work rules, which are far more onerous than the rules in the market sector, forcing developers receiving these subsidies to pay more for labor and materials than their counterparts in the market sector.

The bottom line is this: affordable housing is often saddled with regulations, practices, and hard and soft costs that are above the market sector's base rate. Unfortunately the government programs that are designed to facilitate affordable housing actually make it more expensive. While these are arguably created for the broadest public good, they are now working to the detriment of affordability. This situation can best be addressed with faith-based development.

Faith-based Development Retains a Moral Imperative

In the final analysis, does a faith-based effort add value to affordable housing development? The private sector usually has no interest in building affordable housing unless in doing so they can match their returns in the market sector, whether through subsidies or through protection against risk. The only sector where there is a legitimate interest in building affordable housing, truly affordable housing, is the nonprofit sector, including faith-based organizations. If, however, faith-based organizations consent to the higher costs as a consequence of subsidies, we are complicit in the continued marginalization of the poor. We are enriching consultants at the expense of our neighborhoods.

For faith-based initiatives interested in pursing a large-scale homeownership project, the following are the key things to keep in mind:

1. It takes money, land, and relational power to build affordably. Acquisition of money, land, and power are dependent on the local condition—no recipe, each community has to figure this out within their own context.
2. Economies of scale do not kick in until the project reaches a threshold of 100 units. Think big.
3. The construction and financing systems for building a few houses at a time or even twenty or thirty over a year or more are not sufficient for a large-scale project.
4. Resist the growing trend of municipalities to pass on the costs of predevelopment (e.g. zoning and environmental relief) to nonprofit developers. Particularly with city-owned land, the municipality is in a far better position to clear zoning hurdles and pursue environmental remediation resources than most nonprofit developers.
5. Fight for property tax abatements for affordable homebuyers. The city will reap its return in the form of revitalized neighborhoods and a reduction in crime. The property taxes can be phased in after the first five to ten years.
6. Keep your staff lean. The largest staff ever working on the New York Nehemiah projects was four, and yet 200 or more units were built annually.

We Put Ourselves out of Business!

As South Bronx was rebuilt, the large areas of vacant land that initially allowed Nehemiah to achieve economies of scale became scarce. The land available today is former industrial sites, making development far more complicated and expensive to build. Without land, there is no longer a need to keep Nehemiah Homes alive. The SBC Nehemiah program has been put to bed. Its work is complete. Nehemiah's success in the Bronx has put it out of business. Good news indeed!

PART III

Intangible Structures

This last section of the book seeks to answer two questions: "What can you do to create affordable housing without necessarily building it?" (chapter 16), and, "If you decide to built it, how do you start?" (chapter 17). The models and success factors in these chapters represent the intangibles essential to a successful housing ministry. Chapter 16 enables us to see the big picture, the basic framework from which ministries tend to operate. It provides an opportunity for reflection at the macro level, helping us to define those ministry structures around us—and their ultimate aims.

These last two chapters also provide a microscopic look at proven processes and details that can make or break our projects. The Bible says, "Unless you are faithful in small matters, you won't be faithful in large ones. If you cheat even a little, you won't be honest with greater responsibilities" (Lk. 16:10, NLT)

God cares about both the micro and the macro—those "invisible" foundations built on thousands of small decisions that become a visible public witness to God's love and faithfulness.

If our foundations are not solid and sustainable, those who build on our work will see their efforts fall like a row of dominoes because of the instability we have left as our legacy. We cannot afford to end up with "projects" similar to many of the failed public housing experiments. We must learn from past mistakes, study, and find ourselves approved as honest workmen for God.

Setting the Stage

DARYN KOBATA AND JILL SHOOK

We began this book with Dr. Ray Bakke's words: "Too often our outreach projects are catching bodies as they come over the waterfall, but we don't go up to see what is causing the situation and then seek to prevent it." In this chapter we describe a range of ministry models, from pulling bodies out of the stream to keeping them from falling in. We feature how social services, mobilizing/convening, community development, advocacy, organizing, and social movements set the stage for housing to happen—without necessarily building it. Although these models tend to overlap, the framework on the next page provides an overview of each model's methods, leadership, entry points, and outcomes. Bob Untied, a Pacific Institute for Community Organizing organizer; Mark Lau Branson, a Fuller Theological Seminary professor; and others had a hand in developing the chart.

Social Service Model

Jesus healed the sick and fed hungry people, "catching bodies" along the road. Similarly, over the centuries churches have offered medical help, food, and shelter to those in need, to victims of war, violence, or circumstance.

The Bad Weather Shelter

Sometime between 1986 and 1987, a man died of hypothermia at a bus stop in Pasadena, California. Then three homeless people died on one weekend alone—and five on another. The deaths caused a public outcry. The biblical good Samaritan found the man by the roadside in time, but the Pasadena and Los Angeles faith communities were too late. Bodies were going over the edge, but the church wasn't there to catch them. The deaths coincided with the revitalization underway in Pasadena's Old Town, a former haven for transients. The El Rey and Grand hotels, though

	Social Services	Mobilizing/Convening	Community Development	Advocacy	Organizing	Social Movements
Method	Meet immediate needs; identify assets	Creating events, conferences, utilizing assets in the form of knowledge from experts	Engaging the community to identify and develop their assets, bring outside resources when insiders deem necessary	Standing up for others and/or self, creating networks and coalitions	Listening and developing strong leaders, building networks, coalitions	Large-scale organizing, mobilizing, advocacy
Leadership	Small group, executive director, board or professionals	Self-selecting, with obvious public passion	Volunteer and paid staff	Self-selecting, with obvious public passion	Constant recruitment and development of leaders, a paid lead organizer	Often one charismatic figurehead (MLK, Cesar Chavez) working with a broad network of leaders
Entry Points in Addressing Poverty	Meeting needs, basic resources	Providing knowledge, education	A combination of meeting basic needs, providing resources, awareness of community assets	Providing a voice, being heard by those who can change policy	Providing relational power to rebuild a community, dealing with multiple issues	A combination of mobilizing, community development, advocacy and organizing
Biblical Model	Jesus feeding the 5,000 and healing the sick	Abigail mobilizing her people (1 Sam. 25) and Mt. Ebal (Deut. 27)	Stephen (Acts 6)	Esther advocating on behalf of her people	Nehemiah, Moses	The Early Church
Examples	Bad weather shelter, soup kitchens, rescue missions	Hyepin Im/KCCD; conventions and conferences	Dwelling House Savings and Loan; most models in this book	Charles Suhayda/Hollywood Presbyterian, coalitions and networks	IAF / Mark Fraley; Nehemiah Homes (NY)	Civil rights, apartheid, labor rights, fall of the Berlin Wall, women's suffrage, etc.

flophouses, provided cut-rate "housing stock" that evaporated overnight; now, where they once stood, is a J. Crew.

In response, Joe Colletti and Cynthia Abbott formed a coalition of local churches and service providers[1], including the Ecumenical Council of Pasadena Area Churches (ECPAC), to establish the Bad Weather Shelter. Pasadena's Community Development Commission, the Federal Emergency Food and Shelter Program, and ECPAC funded the effort. Five such shelters were initiated across Los Angeles that year–twenty more the following year.

The churches preferred a locally run program, so in its third year, the Pasadena shelter moved from the Salvation Army to the Pasadena Covenant Church, under ECPAC's leadership.[2] A small staff works with a coalition of twelve churches that take turns hosting their homeless guests in Covenant's basement. When asked what motivates him, Don Bosch, a psychologist who coordinates Pasadena Covenant's turn, says it's Micah 6:8, "To do justice, love mercy, and walk humbly with God." He explains, "We worry about knowing God's will, but his will is obvious. The scriptures lean heavily toward caring for the poor. There's enough to keep us all busy if we just do that." With approximately 1,200 people sleeping nightly on Pasadena's streets (54 percent of them women and children), the shelter averages ninety per night. It's open the entire month of January and other nights when it's below forty degrees or rainy. Host churches are called by noon. Eight or so volunteers arrive by 7:00 p.m. They set up cots and blankets. Each church also provides food for its evening–a sizable contribution given the growing numbers. It was 250 one night. "We see the chronically homeless every year. The ones you see at freeway intersections soliciting," Don says. "But more and more we see families. In fact, one night we had twenty-five children…not the people you expect to be

An Asset-based Social Service Ministry Model

"On the walls of a soup kitchen in Indiana, guests wrote their gifts, skills, and dreams, adding their pictures and names. Sixty people said they loved kids, and thirty-five said they had musical ability. Everybody was reading the walls, and dreams began to happen. A jazz combo emerged. The fifty percent who loved to cook caused the program's whole structure to change. The homeless became the cooks, and the volunteers came hungry, ready to eat. The 250 people were no longer 'us' and 'them.' Twenty people started cooking, and others chimed in: 'I want to do something. What can I do?' You couldn't tell who was who. They were all involved with each other. They began to get uptight about the words *helper* and *helped, client* and *homeless,* changing their language to 'friends, neighbors, and partners.'"—John McKnight, in his workshop, "Asset Strategies for Faith Communities" at the 2003 CCDA conference.

homeless." The Lake Avenue Church, a block south of Pasadena Covenant, hosts an extension shelter specifically for families, initiated by Pastor Andy Bales. Some families have secured long-term housing through this satellite shelter.

Mobilizing/Convening

Throughout history, God has inspired leaders to mobilize crowds to worship, educate, and bring awareness. Here we feature Hyepin Im and Korean Churches for Community Development (KCCD), which mobilizes Korean and other Asian Americans to network and partner with community and government groups to learn how to tap into resources for community and housing development.

The L.A. riots that stunned the nation in 1992 were a major turning point for Hyepin. Of the billion dollars in property damage, Korean Americans sustained half. "It was a devastating event for our community," he says. When millions of dollars came to Los Angeles for rebuilding, very little came to the Korean community. The Korean community needed an advocate to tell its story.

Another turning point for Hyepin was meeting Rev. Mark Whitlock, executive director of FAME Renaissance, the community development corporation (CDC) of the First African Methodist Episcopal Church Los Angeles. (FAME was deeply involved in rebuilding Los Angeles after the riots.) While Hyepin grew up watching her parents find apartments and jobs at FAME, Hyepin witnessed a church with its own numerous affordable housing complexes and a strong employment agency. "I just thought, wow! What a wonderful model!" Hoping to learn more, she embraced an offer to work with FAME to establish Renaissance Capital Partners, a venture capital fund that finances businesses.

Mark urged Hyepin to invite Asian American pastors to a conference held by Churches United for Economic Development (now part of the International Economic Development Council) with former HUD Secretary, Andrew Cuomo. She saw the chance to connect the often forgotten Asian church leaders with mainstream players. "In most conferences and communities," she notes, "when they talk about minorities, they talk about the black and the brown, rarely the yellow." Yet when people speak of the majority, Asian Americans again are often left without a voice—a realization that has frustrated and challenged her.

More than sixty Asian American leaders across the U.S. attended—demonstrating the desire for dialogue between Asians and other groups. The need for an organization to act as a kind of marriage broker between the Korean community and groups involved in community development came into clear view. So Hyepin formed Korean Christians for Community Development in March 2001. Two months later they cosponsored their own summit with HUD's Los Angeles office to unite nonprofit organizations and Korean churches to learn about funding for faith-based economic development. Three days before the conference, only ten participants had signed up. Hyepin asked, "God, is this my idea?" Convinced the event was God's idea, by faith she plunged ahead. God brought 350 participants! With that momentum, Hyepin planned her next move.

In November 2001, just after 9/11, Hyepin planned KCCD's first national faith-based housing and development conference in Washington, D.C., for Asian American pastors with the White House Office of Faith-based Initiatives. With the country panicked over the anthrax scares, they wondered, "Will people come to D.C. at a time like this?" Over a hundred delegates showed! By convening with national leaders, KCCD gave Asian Americans the voice they lacked. As Hyepin puts it, "We seem to be invisible, but God makes visible what's invisible."

KCCD is helping to dispel the mainstream view of Korean Americans as a "model minority." They actually have one of the lowest homeownership rates, lagging behind other minorities. So they sponsored a homeownership fair drawing more than 600 participants, who received bilingual information on the buying process, down payment assistance, building credit, and financing. Initially, some sponsors participated with skepticism, yet by the second fair one sponsor committed $45,000 for KCCD to provide a year-long program. A KCCD's survey found that 95 percent of fair participants had credit scores over 750 but lacked knowledge on the homebuying process and assistance programs. Financial sponsors quickly shifted. Today Freddie Mac and Wells Fargo offer Korean-language seminars, counseling, and follow-up for first-time buyers. So far, over 2,500 people have been educated on homeownership.

To date, KCCD has trained over 1,000 faith-based organizations and nonprofits nationwide through their array of programs: Homebuyer Center, VITA/EITC, Financial Literacy Program, Asian American Healthy Marriage and Family Initiative, Research Institute, Path Builders Technical Assistance Program, Job Training/Placement, Healthy & Wellness Fair, and Small Business Development. A new Workforce Program will target at-risk and adjudicated Asian youth and young adults with a $5 million grant from the U.S. Department of Labor.

Despite the low homeownership rate, a 2001 KCCD survey showed that the sixteen largest Korean churches in Los Angeles had annual budgets of up to seven million dollars not including their land holdings. "If these resources are tapped the right way and leveraged with partnerships," Hyepin says, the possibilities "could be very exciting." Currently, KCCD is partnering with a developer to train these churches to do affordable housing.

Community Development

Continuing up the stream, we find community development, which considers the land, the stream, and its tributaries—the community's assets.

In *Building Communities from the Inside Out* Kretzmann and McKnight show how God is already in the city and that we must discover and redeem its many facets.[3] *Making Housing Happen* has featured many community developers who work through nonprofit CDCs. In the following story, we switch gears, featuring a for-profit community development financial institution: Dwelling House Savings and Loan. Its aim is to generate capital within low-income communities, so they can rebuild themselves.[4] Today Dwelling House has made 1,198 mortgage loans to low-income families, increasing Hill District homeownership from about 13 to 50 percent! This amazing story begins with Bob Lavelle.

Born in 1915, Robert R. Lavelle was a preacher's kid—one of eight—in Pittsburgh. At an early age, his father passed away, and with his mother semi-invalid, the family had no money.

To make ends meet as he was growing up, Lavelle cut grass, shined shoes, and later swept floors at the *Pittsburgh Courier,* a leading black newspaper. Bob began at the *Courier* the same day in September 1935 that Joe Louis knocked out heavyweight champion Max Baer. He worked there for twenty years, moving up to assistant auditor. Working in the Hill District, a booming enclave in its heyday, he saw black people control their own lives and enjoy success—helping him believe he could, too. In 1943 Bob was drafted and trained as an officer, enabling him to attend college on the GI bill—later earning a master's degree. He then went into real estate.

Dwelling House

In 1957, Bob tried repeatedly to finance a mortgage for a black family. But even with one-third down on a $7,500 home, no one would finance it. That's when Bob noticed a sign in a nearby roofing shop: Dwelling House Savings and Loan—open every third Monday from 7:00 to 9:00 p.m. Begun in 1890, the bank once had assets of $500,000, but was now ready to close its doors.

When this small bank refused his loan, he suspected redlining. Frustrated, he spelled out to the bank's directors how they could make the loan and revive the business. The nine-member board had one black director, Norman Hardy, who persuaded the others that Bob was legitimate. When they saw he knew more than they did, after a ten-minute meeting they voted Bob as the board's Secretary (at that time board Secretary was the same as CEO). Bob went in to get a loan and came out as CEO of the bank!

He moved the bank into his realty office. An open house attracted $40,000 in new deposits and raised savers' confidence. But without insurance, growth was slow; deposits totaled just $130,000 by 1968. Since the bank was known to make high-risk loans, becoming insured wasn't easy. But with ramped up efforts to meet the Federal Home Loan Bank's[5] fifteen requirements, (including a minimum of 750 savers and $100,000) on July 31, 1970, with over 900 savers and $534,000 in assets, Dwelling House was insured. By year's end, they had $1,528,642 in assets; by December 31, 2002, its assets were $21,682,214, with 6,799 savings accounts.

Secrets to Dwelling House's Success

By providing discounted home loans to low-income families, Bob helped to revitalize his community. His saga, told in an economics textbook *The Transforming Story of Dwelling House Savings and Loan: A Pittsburgh Bank's Fight to End Urban Poverty*, describes how Bob defied traditional business rules and still made the numbers pencil out by putting people first. As Georgia Beverson put it, "Although the sign says 'Savings and Loan,' Lavelle's major business is investing in people."[6]

Like Jesus, who came to dwell among us and who didn't flaunt his power, Bob deliberately located the business in the ghetto, foregoing the standard metal grilles over the windows. By limiting obvious security, he tells the community, "I am not afraid. I do trust them. I'm trying to help them see that. Because I love them, I trust them. My very vulnerability is my protection."[7] Bob gets to know applicants face-to-face. "In many instances, I've been in their homes and know their situation, the sporadic employment and their domestic relationships," he says. He writes personal notes on delinquent loan notices and visits clients on weekends. He exhorts them:

> You signed that you would pay on the first of each month. Now you're providing [your children] with housing and that's fine, and they do need this roof over their heads, but they need something more than that. They need a parent with integrity, who's going to be an example of honoring his obligation, keeping his word.[8]

Despite the high level of trust and care, Dwelling House has been held up fourteen times. "That cost us," Bob says. "We have to provide market rate interest and follow the same regulations as the big banks, but we depend solely on our loan interest for income. Big banks charge fees, but we don't." The business holds only $21 million in assets, a very small amount for banks today–part of Bob's less-is-more philosophy.

"The institution that lends to your need and not our greed" is Dwelling House's motto. Although its delinquency rate is 30 percent (the average is 2 percent), its financial prudence and high reserves exceed federal guidelines–earning the organization a four-star "excellent" rating from Bauer Financial Reports, Inc.[9] (Investors who believe in Bob's mission help him keep the reserves high.)

Helping people with basic needs such as shelter, Bob explains, helps them build stability in other areas, including a spiritual life. He believes both personal growth and financial equity are vital assets in breaking the poverty cycle. He would say the most important asset is a relationship with

Jesus. But he didn't become a Christian until age 47. Although he taught Bible classes, he didn't know Christ personally. "You need to know Jesus," his mother would say. "Only he has the peace that passes understanding." "I had quit doing all the things you were supposed to quit doing," Bob recalls. "I did good things. But I didn't have peace."[10] Today, he is unashamed to talk about his Savior.

Dwelling House Savings and Loan continues to be Bob's calling and ministry. At 90, he still serves as executive vice president to his son, Robert M. Lavelle, now CEO. He loves God by helping his neighbors qualify for and maintain their mortgages...and come to know Christ.

Advocacy

Moving further up the stream, we look at advocacy, summed up in Proverbs 31:8: "Speak up for those who cannot speak for themselves; ensure justice for those who are perishing" (NLT). God placed Moses in a position to implore Pharaoh to deliver the Israelites from Egypt. God used Esther to speak against an evil law that would destroy her people. Effective advocacy provides a voice. Someone speaking for the poor must also listen to them or help the poor to speak up for themselves. Charles Suhayda, a pastor of First Presbyterian Church of Hollywood, California, helped homeless people become advocates.

Charles Suhayda and HCAN's Beginnings

As a former refugee, Charles knows the struggles of feeling like an outsider. Born in Hungary, he left with his parents at age three when revolution swept the country in 1956. On a mission to China in 1992, he learned to receive love from people very different from himself. While working with World Vision in Cambodia, he visited the infamous Killing Fields, where thousands were tortured and murdered. These experiences created a foundation for compassion and mercy and the kind of respect needed to help disenfranchised people find their voice.

It started with listening to understand Hollywood's complex urban community: the business sector, the tourist population, immigrants, those with wealth, and those in poverty. Hollywood Presbyterian's "The Lord's Lighthouse" assists local homeless and low-income people with food, clothing, healthcare, employment assistance, and spiritual care. In the late 1990s, Lighthouse guests complained of harassment by law enforcement due to redevelopment activities in Hollywood that brought increased security measures. The Lighthouse guests felt unwanted.

With Charles's commitment to listen and his scientific Ph.D. background, conducting research was a logical step. In May 2000, The Lord's Lighthouse surveyed 115 guests regarding food, housing, income, and community interaction. The results: one third, primarily middle-aged (30–60) single men, had experienced numerous negative contacts with police and security. "We knew we'd touched a nerve because people were really interested in the results," says Charles. In groups, about sixty Lighthouse guests discussed the survey. The first few sessions were very intense, venting grievances, how they felt disrespected and angry at security, and, perhaps, angry with themselves. At one meeting, Pete White of the L. A. Community Action Network joined them, saying, "Look, you can get as mad as you want. You can go around and kick trees. But if you're not going to do anything about it, nothing's going to change. You have to make a decision: Are you going to come together and form a group or not?" Taking up the challenge, a dozen Lighthouse guests formed Hollywood Community Action Network (HCAN). In their mission statement, they decided homelessness was not the core issue. The real issue was a lack of affordable housing. So they set out to meet with leaders from the Southern California Association of Nonprofit Housing, the L.A. Coalition to End Hunger and Homelessness, and various social service providers. They came up with a plan. Since it was an election year, HCAN hosted an Affordable Housing Forum at Hollywood Presbyterian for candidates for the Los Angeles City Council 13th District seat. But the community's reaction at the Forum was negative. Charles notes, "Affordable housing is kind of a bad word in some places. The reaction was, 'We don't want that in our neighborhood.'"

Meetings with Councilmember Garcetti

HCAN members met with Eric Garcetti, the 13th District winner, and he spurred them to assess the housing need; the potential for housing–even though many believed no space or funding existed; and to elicit support from the community. To assess the need HCAN surveyed 180 Lighthouse guests. This second survey provided a clear snapshot: one third homeless; another third with temporary shelter, such as staying with a friend part-time; the last third renters. (Three-fourths had annual incomes of $10,000 or less.)

Next, to ascertain the potential for housing, HCAN identified and catalogued nearly all the vacant lots in the 13th District. They researched

The percentage of households in California able to afford a median-priced home sank to 16 percent in June 2005 according to a report released by the California Association of Realtors. The minimum household income needed to purchase a median-priced home at $542,720 in California in June was $125,870, based on an average effective mortgage interest rate of 5.71 percent and assuming a 20 percent down payment. By contrast, the minimum household income needed to purchase a median-priced home at $219,000 in the United States in June was $50,790. (Statistics found at http://home.businesswire.com/portal/site/google/index.jsp?ndmViewId=news_view&newsId=20050811005191&newsLang=en.)

funding streams and discovered part of the problem: While many sources of funding are available for seniors, the disabled, and families, there was little funding for housing development aimed at single, middle-aged men.

They gained support from the Hollywood Business Improvement District and other groups by explaining how providing affordable housing was in their best interest. The Hollywood Community Housing Corporation agreed to set aside 15 percent of the units in their Palomar project. Armed with survey results, letters of support, and testimonies of people living in dilapidated units, residential hotels, and on the streets, HCAN again met with Garcetti. The result: He pledged to help get L.A.'s one hundred million dollar affordable housing trust fund approved. On March 1, 2002, HCAN members stood before the full city council, urging them to pass the proposal. In a historic vote, it was approved!

Going to the State Capital

In May 2002, in conjunction with the L.A. Community Action Network, HCAN conducted a workshop at a statewide affordable housing conference in Sacramento. Telling HCAN's story—a group of homeless and near-homeless educating themselves on the issues and transforming their knowledge into a campaign for permanent housing—they thus inspired others to form their own local housing movements. "I was very proud of them," Charles says.

Part of the conference involved lobbying at the capitol for Proposition 46, the Housing and Emergency Shelter Trust Fund Act of 2002—a $2.1 billion bond measure to fund a spectrum of housing, from shelters to median-priced homes. When they returned from Sacramento, they studied the bond measure in depth and set up a booth to promote it at Hollywood's Farmers' Market. And California voters passed it!

Tyrone Roy went on to join the board of the Los Angeles Homeless Services Authority, representing area homeless. Another guest recently took membership classes and joined the church. Hollywood Presbyterian is primarily a commuter church, with the average attendee living twelve to fifteen miles away. But the Lighthouse is about rebuilding grass-roots contacts in the immediate vicinity. Not only has Charles become an advocate for the poor, he also helps the church members to become advocates. He explains, "I talk about the housing pressures, not just on low-income people, but also on middle-income wage earners...that gets their attention." Charles sees both congregants and staff identify personally with the issue.

Community Organizing

Still further up the stream, we consider why people "fall in" the water to begin with. Nehemiah was both an excellent community developer and organizer. Our Lord himself was a master organizer, with clear goals and methods in training his disciples. The previous chapter described organizing efforts in New York by the Industrial Areas Foundation (IAF), with miraculous results. Other groups like the Pacific Institute for Community Organizing (PICO), Gamaliel, and Direct Action and Research Training (DART) have also made significant gains in issues like affordable housing, healthcare, and education. Here, we feature Mark Fraley, lead organizer of Action in Montgomery (AIM), an IAF affiliate.

Mark's Story and AIM

Community organizing became Mark Fraley's ministry and calling, and now, in Montgomery County, Maryland, 2.5 percent of the property tax or $16.1 million (whichever is greater–in 2005 the 2.5 percent came to 18.4 million) flows each year into the Housing Initiative Fund. This annual sum preserves and expands the county's affordable housing stock.

Raised in the church by a politically aware family, Mark first encountered intense poverty in high school while helping to build a home in Mexico. His teachers encouraged questions, and Mark had many, such as, "What is the role of the church with the poor?" Majoring in political science and American literature at Miami University, he learned much about the U.S. civil rights movement. While teaching in one of the poorest schools in Baton Rouge, Louisiana, Mark learned of IAF, a pioneer in community organizing since the 1940s.[11] Later, attending graduate school in Delaware, he witnessed churches successfully bring more effective law enforcement to their city through organizing. Through his church, Mark attended IAF training sessions and spirited rallies, learning the organizing process and watching God bring justice to cities across the country. He joined IAF full time in 1997.

Concerned over numerous social justice issues, in the mid-1990s a core of seven pastors in Montgomery County contacted IAF. By February 1998, they invited Mark to be their Lead Organizer. Soon, Action In Montgomery (AIM) was established as an IAF affiliate–a grass-roots network of twenty-eight churches, synagogues, and other faith-based groups. To sustain AIM, each institution contributes one percent of its own budget.

Building Relationships

The pastors gave Mark names of potential leaders within their congregations and spheres of influence. He met with these leaders, and just as Jesus expressed anger over injustices in his day, they shared their reasons for anger over injustice; and Mark told of his own. Those people then met with others, growing the network exponentially. A year-long individual

"Rather than seek to impose an outsider's view of what a community needs, IAF helps citizens to organize into trusting relationships and to develop the tools they need to exercise power on their own behalf."—Ernesto Cortes

meeting campaign eventually identified 1,800 leaders from forty congregations. These leaders in turn met with nearly 3,000 congregation members to discuss their concerns about the quality of life in Montgomery County. A retired woman described how her rent had jumped 30 percent in the last two years, while her income rose just 2 percent; a family shared that commuting to D.C. took an hour each way because housing costs forced them to live in a faraway suburb. Again and again, congregation members kept describing how extreme housing costs were creating financial and social hardships. "People don't know how powerful their stories are until they are asked and can tell them," Mark says with passion. "The power comes when we weave all the stories together to create a new story."

Constant leadership development sustains community organizing. Mark defines a leader as "someone with a following." Often, leaders are choir members, Sunday school teachers, or youth leaders, people with constituencies that reflect a congregation's diversity. Leadership teams emerged from each sponsoring congregation. In early 1999, hundreds showed up for workshops to develop leadership skills. Soon, AIM held its first Internal Action—an organizational meeting attended by over 300 leaders. At this "Action" leaders agreed to have fifty house meetings in which eight to ten people would gather for ninety minutes. The rules were simple. First, listen and probe for people's concerns and stories, as deeper questions are raised: What causes such disparity between housing costs and income levels? Why can't families afford housing? Second, evaluate each meeting. Third, identify more potential leaders. The campaign reached approximately 800 people in more than eighty meetings—exceeding their goal of fifty! From there, eighty leaders attended a training retreat, where research-action teams met to explore emerging issues: housing, after-school care, quality of life for seniors, neighborhood issues, and schools and education.

The Founding Convention: It rained all day, stopping just before the meeting. One A.M.E. pastor read about it in *The Washington Post* and decided to attend. Figuring the crowd would be small, he and his wife arrived only five minutes early. But they were shocked at the size of the crowd. With so many cars, they had to park a mile away. The goal of 500 was exceeded, with 726 people attending, including the county executive and three out of nine county council members. People kept arriving. The chairs ran out. Community members began with their stories. One couple couldn't afford the $4,000 per month for their parents' assisted living costs. A police officer served in Montgomery County but had to live in Prince George's County because of high housing costs. At the end, an altar call was held for those interested in being trained as leaders. The goal was 50 new leaders, but 150 came forward!

Going Public

In 2000, AIM research teams met with housing experts, for-profit and nonprofit developers, and government officials. Their goal: to understand why there was a lack of affordable housing. They learned of the lack of capital to build it and that the zoning process was too long and cumbersome—it took eight years to get a proposal off the county desk! They decided to focus on the first item. So at AIM's founding convention—boasting 800-plus leaders—they finally unveiled publicly their fourfold agenda. One item was for a dedicated affordable housing trust fund of 2.5 percent of the annual property tax.

AIM leaders presented their proposal to Doug Duncan, the County Executive who designs and proposes the county budget—subject to approval by a nine-member county council. They asked, "Will you commit to this?" When Mr. Duncan asked for a month to think it over, in their debriefing they decided to trust him and wait, but also to prepare Plan B. Mark describes the follow-up with Mr. Duncan a month later: "Twelve pastors and a rabbi were around the table. 'What do you think?' Mr. Duncan asked as he passed around a document, asking our leaders to carefully read it...He had taken our proposal word for word and was sending it to the Montgomery County Council for a vote! AIM had secured the most powerful political figure in the county as its major ally."

To secure sufficient votes, AIM's efforts snowballed in a flurry of meetings with stakeholders, testifying of the county's housing needs. Momentum and enthusiasm grew as people gained clarity on what they wanted and how to ask for it. At the group's second annual convention in May, over 800 leaders challenged council members to support the proposal. Mark recounts, "As each council member comes forward, we ask 'Will you commit to a dedicated funding of $15 million?' With a giant scorecard, a stoplight, and a roving microphone, we scored each 'yes' or 'no.' Each councilperson had two minutes to talk, stopping when the red light went on. Eight approved a one-time $15 million contribution into the trust, but only one supported a dedicated funding source." The lack of council votes for a permanent funding source forced developers to piece together funding packages every year, taking an enormous amount of time and additional expense. After listening, checking, and rechecking, the people of Montgomery County still wanted a funding source that wouldn't require annual renewal. Winning the $15 million alone wasn't enough.

Election Year

In response to the previous year's defeat, in 2002 AIM launched a Sign Up and Take Charge campaign, recruiting 7,600 county voters to support the dedicated trust. Meanwhile, AIM leaders held individual meetings with each of the thirty candidates running for the County Council. Each candidate received the signed petitions in front of 750 AIM members from their districts. The power of people's stories was evident that night. In five of the nine council districts, candidates publicly pledged to dedicate 2.5 percent of the property tax to the housing fund and AIM's other agenda items.

2003—The Win!

After the election, AIM leaders met with Council President Steve Silverman, asking him to introduce the joint resolution for dedicated funding to the newly elected council. Over the next month eighty AIM leaders met with County Executive Duncan, Mr. Silverman, and five council members, and attended council hearings. But the Management and Fiscal Policy Committee voted the proposal down, two-to-one.

With AIM's resiliency, like that of the woman in Luke 18 who kept knocking on the unrighteous judge's door until she finally got what she wanted, the group was not about to give up. At a County Council meeting later that month, fifty AIM leaders again asked for the dedicated funding. Finally, the resolution passed six-to-three! Through steadfast resolve and tireless labor, AIM brought more affordable housing to Montgomery County residents! Just as important as the win is the process—engaging people of faith to acquire and practice leadership skills and to come together in a powerful democratic process transforming them and their county. Everyone wins.

Movements

Last, our chapter ends with hope for a movement. Movements reshape the very landscape, deal with causes, and prevent bodies from falling. As Jim Wallis would say, "We need to change the course of the wind."[12] God, who owns it all, is already transforming society—we just need to recognize his hand and join. Here we will look at Jane Addams and the Settlement House Movement—how one woman initiated housing policy and transformed our country's cityscapes.

Born in 1860, Jane Addams grew up in privilege, raised mostly by her father, a Quaker minister, whom she adored. Rather than following an erudite path, she found herself drawn to the poor. On several European tours, she visited Toynbee Hall, a center offering Christian love to London's poor.[13] In Chicago in 1898, Addams patterned the first U.S. settlement, the Hull House, on European models. Its goal was to transform poor immigrant communities *with* (not *for*) the residents by providing classes in subjects such as yarn spinning, an old-world talent taught by elderly, babushka-clad women. Valuing their skills as an art form restored their dignity and social standing in the community. Settlements helped poor communities recognize their strength and beauty.

Activists who "settled" with Jane into Chicago's slums became our country's first social workers. Their approach involved careful documentation of working class conditions. Before long, 2,000 people daily entered the Hull House mansion, which became a clearinghouse for every imaginable social service, an experimental lab for social reform, art, music, drama, English, and citizenship education. Addams's work with youth led to playgrounds in schools and the first U.S. juvenile courts. Research on infant deaths and diseases in the tenements led her to purchase a local garbage collection service, demonstrating to the city a well-run service—in turn improving collection throughout Chicago. This same research also led to building code legislation to improve ventilation and open space in disease-breeding tenements. For her visionary efforts, Jane Addams received the 1933 Nobel Peace Prize.

By 1918, 400 settlement houses stretched across the country, igniting the involvement of such notables as John Dewey and Eleanor Roosevelt. In 1931, the settlement house movement spawned what is now the National Housing Conference (NHC), the first U.S. housing advocacy group—still a strong leader in the fight for decent, affordable housing.

————

God is using the housing crisis to reignite the church to its call to both personal and public witness of his love. We believe God desires a housed community with livable wages and sufficient dwellings for all income levels. God is up to something today, evidenced in a hundred ways—not only by the models featured in this book crossing denominational and ethnic lines, but by hundreds of other churches, nonprofit organizations, and even for-profit groups building affordable housing. We have a long way to go. With out-of-control homeless populations in every major city and two-salary couples unable to purchase homes, we must—and can—do something. Areas of Europe and Canada; New York; Maryland; and Sumpter County, Georgia, have made great strides in providing adequate affordable housing. Let us take that step of faith, believing that God can do likewise in our communities—let us unite and be transformed in the process.

Getting Started

ANDY KRUMSIEG WITH JILL SHOOK

And what does the LORD require of you?
To act justly and to love mercy
and to walk humbly with your God.
—Micah 6:8, NIV

When our family moved into our target area on Avers Street, it was then dubbed "the worst drug block" in Chicago, twice making it onto the front page of the *Tribune*. It was so bad that neighbors couldn't get to their apartments without being blocked by lines of drug buyers. Children couldn't play outside. Gunfire was common. Yet, God directed us to start our housing ministry on that very block. No one wanted to move into the homes we were rehabbing. So my wife and I and Dale and Reecie Craft were the first to make that our home—our oasis. That was the beginning of six buildings that we rehabbed on that block. Five years later, many in the church wanted to move onto Avers Street! The kids were out in the street playing again.

This book leaves us with a challenge. The question is, what kind of response will we have? This chapter explains how to get started. Given each community's uniqueness, cookie cutter approaches are inappropriate. But there are success factors that result in beautiful, sustainable, tangible structures, as well as the intangibles—housing that rebuilds people, congregations, and communities in which love and nurture reside.

These chapters have featured leaders across the nation fulfilling God's purpose "to act justly and to love mercy"—the outward expression, "and to walk humbly with your God"—the inward expression of faith. Maintaining a balance of both public and private expressions of faith authenticates our work and our message.

Additionally, our work cannot be separated from the way we accomplish it. When Moses judged Israel and when David brought the ark back to

Israel, they were doing the right things, but in the wrong way, with dire consequences. As Kathy Dudley says, "There was a prescribed way that God wanted Israel to transport the ark, but they hadn't taken the time to investigate or obey this instruction."[1] There is no one better to mentor us on God's prescribed way than Nehemiah—a master community developer and organizer.

In this chapter Jill and I seek to show some of God's prescribed ways. We will move back and forth between the inward and outward aspects of Nehemiah's life and my own journey into affordable housing development. The success factors that unfold in this chapter are: know the vision, do research, obtain and manage resources, plan the right structure, deal with realities, and practice reflection. Each of these contains nuggets of gold that can make or break our housing ministries.

Know the Vision

Know the Vision by defining your target.

Nehemiah's mission was clear—to rebuild the wall. Everyone could easily visualize and state this. We must prayerfully choose a well-defined target area—be it a wall, one block, a city, or entire region.

In 1986, a businessman offered us a low-interest loan of $40,000 for our second housing project, but with one caveat: "You've got to buy a house on the same block where you are already working." While our sights were set on another block, God used that donor to help us start small, with a narrow concentrated focus. This helped us to develop strength and stability. We eventually did six buildings on that block before branching onto neighboring streets. We demonstrated that even on one of the worst drug blocks in Chicago, positive change could occur without displacement and gentrification. This brought great credibility to our vision; and it built our team, our skills, and our knowledge base for later successes.

QUESTIONS: Where and what is the greatest need? Is the need for housing or something else? Does your church have a geographical area they are seeking to target? Do you have relationships or partnerships there? Is it close to available jobs and public transportation?

Know the Vision by asking and listening for both the needs and the assets.

"I asked them about the Jews who had survived captivity and about how things were going in Jerusalem." (Neh. 1:2b) Nehemiah did primary research, asking people with firsthand knowledge of the situation. Questions are powerful—especially if we honor those people we are asking by giving them time to answer and be heard. In the section that follows, Lula Ballton, executive director of the West Angeles Church of God in Christ's community development corporation, tells about her first attempts to listen and hear what people wanted.

Community Needs and Assets Assessment

Learning how to listen was one thing—having some social arrogance that needed to be taken down a peg was quite another. I thought I was good at listening and knowing people's felt needs. I decided child care was needed over in the Crenshaw area. There at the check-cashing place were all these girls and their little ones. One day I was saying, "I want to provide child care, and I want you to talk to me about it." I was just shocked when they responded, "Child care? I need a job!" So we responded to that and got those people jobs, including getting Albertson's to move to the city. That was the first store they had ever built in the city; they had always built in suburbs or moderate-size towns. All of their new hires for our new local store were from the community. That was very exciting.

Later, walking through a different neighborhood, we talked to people about jobs. Their response: "Jobs? Who's going to take care of my baby? I can't work." Just the opposite! And these two locations were only three miles apart.

In the area in which we ended up building our first affordable housing, the needs were again altogether different. So that caused me to listen more carefully to what people wanted. We developed an instrument that focused on the assessment of needs and assets with questions like: What is the best thing in the neighborhood? They mentioned public assets such as schools, colleges, artists, musicians, and historical figures. We also asked, what can we do to make it better? But instead of distributing the survey (figuring people wouldn't read it), we chose a nonthreatening group to conduct it—high school students. They kept hearing the need for good housing where parents could watch their children play, have enough space to do homework, and have access to a computer. So that's how our housing started to take shape. We didn't have any money. We didn't have any expertise. We had only filled out the forms to become a Community Housing Development Organization (CHDO)—a licensed developer in the city of Los Angeles. God came though in miraculous ways. Our first housing was for large families and featured yard space for children and state-of-the-art computers with Internet access in every unit. West Angeles has gone on to become a national example of church-based housing, in a large part due to their approach of listening for both the needs and the assets.

A community defined only by its needs can take on a negative identity that destroys its soul. For years the people of the Bronx, stigmatized by negative assessments by outsiders and the media, internalized this negative identity. In Jerusalem in Nehemiah's day, "...the people were making due as best they could among its ruins."[2] They had lost much of their Jewish identity and spiritual bearings. Contributing to this negative identity is victimization. The poor are often victims of higher interest rates, expensive groceries, check cashing stores, and scams.[3] They are vulnerable to segregation, social isolation, lack of information, misinformation, and predatory lending.[4] Injustices erode their hope and will to keep trying—driving them deeper into poverty. Nehemiah understood this seemingly endless cycle; he didn't condemn the people for their plight or for giving up on the wall years earlier (Ezra 4:7–23). Rather, he used a strategy that began to break the cycle. The very process of listening caused the people to hear their own dreams and believe again.

QUESTIONS: What questions do you need to ask in your target area to determine the needs and assets? Who will you ask? And who will perform the assessment?

Know the Vision by identifying with those whom you are called to serve.

Nehemiah allowed the people's disgrace, pain, and frustration over their plight to become his own. Though he was 800 miles away, he still identified with them in his prayers:

> I confess that *we* have sinned against you. Yes, even *my own* family and *I* have sinned! *We* have sinned terribly by not obeying the commands, laws, and regulations that you gave us through your servant Moses. (Neh. 1:6b–7, NLT, author's emphasis)

Chuck Swindoll says, "For more than 160 years, Jerusalem was little more than a pile of debris, a huge dumping yard."[5] Political circumstance contributed to their reasons for an unfinished wall. But the root reason was spiritual. Upon hearing of Jerusalem's "great trouble and disgrace" with a torn down wall and burned gates, Nehemiah wept, fasted, mourned, and prayed day and night, seeking God's will and vision for the city (Neh. 1). No doubt, Nehemiah's genuine care and tears jarred them into seeing the seriousness of their situation. Moved by a passion for obedience to God's law and by mercy for a vulnerable, unprotected people in a politically volatile climate, Nehemiah was called by God to do something about it. While Nehemiah simply could have sent money and materials and let others to do the project, he chose to identify with the people directly—he sent himself. His God-ordained vision for Jerusalem required that he leave the plush palace of Persia to get dirty in the streets with people he had never met, in a ruined city 800 miles away.

Know the Vision by listening to God.

While attending an urban sociology class at Wheaton College, I had tingles going up and down my spine when we discussed the poor, the city, and housing issues. My wife and I were planning to be missionaries in

Africa. I remember thinking, "If we're going to be good missionaries overseas, we should not divorce ourselves from the poor in our own country." A friend put me in touch with Pastor Wayne Gordon of the Lawndale Community Church in Chicago (chapter 10). We volunteered six months; then, rather than go to Africa, God redirected us to live in an African American neighborhood. We dreamed of starting a housing ministry.

If I want my home to be an oasis, to obey the great commandment I should also want that for my neighbors. To love my neighbors as myself, I am moved to actively seek adequate, affordable housing for those who don't have that oasis. I did not dream up this new direction for our family, nor did Nehemiah dream up his calling. Our two-year commitment to Lawndale turned into eight. God then moved us to St. Louis to help start Jubilee Community Church alongside Pastor Leroy Gill and Jubilee Christian Development Corporation, which includes housing and economic development enterprises.

To accomplish affordable housing, many things must be learned: networking skills, project management, leadership development, organizational management, and fundraising. But it is nearly impossible to teach passion and calling. They are born of God. The "tingling" feeling that I sensed years ago still hits me today. That passion is what attracts other people to the vision.

Every generation includes people who recognize God's vision, like the practitioners introduced in this book and countless others who bring life in hurting places around our globe. "Where there is no vision, the people perish" (Prov. 29:18, KJV). Only with vision can we see what doesn't yet exist and exercise true faith with the "conviction of things not seen" (Heb. 11:1). When Nehemiah finally made the vision public, he was so sure of God's leading that he stated plainly, "The God of heaven will help us succeed" (Neh. 2:20a, NLT). As the vision grows and takes shape, it must be stated and restated until it is embedded in the very soul of the organization. Nehemiah was a catalyst to restore Israel's belief that they could do something about their plight. Faith grew as the wall went up—as they put their faith into action.

QUESTIONS: When in your life have you felt that "tingle"? What do you do that you can hardly keep from doing because you enjoy it so much? Are you asking questions of the community, of yourself, and God? Are you listening for answers? What is the vision God is giving you and others? Does everyone in your organization know the vision?

Know the Vision through teamwork and timing.

The road to affordable housing includes building a team of passionate, "like-visioned" players with whom we can work. But like Nehemiah, we must be sensitive to the right timing while eliciting the support of team players and stakeholders. Nehemiah carried the dream for over four months before telling the king his plans. No doubt he had many opportunities to tell him, as he daily tasted his wine, but he chose to wait until the time was right.

> When a man grows aware of a new way in which to serve God, he should carry it with him secretly, and without uttering it, for nine months, as though he were pregnant with it, and let others know of it only at the end of that time, as though it were a birth.–Martin Buber[6]

Too often we run ahead of God, leaving our team in the dust in our eagerness to accomplish a task. Timing and process must be honored if we expect God to bless our efforts. We must honor people by allowing sufficient time for God to impart the vision into their souls. Yet we cannot become so bogged down in discerning God's will that we become paralyzed.

Ideas can be ahead of their time. Over the years, the people of Atlanta no doubt considered many ideas on how to deal with the former Stockade Prison. It wasn't until God ignited Bob Lupton and Renny Scott that it became GlenCastle. The time was right. Their organization was linked with both the poor and with the influential. Their track record of dependability and service in the neighborhood gave them credibility. The people of Atlanta could trust them to accomplish the vision.

QUESTIONS: Are you willing to work with a team of imperfect people to whom God has given this same vision and calling? Are you willing to discipline yourself until the time is right?

Do Research

Do Relational *Research.*

After arriving in Jerusalem, Nehemiah quietly surveyed the city by night and formulated tentative strategies.[7] He didn't pay someone to conduct a study; he did the research himself. This hands-on approach built credibility and relationships.

Nehemiah said, "I regularly fed 150 Jewish officials at my table, besides all the visitors from other lands!" (Neh. 5:17, NLT). We need good relationships with officials, city staff, banks, developers, and nonprofit organizations. We need a broad spectrum of people around our tables to learn all we can about how to house the most vulnerable. As in the discussions around the tables at the Potter's House in Washington, D.C., and the Stranskes' approach in Denver, an ever-expanding circle of relationships and information must be part of our ongoing research and reflection. Get placed on mailing lists, attend housing workshops and conferences, conduct "vision" trips to housing ministries, and read periodicals.[8]

As we cultivate relationships, we become aware of the needs and assets of the community, including officials and businesses, banks, and nonprofits.

The church, parachurch organizations, relief and development organizations, mission agencies, faith-based and secular nonprofit organizations, and even for-profit developers all have the capacity to do affordable housing, but some are better suited to carry out the task. Linking with one of these groups may be the best way to develop housing, but the partnerships should enhance and support the church's mission and vision. Research findings are then incorporated into ministry plans, strategic plans, and business plans—consistent with the vision.

QUESTIONS: Are you seeking out relationships with the people you are seeking to serve? Are you developing partnerships without taking the time to first build a trusting relationship?

Do Research on the appropriate housing model.

The appropriate housing models emerge with the research on community needs and assets. What kind of housing does the target area need and want? Do you need to create walking spaces that provide a sense of community with a healthy racial and economic mix? Is it close to shops and jobs so as to limit traffic and heavy car reliance? What is appropriate for the neighborhood—mixed-use, multi-family, low-rise, high-rise, or single-family detached homes? Will the housing's organizational structure be cooperative, co-housing, a community land trust, tenant-owned, or a newly envisioned model?

Starting out, it is critical to focus on one model. With vacant lots, new construction is an obvious choice. With abandoned buildings, you will likely choose rehab or adaptive reuse. Owner-occupied properties create stability, but not everyone is ready for homeownership—other good options should be available. If low-income families don't own or rent a price-controlled property, with gentrification they lose out. Some ways to create renewal with justice are through rent stabilization, cooperatives, community land trusts, and inclusionary laws. We must use these options and come up with new ones.

QUESTIONS: What is the stated mission of your housing? Are you using the housing models that fit your vision and the neighborhood's desires and needs?

Do Research to identify a good property management system.

Nehemiah's role changed from a visionary wall builder to governor. The skills used in management (governing) are very different than in visioning. If a church chooses a rental model, a sustainable management system is paramount. As DarEll Weist aptly says, even a property management company must be managed. Insufficient screening and bending of rules can destroy the living environment and give the church a bad name. Perhaps the answer is to create jobs by starting a property management company, as did Richard Townsell in Lawndale. Jerome Garciano, who leads the

National Fellowship of Housing Ministries, establishes property management training within universities, seminaries, and Bible colleges.[9] His goal is to train and equip people of faith to share God's love as on-site property managers.

The Property Management Vision of Community Baptist

In a day when public housing is often torn down, King's Village was resurrected—a Section 8 property encompassing thirty-three acres across from the Community Baptist Church in Pasadena. The landlord neglected it for twenty-nine years, not spending a cent on its upkeep. Even the police would not enter the area. Jean Burch grew up at Community Baptist with her father as pastor. After working in the corporate world, Jean answered God's call to return as its pastor. She and Harold James, the founding president of the church's Northwest Pasadena Development Corporation, reignited the church's original vision to provide low-cost housing. Through tax credits, a limited partnership was established, and all 314 units of King's Village were refurbished without displacing its 1,200 residents![10]

The church used its influence as the limited partner to find a management company that would work in tandem with the church's mission of life transformation. Winn Residential fit like a glove. Because the people's pleas for repairs and help had not been heard for years, the residents needed to be part of the process, so a resident council was born—a body consisting of King's Village residents, church members, police, and even residents from the surrounding neighborhood. This allowed all sides of the issues to be heard.

Anna Schultz, Winn Residential's property manager, won numerous awards during her tenure at King's Village: "Manager of the Year" for 2003;[11] The National Leadership Award, given by President Bush in 2004; and "Business Person of the Year" by the National Republican Congressional Committee. What is Anna's secret of good property management? "Integrity and reputation are all you have. If you have a wall full of awards, it means nothing if you can't back it up." If someone tries to talk her out of paying rent, she says it is unacceptable, but also negotiates, "How can we make this work for you?" Considering all sides of the situation, she recognizes that nothing is all black or white. Anna is diplomatic, yet stands her ground. She diligently complies with all the government reporting.

Today, state-of-the-art computer centers, libraries, tutoring, mentoring, Bible clubs, Boy and Girl Scouts, a food pantry, and holiday parties give hope at King's Village. Community Baptist continues to grow.

The Gautreaux lawsuits proved that scattering low-income housing throughout cities is the best way to strengthen society. But once through the lengthy approval process, especially if built in wealthy or gentrified areas, all efforts can be shattered if a good management system is not in place. On the other hand, if good management is in place, NIMBY attitudes can be shed. Sister Elaine Sanchez in San Jose, California, reports how the wealthy neighbors that surround the six acres of affordable housing their congregation helped to create are now grateful for their neighbors and even employ a number of them. Like Nehemiah, who envisioned and governed well, good management can serve to build bridges between economic disparities.

QUESTIONS: Have you determined the long-term sustainability of your project? Have you done your research on management systems that work? Are residents part of the decision process?

Obtain and Manage Resources

Obtain and Manage Resources by beginning small and relational.

The Jews saw that to succeed they desperately needed a friend in high places. When Nehemiah learned of Jerusalem's disgrace, he risked being sad in the king's presence—an act with grave penalties. When King Artaxerxes noted his sadness, Nehemiah was ready to negotiate the needed permissions, resources, and release from his duties. For reinforcement, he shared his vision with the queen. He dreamed big, but it began with one small step of faith at a time, first risking these conversations.

Starting out in St. Louis, we had opportunities to pursue a twenty-unit apartment building and acquire several two- and four-unit abandoned buildings in the neighborhood, but we chose to rehab a single-family house. Kevin and Pat Huntspon, a family in our church, put in the "sweat equity" necessary to obtain ownership. It was a step of faith, yet within our reach.

The first project should be of manageable size and time span—finished in less than a year. If things drag on, the vision can deteriorate, like blowing up a balloon and letting it sit there—it eventually loses air all by itself. Nehemiah bit off a huge job, but the work was divided into manageable pieces. Like the blitz builds of Habitat, Nehemiah set a short time frame: "So the wall was finished...in fifty-two days"(Neh. 6:15). That was less than two months!

QUESTIONS: What small steps of faith are you taking? Are you willing to forgo large opportunities until you have some successes with smaller ones?

Obtain and Manage Resources with a community building strategy.

Nothing indicates that Nehemiah designed the strategy (Neh. 3). The text implies that the people came up with the plan. Catching his vision, they replied, "Let us start rebuilding!" (Neh. 2:18). Nehemiah didn't do what they could do for themselves. Too often a leader asks followers to embrace the leader's strategy, then wonders why the people are not committed and engaged.

What was their strategy to rebuild the wall? They divided the work into doable portions with various leaders at each section, with a vested interest in securing the wall close to their homes. This strategy rebuilt the wall with their most precious resource: people. John Perkins says, "Nehemiah 3 lists forty-two groups of people who built the wall. Priests and Levites, governors and nobles, men and women, young and old, worked shoulder to shoulder, side by side, to complete the task. Men came from Jericho forty miles away to help."[12] Like Jimmy Carter's involvement with Habitat, it was not beneath the nobles to work alongside commoners. No doubt this mixing of socioeconomic groups along the wall went a long way in reweaving the relational strength of the community.

When the wall was finished and the city secured, the people moved from a survival mentality to seeking a renewed spiritual life. That's when Ezra got involved. This was also Nehemiah's goal, but Nehemiah knew his gifts, strengths, and limitations—giving space for Ezra's gifts to be unleashed.

QUESTIONS: Do you respect your own and other's gifts and limitations? Do you trust God to work through others? Does your plan build corporate faith relationships across unlikely boundaries?

Obtain and Manage Resources by seeking relationships—not money.

Housing is money-intensive. There's no way around it. The money comes from donors, grants, assets, loans, tax credits, donated services, and sometimes even by raising support for workers—similar to a mission agency. We must get money, but funding that is in line with our vision. Funding is often a confirmation of the vision—but it should not determine the vision.

We must create a pipeline of people to sustain the work. The work begins because the people call for it, the people need it, and the people want it. Creating a pipeline is about giving others entry into the process. I do that by inviting people to see our work. When they see the quality of our work, they often get involved. Our last home build had about 400 volunteers—all potential donors. But don't be after their money. Money comes as a product of relationship, partnership, and vision sharing. Funding is a challenge that should not be underestimated, but it can also be a great encouragement. People will give money to a vision and to people they believe in. Initially, individual donors are the primary source of funding. Ongoing communication, newsletters, and follow-up are important tools. Sometimes money comes from those we least expect.

When Jim Rouse watched Church of the Saviour begin to rehab The Mozart and its 940 code violations, he got involved financially. Inspired, he created the Enterprise Foundation—today, the largest nationwide technical support group funding affordable housing. Before we began our first housing project in St. Louis, we knew we had insufficient funds; but we also knew God wanted us to start. At every step the finances were there. Funding is about relationships, and—bottom line—it is mostly about our relationship with God.

QUESTIONS: Have you considered a broad spectrum of funding options? Are you opening up a pipeline for people interested in volunteering and/ or donating? Are you taking into account the people and resources already present in the target area?

Obtain and Manage Resources by leveraging power.

Nehemiah understood that the assets of his integrity and his high position as cupbearer could be leveraged to obtain other assets—even relationships with other powerful people. Nehemiah's handling of money and resources were exemplary—and rare! He never took advantage of his daily ration of food—even though he regularly fed hundreds of guests. He determined not to exact any burden from the people, and he made sure no one else did either. He confronted the Jewish nobles in public and called them to account for charging interest to their fellow Jews, a practice that forced the poor to to sell their land and become slaves—illegal practices in Israel. Holding leaders accountable created a more equitable use of community resources.

Matthew's gospel makes it clear that not just the church, but all nations will be accountable for how we treat the most vulnerable (Matt. 25:31–46). Sometimes we need to wisely hold our officials accountable to what they are already supposed to do—maybe a mere reminder of the Fair Housing Laws. By expecting our government to be accountable, we, too, must follow suit. Are we complicit in a value system in which the highest-paid CEOs' salaries are about 431 times that of the lowest-paid worker?[13] Some top company leaders are now capping executive salaries, including their own. To obtain and manage resources, we must leverage the power of our positions, our integrity, and our moral imperatives.

QUESTIONS: Can you appropriately enlist the support of those in authority over you? Do you need to call them to account to uphold policies? Are you willing to live out justice in your own lifestyle choices and integrity?

Plan the Right Structure

Plan a Structure in which the church plays a significant role.

After researching possible partnerships with existing groups, if none fit the vision, the government gives us the option to start a separate 501(c)3 nonprofit organization. Within the various nonprofit options, it must be decided which option best fits. Mission Waco in Waco, Texas, known for their affiliation with Church Under the Bridge,[14] utilized a Community Housing Development Organization (CHDO, pronounced "chodo"). This structure allows access to the 15 percent of HOME funds set aside for CHDOs. A CHDO's mission is exclusively housing development, and a third of the board must be residents of the neighborhood being served. Mission Waco has now moved faster to masterplan their target neighborhood–twelve blocks with 1200 homes and 220 vacant lots.

Mission Waco believes in the centrality of the church in their development work, as we do in St. Louis. Connection to a church cannot be minimized. The church dedicates, baptizes, marries, buries, and leads followers of Christ though a lifelong commitment to personal growth. The church provides the kind of structure, stability, and spiritual resources necessary for personal transformation that can break long-held cycles of poverty. As much as we believe in the importance of the church, we also see the value of protecting our church from liabilities by working through a separate nonprofit organization. Housing in particular can result in high liability.[15]

QUESTIONS: What is the role of the local church in your housing strategy and plan? Does the mission include both personal and public transformation? If you begin a nonprofit organization, what type of nonprofit is the best match for your vision?

Plan a Structure with the right board members.

Nehemiah knew how to discern people's character. He knew whom he could trust and made no attempt to listen to those he could not, like Sanballat and Tobiah. If a separate nonprofit organization is created, this will involve developing a board of trusted people–sometimes both a governing and an advisory board. The right board members can make or break a housing ministry.

Who goes on a board? If it's a ministry of the church, then a high percent should be church members. Members of the target neighborhood should be included. When we set up our St. Louis board, all but one of the eleven members were either part of our church or from the target neighborhood. Our purpose is a neighborhood-driven vision. Filling a board with experts: fund-raisers, financial experts, construction specialists, architectural designers, and generous donors will get the housing built– but the community no longer owns the vision and has not grown in their skills and capacity.

An advisory board is a good place for the experts. Choose those worthy of your trust, who see the vision and are willing to share their expertise, resources, and networks to accomplish the vision. Even if board members come with a level of expertise, board training is essential. Nehemiah made "certain that each person knew his work" (Neh. 13:30, NLT), In addition to board development, regular communication must take place between the boards, the church, and the community.

QUESTIONS: Does your choice of board members match your vision? Are you empowering the board, the church, and the community?

Plan a Structure for organizational management.

Some of us like to fly by the seat of our pants (and we may even be good at it), but eventually the need for administration arises. Hours in the office can bog us down. When that time comes, gifted administrators must be on our team.

The key is sufficient structure to accomplish the vision, without suffocating it with undue administration. The organizational structure we start with will probably need to be adjusted as the housing ministry grows. Nehemiah's role and organizational structure changed several times. With growth, the tendency is to become a bureaucracy, but bureaucracies sometimes forget that the ultimate aim is to serve people—not for people to serve the organization.

Conflicts can increase when change occurs, either leading to the organization's demise, or to its maturing. Listening to those we work with and serve will help discern needed adjustments. The U.S. is so task-focused that we jump into the work and forget that doing the work also involves consensus building, evaluation, reflection, and accountability to a board. Time spent involving people in decisions saves time.

QUESTIONS: Have you built consensus on your process for decision-making? Are you keeping flexible organizational structures while not losing the vision? Are you making decisions *for,* or *with,* the poor?

Deal with Realities

Deal with Realities by openly addressing tough issues—such as race.

Nehemiah addressed sensitive racial issues and economic injustices head on (Neh. 5, 13). Many people are tired of discussing race. They see it as a non-issue, no longer relevant, and that today it's a matter of reconciliation across economic disparities. Actually, more Caucasians are below the poverty line than people of color, simply because there are more in our population. But those of us who are Caucasian are often isolated from the unacceptably high proportion of people of color in poverty. This cannot be ignored.

Even with strides made in the civil rights era, most cities still have racially segregated neighborhoods. And the church is the worst culprit—the most racially segregated institution in our country. Race, indeed, plays a factor in housing. We cannot expect our communities to integrate if our leadership does not lead the way—including church leadership.

We can learn from the example of the Antioch Church, with racially mixed leadership (Acts 6). Their initial structure was falling short, but they found the right racial mix of godly leaders, enabling the body of Christ to function equitably.

QUESTIONS: Do people of a different ethnicity sit on boards and teams just so your organization has an appearance of racial integration, or are you truly hearing their perspective? Are you willing to submit yourself to the leadership of people of a different color and ethnic background than your own? Does your housing promote or prevent racial and economic segregation?

Deal with Realities by being vigilant in adversity.

If we are serious about affordable housing, then we can expect adversity. The moment Nehemiah declared his vision to the stakeholders, Sanballat, governor of neighboring Samaria, gathered his cohorts and scoffed contemptuously, "What are you doing, rebelling against the king?" But Nehemiah replied, "you have no stake or claim in Jerusalem" (Neh. 2:19–20, NLT). Nehemiah knew the facts regarding the government structure—that indeed they had no claim on Jerusalem—and he knew the depths of human deception. Head on, he consistently confronted his enemy's spiritually disguised smear tactics and intimidations. Four times he sent messages saying, "I am doing a great work! I cannot stop to come and meet with you."(Neh. 6:3, NLT). Frustrated, they delivered an open letter in person—supposedly a prophecy—accusing Nehemiah of building the wall to incite a rebellion and become their king. He simply said, "You know you are lying. There is no truth in any part of your story"(Neh. 6:8, NLT).

Nehemiah's calling took strength of character. Repeated references to his prayer life show utter dependence on God, no doubt where he gathered courage to keep his boundaries clear. He never played into his detractors' threats or resorted to speaking against them—only against their actions, which he saw for what they were: evil.

Even with Nehemiah's resistance to underhanded politics, his workers were ready and armed. What does this have to do with housing? John Perkins says, "Justice is eternal vigilance."[16] It is easy to arm ourselves with swords, but much more difficult to arm ourselves with "eternal vigilance." Every day city councils and Congress make decisions that affect housing affordability. Passivity is a greater enemy than the sharp tongue of the Sanballats of this world. In the meantime, the rich keep leveraging assets to purchase more homes subsidized by huge tax breaks while HUD budgets decrease—and the poor go homeless, inadequately housed, or severely cost burdened. Or they leave. They silently exit gentrified neighborhoods. Few notice until ethnic churches and public schools depopulate. We were not vigilant. We must be armed and ready like Bob Lavelle.

> In 1948, white real estate agents began forming multiple listing services (MLS) that included all available homes in an area, giving them control of the market—but they excluded non-whites. Numerous times, Bob paid $500 to join an MLS service, but afraid he would bring black families into their areas, every year the service

returned his fee. They said he didn't receive enough votes. Therefore, almost no homes existed that he could sell. He told them, "I have the same license you do, but you are preventing me from making a living."[17]

The assassination of Martin Luther King Jr. on April 4, 1968, was a turning point for Bob.[18] When the riots caused property values to go up in flames, such a political climate enabled Bob and other plaintiffs to win a class-action lawsuit under the Sherman Antitrust Act. They chose a federal law, so it would be applied nationally.

When Bob's opponents accused him of unspecified immoral behavior, he stood up in court, to his lawyer's chagrin, and demanded to know the accusations against him. The case was delayed a week during which time, due to Bob's attention to detail, he noticed someone missing from the list of plaintiffs—the one they ended up bribing to discredit Bob's character. Bob's vigilance uncovered the bribe. The suit was dropped, and agents of color were ensured equal access into multiple listing services nationwide.

Because the 1949 Housing Act failed to include the poor in decisions about their lives, whole neighborhoods across our land were demolished. In the mid-1950s, Pittsburgh displaced 8,000 residents of its Hill District. With righteous anger, Bob recounts, "I stood in front of bulldozers to keep houses from being demolished."[19] But his efforts failed, and the area slid into a decades-long decline.[20]

Affordable housing often challenges the status quo. Nehemiah and Jesus both confronted the established elite. They both cleansed the temple, both faced detractors who paid to have them discredited—and both turned adversity into opportunities.

QUESTIONS: How do you respond to opposition and adversity? Are you aware of and resistant to the dirty tricks of your opponents? Do you maintain your integrity so that there can be no ground for accusation against you?[21]

Deal with Realities by dwelling among the people.

Once the wall was rebuilt, Jerusalem had everything but the most important ingredient—people. "At that time the city was large and spacious, but the population was small. And only a few houses were scattered throughout the city."(Neh. 7:4, NLT). Officials needed to live there—but few others wanted to. It is estimated a million or more people lived in Jerusalem's "suburbs."[22] Therefore, "a tenth of the people from the other towns of Judah and Benjamin were chosen by sacred lots to live there, too, while the rest stayed where they were." (Neh. 11:1, NLT) The few that volunteered to move to this desolate inner city were commended for doing so. God didn't call everyone to move into Jerusalem, only one in ten. If too many people move from the suburbs, gentrification soon follows. The goal of a housing ministry is not to displace the poor. God called Nehemiah and those featured in this book to live in the neighborhood they served. God also led Jill Shook as well as my own family to move into the heart of urban America.

By living in the community, the problems are no longer "theirs," but our problems and our solutions. We are no longer do *for,* but *with,* the neighborhood. We see the neighborhood assets. We meet carpenters, electricians, and plumbers. They need jobs, and we need their skills as we rebuild our community together. As we affirm people's dignity around their strengths, loving them as ourselves, we notice how God was already there, bringing about redemption. An oft-quoted Chinese poem describes the goal of this process:

> Go to the people
> Live among them
> Love them
> Listen to them
> Start with what they know
> Build on what they have
> But of the best leaders, when their task is done
> The people will say, 'we have done it ourselves.'[23]

QUESTIONS: Are you willing, should God call you to move? If you don't live among those you serve, what strategies can avoid the "we-they" scenario? If you have moved into a poor neighborhood and find yourself contributing to gentrification, how can you stop the exit of poor from your neighborhood?

Practice Reflection

Practice Reflection by celebrating and thanking.

In the repopulated Jerusalem, the people gathered and wept over their sin when Ezra read the rediscovered law. They spent hours confessing their sins. They could then celebrate because they had made things right with God; they were free to rejoice with a whole heart. At that point in their reflection Nehemiah charged: "Go and celebrate…This is a sacred day before our LORD. Don't be dejected and sad, for the joy of the LORD is your strength" (Neh. 8:10, NLT).

Nehemiah gathered people from surrounding villages to dedicate the wall. He led choirs up though the crowd onto the wall from one direction, while Ezra led choirs from the opposite direction, meeting on top for a breathtaking ceremony.

When Harold James—the man who envisioned with Pastor Jean Burch the dramatic transformation of King's Village into a village that truly honors the King of kings–passed away, not all the residents were able to attend his funeral. So Anna Schulz organized the residents to stand on Fair Oaks, the principal street running next to their housing complex, as the funeral precession passed. Everyone wore black and took off their hats as the hearse passed by. They paid their respects to a man who had shown them such deep respect.

When the task is completed and all the tools are put away, it is essential to celebrate the living and those departed who have changed our lives and cities. We worship the One who restores walls, burned-out buildings, and people. People need to be recognized and thanked. At times volunteers can be a mixed blessing, but without them many of our ministries would not exist. Because of the people who believe in the vision, we can live out God's calling. Showing appreciation for our team cannot be minimized, be it a formal ceremony, public recognition, or a simple "thanks"–these gestures go a long way. Celebrating people and our milestones serves as a reminder to us of God's love and goodness.

QUESTIONS: Do you take time to celebrate the milestones? Do you regularly call or send notes with no other reason than to thank people? Do you thank God for the task and the joy of serving? Do you thank God even in the challenges and hard times?

Practice Reflection by thorough ongoing evaluation.

The book of Nehemiah ends passionately, reevaluating the vision of God's holiness. Nehemiah used scathing language and action to purge those things displeasing to God. He reassigned tasks and challenged the status quo, asking God at interludes to remember this zeal as a "good deed." In today's culture, such "good deeds" may look very different. But passionate reevaluation and accountability are essential. Are lives and communities being transformed–including our own? Even the best of ministries always have room for improvement. If done right, a good evaluation process creates a place of affirmation and a sense of community as people's feedback is asked for, heard, honored, and respected.

Everyone should have an opportunity to provide feedback: partners, stakeholders, residents, the community, and your team. This can be formal–bringing in professional evaluators–or as simple as taking a few minutes after each meeting to ask, "How would you evaluate this meeting on a scale of one to ten?" and then discuss one or two reasons for high or low ratings. Less formal evaluations can be "conducted" by just hanging out in the neighborhood. We need to know what the community is saying about us. Often, the community won't tell us what they think; but it's in the grapevine, and we need to listen. Often blind to how we are perceived, we need others to be our mirrors. Be courageous enough to evaluate yourself and your leadership, asking for honest feedback. Has your passion fizzled?

Who will ask you the hard questions? Do you stick to the vision, or do you get sidetracked?

No matter what evaluation tools are used, be it listening to the grapevine, a weekend away with the team, or just meeting over coffee, the important thing is that ongoing evaluation takes place at all levels and that everyone has a chance to be heard.

As you reflect on your overall vision and housing ministry, the questions in this chapter are a good place to start. God is challenging us deeply to look at the inward and outward expressions of our faith. We cannot neglect any part of the command to "act justly, love mercy and walk humbly with your God"–these three must work in tandem if we want success. We must be faithful to that still, small voice–from the microscopic details that challenge the core of our integrity and patience to the macroscopic grand scheme indicated in Jesus' prayer for "Thy Kingdom to come, Thy will be done on earth as it is in heaven" (Mt. 6:10, KJV). The One who owns, redeems, and sustains our dreams, our communities, and the world has a vision that includes us. What is your part?

Details of the state of affordable housing in the United States fluctuate constantly. See www.makinghousinghappen.com for the latest statistics and other updated information concerning the need for affordable housing and efforts to meet that need.

Notes

Introduction—Falling Bodies

[1]From lecture on "Transformational Leadership for the Global City," in Guangzhou, China, January 17, 2003.

[2]Henri Nouwen, quoted in Charles Ringma, *Dare to Journey with Henri Nouwen* (Colorado Springs: Peñon Press, 2000), taken from reflection 47.

[3]Jim Wallis, *Faith Works: Lessons from the Life of an Activist Preacher* (New York: Random House, 2000), 306–7.

[4]Raymond Bakke, *A Theology as Big as a City* (Downers Grove, Ill.: InterVarsity Press, 1997).

Chapter 1—Our Nation's Housing Crisis

[1]Joint Center for Housing Studies of Harvard University, The State of the Nation's Housing 2005, (Cambridge, Mass.: President and Fellows of Harvard College, 2005), 3.

[2]Kathryn P. Nelson, Mark Treskon, and Danilo Pelletiere, Losing Ground in the Best of Times: Low Income Renters in the 1990s (Washington, D.C.: National Low Income Housing Coalition, 2004), 2, 10.

[3]Texas Transportation Institute, 2005 Urban Mobility Study, available at mobility.tamu.edu

[4]National Coalition for the Homeless, "How Many People Experience Homelessness?" NCH Fact Sheet 2 (Washington, D.C., June 2005), www.nationalhomeless.org/publications/facts.html. See also John M. Quigley, Steven Raphael, and Eugene Smolensky, who link the 1980s spike in homelessness to affordability in their abstract, "Homeless in America, Homeless in California," The Review of Economics and Statistics 83, no. 1 (February 2001): 37–51.

[5]"A Bane Amid the Housing Boom: Rising Foreclosures," Washington Post, May 30, 2005, A1

[6]David S. Johnson, John M. Rogers, and Lucilla Tan, "A Century of Family Budgets in the United States," Monthly Labor Review (May 2001): 33.

[7]Lawrence Mishel, Jared Bernstein, and Sylvia Allegretto, eds., The State of Working America 2004/2005 (Ithaca, N.Y.: ILR Press, 2005), 122

[8]Information provided by National Low Income Housing Coalition. For this and other information, see their annual *Out of Reach* report, available at www.nlihc.org

[9]Isabel Sawhill and Adam Thomas, *A Hand Up for the Bottom Third: Toward a New Agenda for Low-Income Working Families* (Washington, D.C.: The Brookings Institution, May 2001), 16–17.

[10]National Coalition for the Homeless, *People Need Livable Incomes*, available through www.nationalhomeless.org.

[11]"Poor and Uninsured Americans Increase for Third Straight Year," *Los Angeles Times*, 27 August 2004, A1, A24.

[12]Barbara Ehrenreich, *Nickel and Dimed: On (Not) Getting By in America* (New York: Metropolitan Books, 2001), 199–200.

[13]Ibid., 25.

[14]Special recognition goes to: Adrienne Schmitz, Suzanne Corcoran, Isabelle Gournay, Matthew Kuhnert, Michael Pyatok, Nicolas Retsinas, Jason Scully, *Affordable Housing: Designing an American Asset* (Washington, D.C.: Urban Land Institute, 2005) for an exhaustive timeline chronicling the history of low-income housing. The book was published in conjunction with the National Building Museum's 2004 exhibit of the same name and was of great help in providing research direction.

[15]Metropolitan Area Research Corporation, *Los Angeles Metropatterns: Social Separation and Sprawl in the Los Angeles Region* (Minneapolis: Metropolitan Area Research Corporation, 2000), 7.

[16]Jim Rooney, *Organizing the South Bronx* (Albany: State University of New York Press, 1995), 49.

[17]Michael H. Schill and Susan M. Wachter, "Principles To Guide Housing Policy at the Beginning of the Millennium," *Cityscape* 5, no. 2 (2001): 7, http://www.huduser.org/Periodicals/CITYSCPE/VOL5NUM2/schill.pdf.

[18]Today, 16 percent of those receiving housing vouchers, and 31 percent of all public housing residents, are elderly. People with disabilities make up 22 percent of all vouchers holders and 32 percent of all public housing residents. Sunia Zaterman, "The Real World of Public Housing" (Washington, D.C.: Council of Large Public Housing Agencies, 2004).

[19]During that same period, homeownership subsidies, in the form of tax breaks, grew by 360 percent. (Budget authority refers to authorized amount of funding for a particular year, regardless of when spending occurs, as opposed to budget outlay, which refers to actual spending during a particular year.) Source: National Low Income Housing Coalition. Calculated from the budget of the United States government, fiscal years 1991 and 1992, Table C-1; fiscal year 1993, Table 24-1; and Special Analysis G, 1993 and prior budgets. 1992 figures form Budget Baselines, Historical Data, and Alternatives for the Future, January 1993, appendix 1, Table 21. 1993-2007 figures from budget of the United States government, analytical perspectives, fiscal years 1995-2004, Table 6-1.

[20]May 2004 interview with Joseph Shuldiner, onetime executive director of the Los Angeles Housing Authority and general manager of the New York City Housing Authority.

[21]Also during this period the federal government established Fannie Mae in 1938 to expand the flow of mortgage money. Fannie Mae become a private, shareholder-owned company in 1968 and was joined by a second government-sponsored enterprise (GSE) with a comparable role, Freddie Mac, in 1970.

[22]Nicholas Lemann, *The Promised Land: The Great Black Migration and How It Changed America* (New York: Vintage Books, 1991), 6–7.

[23]Business and Professional People for the Public Interest, "Public Housing Transformation: Gautreaux," http://www.bpichicago.org/pht/gautreaux.html

[24]Dreier, "Labor's Love Lost?" 338.

[25]Ibid.

[26]Dena Amoruso, "The Housing Act of 1949: 50 Years of The American Dream Celebrated," *Realty Times–Real Estate News and Advice,* March 19, 2000, available at http://realtytimes.com/rtcpages/19991029_hsingact.htm.

[27]HUD's 1973 National Housing Policy Review called the 1949 Act "a commitment without a timetable and without adequate means of accomplishment." See Charles J. Orlebeke, "The Evolution of Low-Income Housing Policy, 1949 to 1999," *Fannie Mae Foundation Housing Policy Debate* 11, no. 2 (2000): 492.

[28]Arnold R. Hirsch, summarized in Robert E. Lang and Rebecca Sohmer, "The Legacy of the Housing Act of 1949: The Past, Present, and Future of Federal Housing and Urban Policy," *Fannie Mae Foundation Housing Policy Debate* 11, no. 2 (2000): 294.

[29]William B. Fulton, Jennifer Rich, Manuel Pastor, Peter Dreier, *Sprawl Hits the Wall* (Los Angeles: The Southern California Studies Center of the University of Southern California; Washington, D.C.: The Brookings Institution Center on Urban and Metropolitan Policy, 2001).

[30]The Fair Housing Act, along with the 1964 Civil Rights Act and the 1965 Voting Rights Act, was part of the legacy of the civil rights movement.

[31]Kelli M. Evans, "Oldsmar: Using Civil Rights Laws to Build Affordable Housing," *The NIMBY Report* (Washington, D.C.: National Low Income Housing Coalition, Fall 2002): 13.

[32]Neil R. Peirce and Carol F. Steinbach, *Corrective Capitalism: The Rise of America's Community Development Corporations* (The Ford Foundation, July 1987), 12.

[33]Harry J. Wexler, "HOPE VI: Market Means/Public Ends–The Goals, Strategies, and Midterm Lessons of HUD's Urban Revitalization Demonstration Program," *Journal of Affordable Housing* 10, no. 3 (Spring 2001): 206.

[34]John F. Bauman, Roger Biles, and Kristin M. Szylvian, eds., *From Tenements to the Taylor Homes: In Search of an Urban Housing Policy in Twentieth Century America* (University Park, Pa.: Pennsylvania State University Press, 2000).

[35]This was, in part, due to an ongoing debate between production advocates and voucher advocates. The Nixon administration came to agree that production was not the solution. Orlebeke laments that "the 1973 moratorium had squashed what was left of the spirit of '68." (Orlebeke, "Evolution of Low-Income Housing Policy," 502).

[36]*Los Angeles Metropatterns,* 7

[37]For a NIMBY tale, see Diane Citrino, Michael Allen, and Kim Schaffer, "Buckeye Goes to the Supreme Court," *The NIMBY Report* (Washington, D.C.: National Low Income Housing Coalition, Fall 2002), 8–9.

[38]"Leaders Spotlight Housing Needs," *Realtor Magazine* (November 2003): 22.

[39]Affordable housing developers often use income bands to determine the income mix in a development. An apartment complex might have, for example, 40 percent of units set at market rate, 20 percent for those earning 80 to 120 percent of median income, 20 percent for those at 50 to 79 percent of median, and the remaining 20 percent for those at less than 50 percent of median. Advocates often fight to ensure that the lowest income bands are not forgotten.

[40]Kim Schaffer and Irene Basloe Saraf, "The Numbers Say Yes, Getting to YIMBY: Lessons in YES In My Back Yard," *The NIMBY Report* (Washington, D.C.: National Low Income Housing Coalition), 2003): 25.

[41]Business and Professional People for the Public Interest, "Myths and Stereotypes of Affordable Housing," September 2003, available at www.bpichicago.org/rah/pubs/myths_stereotypes.pdf.

[42]National Crime Prevention Council, "Strategy: Ensure Supply of Affordable Housing," available through www.ncpc.org.

[43]Bipartisan Millennial Housing Commission, *Meeting Our Nation's Housing Challenges* (Washington, D.C.: U.S. Government Printing Office, May 30, 2002), 112–13.

[44]CDBG spending was reduced by $364 million in FY 2006.

[45]Cushing Dolbeare and Sheila Crowley, *Changing Priorities: The Federal Budget and Housing Assistance 1976–2007*(Washington, D.C.: National Low Income Housing Coalition, August 2002), 8–9.

[46]The 1975 Home Mortgage Disclosure Act uncovered these abuses by requiring that lending institutions with assets over $10 million report all mortgage applications, including race, gender, income, and geographic data.

[47]Various recent policy changes have weakened or threaten to weaken this invaluable tool for development.

[48]Twenty-five percent of those in need receive housing subsidies, according to Michael Stegman, Walter Davis, and Roberto Quercia, *Tax Policy as Housing Policy: The EITC's Potential to Make Housing More Affordable for Working Families* (Washington, D.C.: The Brookings Institution, Center on Urban and Metropolitan Policy, October 2003), 2

[49]We have borrowed the title for this section from an article of the same name by Tufts University professor Rachel G. Bratt, July/August 1997, National Housing Institute, available at www.nhi.org/online/issues/94/bratt.html

[50]Peter Dreier, "Philanthropy and the Housing Crisis: The Dilemmas of Private Charity and Public Policy," *Fannie Mae Foundation Housing Policy Debate* 8, no. 1 (1997): 245–50. The repeal of project-based Section 8 is covered in Orlebeke, "Evolution of Low-Income Housing Policy," 505.

[51]Millennial Housing Commission, *Meeting Our Nation's*, 23–34.

[52]While CDCs have remained politically popular, their perceived role shifted from a *complement* to government in the 1960s and 1970s, to an *alternative* to government in the 1980s, and they lost most of their funding. See Carol Steinbach, "Community Development Corporations in U.S. Civil Society," 2 found at www.ids.ac.uk/ids/civsoc/final/usa/USA2.doc. This change has made community block grants, low-income housing tax credits, and other Congressional provisions crucial. Through these laws and the support of intermediaries, such as the Local Initiatives Support Corporation and The Enterprise Foundation, CDCs have grown to an estimated 3,600 groups that have created 247,000 jobs and 550,000 units of affordable housing. See National Congress for Community Economic Development, at www.ncced.org/aboutUs/faqs.html

[53]Dreier, "Philanthropy and the Housing Crisis," 260.

[54]Remarks of Lee H. Hamilton, *Congressional Record,* Oct. 18, 1989.

[55]As quoted in Dreier, "Philanthropy and the Housing Crisis," 272–73.

[56]NLIHC, "HOME Investment Partnership Program," *2005 Advocates' Guide to Housing and Community Development Policy* (Washington, D.C.: National Low Income Housing Coalition), available at www.nlihc.org/advocates/home.htm.

[57]First established in 1954 and modified as part of the 1986 Act, private activity bonds are used, among other things, to support first-time homebuyer programs and multifamily

housing development. Using mortgage revenue bonds, Housing Finance Agencies have made homeownership possible for more than 2.5 million low- and moderate-income families and they help another 100,000 families per year buy their first homes. See NLIHC, "Housing Bonds," *2005 Advocates' Guide to Housing and Community Development Policy* (Washington, D.C.: National Low Income Housing Coalition), available at www.nlihc.org/advocates/housingbonds.htm

[58]NLIHC, "HOPE VI," 2004 and 2005 versions, *Advocates' Guide to Housing and Community Development Policy* (National Low Income Housing Coalition), available at www.nlihc.org/advocates/hopevi.htm.

[59]*Meeting our Nation's Housing Challenges,* 180. See also Peter Dreier, who cites the following statistics: 1970–6.5 million affordable units for 6.2 million low-income renter households; 1995–6.1 million affordable units for 10.5 million low-income renter households, *Labor's Love Lost?,* 352.

[60]Peter Dreier, "Putting Housing Back on the Political Agenda," in *Housing Policy in the New Millennium Conference Proceedings,* ed. Susan M. Wachter and R. Leo Penne (Washington, D.C.: U.S. Dept. of Housing and Urban Development, 2001), 49.

[61]Peter Dreier, *Rebuilding the Public Sector: Housing* [Draft to Ford Foundation], April 2004, 4.

[62]Dolbeare and Crowley, *Changing Priorities,* 3.

[63]Millennial Housing Commission, *Meeting Our Nation's,* 29.

[64]Dreier, *Rebuilding the Public Sector: Housing,* 8. Dreier also points out that only about 6 million low-income households receive federal housing subsidies, compared to 33 million homeowners who take advantage of tax breaks.

[65]State of the Nation's Housing 2005, 4.

[66]Peter Dreier, "Moving From the 'Hood: The Mixed Success of Integrating Suburbia," *The American Prospect* 7, no. 24 (December 1, 1996), available at www.prospect.org/print-friendly/print/V7/24/dreier-p.html.

[67]State of the Nation's Housing 2005.

[68]NLIHC, "Fair Housing," *2004 Advocates Guide to Housing and Community Development Policy* (Washington, D.C.: National Low Income Housing Coalition, www.nlihc.org/advocates/fairhousing.htm.

[69]*Los Angeles Metropatterns,* 11

[70]Sheryll D. Cashin, "Living Separately and Unequally," *Los Angeles Times,* 6 July 2004, Op-Ed page. In 1997, the average Black student attended a school that was more than half Black and 43 percent poor. The average Hispanic student attended a school that was more than half Hispanic and 46 percent poor. By contrast, the average White student attended a school that was 81 percent White and only 19 percent poor. Source: *Los Angeles Metropatterns,* 11.

[71]Joint Center for Housing Studies, *Strengthening Our Workforce and Our Communities through Housing Solutions* (Cambridge, Mass.: Harvard University; Washington, D.C.: Center for Workforce Preparation, U.S. Chamber of Commerce, 2005), 5.

[72]*Creating Great Neighborhoods: Density in Your Community* (Washington, D.C.: Local Government Commission in cooperation with U.S. EPA, September 2003), 6–7.

[73]Montgomery County, Maryland, blazed the trail in 1973 with an inclusionary zoning law that still exists after more than thirty years. This law, which has resulted in nearly 11,000 units of affordable housing, allows developers a density bonus to offset the production costs for affordable units, permitting them to build up to 22 percent more units than the normal zoning allowance. Source: The Maryland-National Capital Park and Planning Commission, Montgomery County Department of Park and Planning, and Montgomery County Planning Board. See www.mc-mncppc.org/research/////analysis/housing/affordable/mpdu.shtm.

[74]See Rick Jacobus and Amy Cohen, "Creating Permanently Affordable Homeownership Through Community Land Trusts," in *California Affordable Housing Deskbook* (Point Arena, Calif.: Solano Press, forthcoming).

[75]See Unidev's model: http://www.unidevllc.com/why_housing.htm.

[76]Policies vary among cities, but usually allow landlords to raise rents either at the rate of inflation, when their costs increase, or when a unit is vacated.

[77]"A Real Look at Rent Control," *Dollars & Sense* (January 1986), available at www.tenant.net/Alerts/Guide/papers/reallook.html

[78]Henry O. Pollakowski, *Rent Regulation and Housing Maintenance in New York City* (Cambridge, Mass.: Massachusetts Institute of Technology Center for Real Estate, May 1999), 16.

[79]Other models similar to manufactured housing (which is delivered to a site on its own chassis and is the most complete) are modular homes (nearly complete in pre-built, three-dimensional modules), panelized homes (arriving in prefabricated wall sections), and pre-engineered homes (requiring construction of ready-to-assemble precut components). For a beautiful example of a modular home, see "Modern Prefab," *Sunset Magazine* (August 2004): 67–68 .

[80]*The State of the Nation's Housing 2005,* 19.

[81]Dreier, "Putting Housing Back on the Political Agenda," 75.

[82]These and other strategies were proposed by Dreier and outlined in his speech to the Housing Policy in the New Millennium Conference in 2001. Source: Dreier, "Putting Housing Back on the Political Agenda," 67–68.

[83]Cited in Donald W. Dayton, *Discovering an Evangelical Heritage* (Peabody, Mass.: Hendrickson, 1976, 1994), 9–10

[84]Ibid., 116–17.

Chapter 2—Ownership, Land, and Jubilee Justice

[1]Loewen, James W., *Mississippi: Conflict and Change,* ed. James W. Loewen and Charles Sallis (New York: Panthian Books, 1974), 1, 136–37.

[2]Racial segregation is a kind of institutionalized discrimination that separates people based on their race. The separation may be geographical, but is often supported by providing services through separate legal and social structures. The Jim Crow laws of the South, for example, created separate public bathrooms, drinking fountains, and schools for Blacks and Whites. See en.wikipedia.org/wiki/Racial_discrimination.

[3]Without land, former slaves were forced to work out a new relationship with their former owners. Sharecropping offered some freedom to work independently and at first seemed a good bargain for ex-slaves, but quickly proved disastrous for both poor Blacks and Whites. Sharecroppers needed not only land, but seed, fertilizer, and provisions to live on until the harvest. Falling crop prices, high credit rates, and unscrupulous merchants and creditors left Black and White sharecroppers alike in debt after the harvest, eventually tying them into an endless cycle. See www.bchm.org/wrr/recon/p6a.html

[4]Near the end of the Civil War, General William Tecumseh Sherman issued a special field order setting aside 40-acre land parcels for freed slaves. But, caving to political pressure, President Andrew Johnson invalidated the order in favor of the previous White landowners. Former slaves who wanted to stay on the land then had to work for the former slaveholders. Franklin D. Raines, "Forty Acres and a Mortgage," *Sojourners* (Sept.-Oct. 2002), http://www.sojo.net/index.cfm?action=magazine.article&issue=soj0209&article=020920.

[5]Manning Marable, *The Great Wells of Democracy* (New York: BasicCivitas Books, 2002), 226.

[6]Henry George, "Liberation Theology and Land Reform Readings," at www.landreform.org/reading0.htm.

[7]Walter Brueggemann, *The Land: Place as Gift, Promise, and Challenge in Biblical Faith,* 2d ed. (Philadelphia: Fortress Press, 1977, 2002), 1.

[8]Ibid., xi.

[9]Mark Kramer, "Without Place or Power: In Search of a Biblical Approach to Land Rights," *Prism* (March-April 2003): 8–9.

[10]Donald Kraybill, *The Upside-Down Kingdom* (Scottdale, Pa.: Herald Press, 1978, 1990), 95–106.

[11]Ched Myers, *The Biblical Vision of Sabbath Economics* (Washington, D.C.: Tell the Word, 2001), 15.

[12]For a more complete treatment of the Sabbath laws, see ibid.

[13]Henry George, "Biblical Economic: Mishpat–The Laws in Practice," Reading no. 3, at www.landreform.org/reading0.htm

[14]James Putzel, *A Captive Land: The Politics of Agrarian Reform in the Philippines* (Manila: Ateneo de Manila University Press, 1992).

[15]Henry George, "The Church and Land," in *Biblical Economics,* Reading no. 9, at www.landreform.org/reading0.htm.

[16]This remarkable story is told by Charlotte Wiser in *Behind Mud Walls 1930–1970* (Berkeley: University California Berkeley, 1971).

[17]Putzel, A Captive Land.

[18]Henry George, "Claiming the Promised Land: A New Jubilee for a New World," in *From Wasteland to Promised Land,* Reading no. 9, at www.landreform.org/reading0.htm

[19]W. R. Domeris, " *byon," New International Dictionary of Old Testament Theology and Exegisis,* vol. 1 (Grand Rapids: Zondervan, 1997), 228.

[20]Ibid., 229.

[21]We have only scratched the surface of the many Old Testament references to the rich, the poor, oppression, and justice, especially in the prophets. Readers wishing to explore these themes in depth might look up these topics in a Bible concordance and read these verses directly.

[22]From a lecture by Raymond Bakke in Seattle, Washington, for a doctoral course on Transformational Leadership for the Global City, June 2002.

[23]Domaris, *New International Dictionary of Old Testament,* 230–31.

[24]Other biblical authorities add here (or after verse 12) verse 14, "Woe to you, scribes and Pharisees, hypocrites! Because you devour widows' houses and for a pretense you make long prayers; therefore you will receive the greater condemnation" (NASB).

[25]For a detailed discussion, see Richard Horsley, *The Liberation of Christmas* (New York: Crossroad, 1989), 40–51, and Ched Myers, *Binding the Strong Man* (Maryknoll, N.Y.: Orbis Books, 1988), 50–53, 75–82.

[26]Ibid.

[27]Kraybill, *Upside-Down Kingdom,* 667–68.

[28]Sharon H. Ringe, *Jesus, Liberation, and the Biblical Jubilee* (Philadelphia: Fortress Press, 1985), 23, 29–30.

[29]The word *oppression* occurs more than 100 times in the Old Testament, but seldom in the New Testament. It occurs in Jesus' mission in Luke 4:18, quoting Isaiah 58:6; twice in Acts (7:19, 34), referring to the Hebrews' slavery in Egypt; and in James 2:6, referring to the rich who exploit the poor. There are also descriptions of oppression in which the word is not used, e.g., James 5:1–6. When Jesus cleansed the temple, he called it a "den of robbers," because the religio-politico-economic elite had turned the temple's operation into an oppressive system. See "Oppression," *Illustrated Bible Dictionary* (Downer's Grove, Ill.:InterVarsity Press, 1998), s.v. "Justice."

[30]Thomas Hanks, *God So Loved the Third World* (Maryknoll, N.Y.: Orbis Books, 1983), 38 ff.

[31]In fairness to the KJV translators, *mishpat* can be translated as either "judgment" or "justice." The *New* KJV has largely corrected this problem, and the NIV has used "justice" even more. However, there is still a problem in communicating the full meaning of justice in English translations.

[32]Glen Stassen and David Gushee, *Kingdom Ethics* (Downers Grove, Ill.: InterVarsity Press, 2003), 42–43.

[33]Graham Cray, "Transformation," *A Theology of the Kingdom,* vol. 5, no. 4 (1988). Note that the *New Jerusalem Bible* translates, "God's saving justice."

[34]Sidney Rooy, *Righteousness and Justice,* unpublished paper.

Part II—Tangible Structures

[1]Also in the plan are catfish ponds, a park, a prayer center, a retirement community, a wellness center, a family life center, and a tennis center; see www.kingdombuilder.com/templates/cuskingdombuilders/details.asp?id=23260&PID=74173

[2]Mercy Housing, "Annual Report 2003," 21, available at www.mercyhousing.org/resources. Representatives from thirteen Catholic Sister organizations, spanning the U.S., are cosponsors of Mercy Housing. They address the need for quality housing as well as tools for self-improvement.

[3]ECHC was formed when Sister Donoghue helped residents near St. Vincent's Church successfully oppose the development of *another* garment factory on the site of a previous one.

Later, in partnership with the Los Angeles Community Design Center, they purchased the original garment factory site and built thirty-three units of affordable housing, including childcare services and a neighborhood center.

⁴Jude Tiersma-Watson and Charles Van Engen, eds., *For God So Loves the City* (Monrovia, Calif.: MARC Publications, a division of World Vision, 1994).

Chapter 3—Habitat for Humanity and Preachtree Presbyterian Church

¹Community Housing Improvement Systems and Planning Association, founded by Moncrief in 1980. *CHISPA* means "spark" in Spanish.

²Fuller's book, *Love in the Mortar Joints* (Chicago: Association Press, 1980), dedicates a chapter to the term and explains that it embraces five principles. 1. Christ can multiply the miniscule to accomplish the gigantic, as in the feeding of the multitudes. This teaches us that when we move out in faith, God moves, too, and miraculously multiplies our supplies to fill the need. 2. We do not place value on profit or interest, but on meeting human need. Christ will show us how to face the challenges of inflation, indifference, opposition, or lack of resources. 3. Christ expects us to put the resources we receive into meeting human needs, and not to hoard them. 4. Every human life, no matter how insignificant it may seem, is priceless. 5. We acknowledge that people's needs are paramount and that our response is not connected in any way with people's usefulness or productivity. "Grace and love abound for all," as Fuller states.

³In the case of Penn-Craft, cooperative relationships blossomed far beyond the construction of housing. A series of cooperative ventures in housing, farming, and manufacturing is still thriving today, almost seventy years later.

⁴American Friends Service Committee, Statement of Values adopted by its Board of Directors, June 19, 1994, as reflected on its Web site.

⁵Woody Guthrie, "Pastures of Plenty."

⁶The fertile land assigned to the Israelites in Egypt (Gen. 45:9–11; 46:27–30; 46:33–47:7; 47:26–28; 50:7–9; Ex. 8:21–23; 9:25–27).

⁷The Sumter County initiative "Victory House" was dedicated in Fall 2000.

⁸Millard and Linda Fuller left Habitat for Humanity in January 2005 and are no longer actively involved with this organization.

Chapter 4—Jubilee Housing

¹From Potter's house Web site: http://www.pottershousebooks.org/HTML/ origins.html#, which provides excerpts from the out-of print Elizabeth O'Connor, *Call to Commitment: An Attempt to Embody the Essence of Church* (Washington, D.C.: Servant Leadership Press, 1994.).

²Ibid.

³Ibid.

⁴Bill Haley, *Staying Small, Going Deep Building the Kingdom: Lesson for Transforming Churches from The Church of the Saviour.* Out of print.

⁵Ibid., 10.

⁶Ibid. ,13.

⁷Ibid. ,18.

⁸Jeff Bailey, *Journey Inward, Outward & Forward: The Radical Vision of the Church of the Savior* (Washington, D.C.: Tell the Word, 2001), 10.

⁹ Haley, *Staying Small.*

¹⁰In 1976, six churches formed around various areas of interest: housing (Jubilee), children (Seekers), hospitality (Potters House), polyculturalism (8th Day), public policy (Dunamis) and retreat (Dayspring). Gordon continues preaching at the ecumenical service, where many visitors come. Membership in Church of the Saviour means joining one of the little churches. Dunamis ended, and five more churches have been born from calls confirmed in mission groups: New Community (renewing the neighborhood at 16th and S), Christ House (health care for the homeless), Lazarus House (post-AA recovery), Festival Church (Servant Leadership School), and Church of the Servant Jesus.

¹¹From Church of the Saviour and Seeker's Church website: http://www. seekerschurch.org/general/saviour.htm

[12]We acknowledge here a great debt of gratitude to Elizabeth O'Connor, who was intimately involved with Jubilee Housing. Much of the text presented in this chapter has been adapted, with permission, from the third chapter of her book, *The New Community: A Portrait of Life Together in Words and Pictures* (New York: Harper & Row, 1976). Where necessary, we have made minor changes.

[13]Pamphlet, *Jubilee Ministries* (Washington, D.C.: Tell the Word), 11.

[14]Interview with Terry Flood.

[15]*An Invitation to Jubilee:* Jubilee Ministries, 1640 Columbia Rd. NW, Washington D.C. 20009.

[16]Bailey, *Journey Inward,* 4.

[17]Information from http://www.enterprisecommunity.org/index.html.

[18]Information from http://www.charitablechoices.org/charities/JubileeJobs/default.asp.

[19]Interview with Terry Flood.

[20]Taken from interviews with Jim Knight, executive director of Jubilee Housing.

[21]Information from www.mannadc.org.

[22]Over a three-year period they were able to fully fund it from a percentage of the transfer and recordation fees the city collects every time a property is sold in Washington, D.C. Manna Web site: http://www.mannadc.org.

[23]Ibid.

[24]O'Connor, *The New Community,* 37.

[25]Ibid., 38.

[26]Ibid.

[27]Ibid.

[28]Bailey, *Journey Inward,* 2

[29]Ibid.,16

[30]O'Connor, *The New Community,* 36.

[31]Ibid.

[32]Ibid., 53.

[33]Ibid., 53–55.

[34]Quoted in "Musings on the 30th Anniversary," *Grapevine Express* 1, no. 2 (February 2004). *Grapevine Express* is a newsletter for Jubilee Housing residents.

Chapter 5—An Ex-Prison and an Abandoned Hospital

[1]Using hand tools and castoff materials (broken glass, sea shells, tile) Italian immigrant Simon Rodia worked from 1921 to 1955 to build a monument to his adopted country and to the spirit of individuals who make their dreams tangible. See www.wattstowers.net

[2]Jonathan Cohen, "Preservation, Mixed Use and Urban Vitality," *Periferia,* Internet Resources for Architecture and Urban Design in the Caribbean; accessed in January 2006 at www.periferia.org/publications/cohen1.html

[3]"Maxxon Level-Right Lends a Hand in Adaptive Reuse," accessed in January 2006 at www.dcd.com/bpr/bpr_ja_2_2003.html

[4]To adapt and reuse buildings, labor-intensive "conservative disassembly" techniques are required to dismantle buildings in such a way that as much reusable construction material as possible is salvaged.

[5]Janice E. Kirk and Donald R. Kirk, *Cherish the Earth: The Environment and Scripture* (Scottdale, Pa.: Herald Press, 1993).

[6]Ibid.

[7]Raymond Bakke, *A Theology as Big as a City* (Downer's Grove, Ill.: InterVarsity, 1997), 35.

[8]Headline on January 8, 1990 *Crain's Chicago Business* newspaper.

Chapter 6—Build a Community

[1]Interview with Rev. Dr DarEll T. Weist in 2003.

Chapter 7—Change from the Inside Out

[1]Martin Luther King Jr., *The Trumpet of Conscience* (New York: Harper & Row, 1967) Nonviolence and Social Change.

²Mutual housing is a type of shared ownership where residents buy shares of stock (rather than equity) in a project. Although the Cambria Apartments are not mutual housing, since there are no shares and the residents didn't purchase anything, the communal ownership made it appealing to SCMHA (Southern California Mutual Housing Association). (

³We hired Nancy Lewis as our financial consultant, Luis Hoyos (of Castro-Blanco, Piscioneri & Associates) and Judith Sheine as architects, Allen Sanderson as general contractor, and Solari Enterprises as property management agent. In addition to these lead roles, many other people, ranging from construction supervisors and toxic monitoring companies to security companies, also worked on the project.

⁴Grants from the California Community Foundation, Local Initiatives Support Coalition, Liberty Hill Foundation, and Low Income Housing Fund provided seed money.

⁵The city financed the project from a block grant it had received from the Department of Housing and Urban Development for low-income housing.

⁶In addition, 6 percent of our funds came through Citibank from the Federal Affordable Housing Program.

⁷The building is actually owned by a limited partnership in which Comunidad Cambriaas general partner, makes most operational decisions. Certain limits are imposed by our partnership agreement with CEF (California Equity Fund), our loan agreements with the City of Los Angeles and Citibank, and our regulatory agreement with the Tax Credit Allocation Committee.

⁸Construction costs for rehabilitating forty units were about $2 million. We spent roughly another $2 million on the building purchase, toxic abatement, carrying costs, consultant fees, and reserves. Legal Aid, Inquilinos Unidos (Tenants United in English), and outside members of our board donated their services.

⁹We were influenced by John Perkins's "three R's" of Christian community development: relocation, reconciliation, and redistribution.

Chapter 8—The Point

¹Brian Leary (vice president of design and development at Atlantic Station), "Home Is Sweet for Mixed Use Facilities," in *Building Operating Management,* September 2003 ; accessed in January 2006 at www.facilitiesnet.com/bom/article.asp?id=1612

²Jay Walljasper, "Jane Jacobs: Defender of the Urban Neighborhood," in *Conscious Choice,* May 2002, accessed in January 2006 at http://www.consciouschoice.com/2002/cc1505/citizen1505.html.

³Jane Jacobs, *The Death and Life of Great American Cities* (New York: Random House, 1961, 2002).

⁴Ibid.

⁵Nancy A. Miller and Jeff Miller, "Defining Mixed Use Development," Design Center for American Urban Landscape, College of Architecture and Landscape Architecture, University of Minnesota, 2003, accessed in January 2006 at www.designcenter.umn.edu/reference_ctr/publications/reports/pdf/DPmixed_usetext.pdf

⁶Raymond Bakke, *The Urban Christian* (Downers Grove, Ill.: InterVarsity Press, 1987), 78.

⁷At the same time that "no growth" policies are touted, "usually in the form of onerous or arbitrary zoning restrictions, they create artificial housing shortages and inflation of land values." Jonathan Cohen, "Preservation, Mixed Use and Urban Vitality," accessed in January 2006 at www.periferia.org/publications/cohen1.html .

⁸Ibid.

⁹Ibid.

¹⁰Allan Kingston, "L.A. Must Find Room for Working Class," *Los Angeles Business Journal* (March 5–11, 2001).

¹¹Philip Nyden, John Lukehart, Michael Maly, and William Peterman, "Racially and Ethnically Diverse Urban Neighborhoods," *Cityscapes: A Journal of Policy Development and Research* (1998): 4.

¹²Not actual names.

¹³See Leviticus 25.

¹⁴Denver's transit organization.

¹⁵Five Points historically had many Latinos and Anglos, though the majority was African American (the a popular myth in Denver was that it was *all* African American, but the 2000

census data showed a demographic shift to 43 percent Latino, 27 percent White and 26 percent African American.

[16]Juneteenth is a celebration commemorating the ending of slavery in the United States.

[17]We filed a condominium regime for the whole project so funds restricted to a specific use could be isolated. For example, tax credit funds for the thirty-five affordable rental units were restricted to only that part of the project. The retail required its own financing, a low-interest loan from the City of Denver and a bank loan paid from tax increment revenues. The for-sale condos and office space received financing from purchasers.

[18]HUD publishes income limits for affordable housing annually, based on median incomes and family size in geographic areas. These serve as a guideline for developers. With The Point, tax credit rules restrict only twenty-one units, or 60 percent, of the rental units. HUD Home program rules restrict the rest.

[19]Tax credit rules require that the building be placed in service two years after obtaining a carryover allocation, which must be obtained by the end of the year of application.

[20]From a sermon delivered by Gordon Cosby to the congregation at Church of the Saviour in Washington D.C. circa 1980.

Chapter 9—My Friend's House

[1]JM Services/Construction also teams up with other churches and nonprofit organizations that minister to former alcoholics and felons: the Catholic Rainbow Outreach, Teen Challenge, and Victory Outreach.

Chapter 10—Raising Lazarus from the Dead

[1]With permission, from Bob Lupton's *Urban Perspectives* 4/04 edition, a communication from FCS Urban Ministries, Atlanta, Georgia.

[2]The full story is told by Wayne Gordon, *Real Hope in Chicago* (Grand Rapids: Zondervan, 1995).

[3]CDCs are not exempt from real estate taxes.

Chapter 11—Mustard Tree Co-op

[1]From the National Cooperative Bank Web site: (*http://www.ncb.coop/*)

[2]A partial list of co-ops include food stores, pharmacies, clothing outlets, bookstores, and service stations. In the U.S., rural utility co-ops power over 80 percent of the land, and telephone co-ops and credit unions serve 71 million members. See www.coopfoodstore.com/html/about_coops.html or www.1strochdalenyc.coop/about.htm

[3]With sales in the U.S. of $3 billion in 1991, it is one of the largest companies in Spain. Its 160 co-ops and 23,000 member owners provide services including healthcare, housing, social security, education, and unemployment insurance. See www.iisd.org/50comm/commdb/desc/d13.htm.

[4]Ibid.

[5]National Association of HousingCooperatives. See www.coophousing.org/starting_new.shtml.

[6]In Michigan, "Land contracts allow for a sale directly between buyer and seller without a third party lender. The owner provides the financing, causing interest rates to be somewhat higher. Land contracts are typically no more than 10–15 years." From Richard Cannon, in a communiqué of July 22, 2004.

Chapter 12—Temescal Commons

[1]Its master developer, Wonderland, is planning a community with twenty affordable units.

[2]Text of the "Essentials," accessed in January 2006 at http://www.fuller.edu/sot/faculty/branson/cp_content/RUMCessentials.htm. The church's discipleship and missional structures are discussed in Mark Lau Branson, "Forming Church, Forming Mission," *International Review of Mission, Vol. XCII*, No. 365 (April 2003) : 153–68; and in Lois Barrett et al., *Treasure in Clay Jars: Patterns in Missional Faithfulness* (Grand Rapids, Mich.: Eerdmans, 2004).

[3]Katherine M, "Working with a Religion-Based Community," *Co-Housing Journal* (Spring 2002): 23.

[4]J. R. Bergdoll, *Co-housing Journal* (Summer 2000): 48.

[5]Tom Prince and Mark Lau Branson, "We Created an Ecofund for Temescal Co-housing," *Co-Housing Journal* (Spring 2002): 22–24. Environmental choices that did not cost extra were part of the group's standard budget.

[6]Danny Morris and Charles Olsen, *Discerning God's Will Together* (Nashville: Upper Room Books, 1997).

[7]From personal interview with Tom Prince in February 2004.

Chapter 13—Vista Hermosa

[1]National Building Museum, "Affordable Housing: Designing an American Asset," script for an exhibition on display from Feb. 28 to August 8, 2004, accessed in January 2006 at http://www.nbm.org/Exhibits/current/Affordable_Housing.html.

[2]From Bob Lupton, "Another Tale of Two Cities," *Urban Perspectives* (March 2004), accessed in January 2006 at http://www.fcsministries.org/up/.

[3]Carol A. Bell, "*Workforce Housing: The New Economic Imperative,*" *Fannie Mae Foundation Housing Facts and Findings* (2004), accessed in January 2006 at http://www.fanniemaefoundation.org/programs/hff/v4i2-workforce.shtml.

[4]Bobby Rayburn, "Building a Foundation for Workforce Housing," in *America's Working Families: Where Will They Live,* an online publication from the National Homebuilders Association's December 2004 "Close to Home: A Symposium on Workforce Housing." Accessed in January 2006 at http://www.nahb.org/fileUpload_details.aspx?contentTypeID=7&contentID=481

[5]Bell, *Workforce Housing.*

[6]Ibid.

[7]Ibid.

[8]Acting as an intermediary between government and developers, the Partnership works with the city to obtain donated land, subsidies, and necessary infrastructure improvements, including reduced taxes slowly growing to market rates over a period of twenty years.

[9]Jane Adler, "Affordable Housing Success Stories," *Realtor Magazine* (May 1, 2003), accessed in January 2006 at http://www.realtor.org/rmomag.nsf/pages/featuremay03hsg.

[10]Ibid..

[11]Cheryl Broetje, "Servant Leadership Blossoms at Broetje Orchards," from the Greenleaf Center for Servant Leadership Web site, accessed in January 2006 at http://www.greenleaf.org/leadership/read-about-it/articles/Servant-Leadership-Blossoms-at-Broetje-Orchard.htm.

[12]Ibid.

[13]Earl Roberge, "First Fruits–Broetje Orchards," *Washington Business Magazine* (Summer 2002).

[14]U.S. Department of Labor Report to Congress: "The Agricultural Labor Market–Status and Recommendations" (December 2000), accessed in January 2006 at http://migration.ucdavis.edu/rmn/word-etc/dec_2000_labor.htm.

[15]Jim Rice, "Core Values," *Sojourners* (November-December 2000).

[16]They divided the daily costs of child care between Broetje Orchards and their employees, on a 2/3 to 1/3 ratio respectively. At today's rates, employees pay approximately $7 per day for the education and care of their pre-kindergarten children, as compared with a local average of $28 per day.

[17]Cheryl Broetje, "Servant-Leadership Blossoms."

[18]In 1990, median family income in Walla Walla County was $25,840 (according to the 1990 U.S. Census of Population and Housing).

[19]Pasco City Ordinance No. 3423, 3424, and 3428, dated July 17, 2000.

[20]The Vista Hermosa Foundation is a family foundation, started in 1991 by the Broetjes. The larger mission of the foundation is to use proceeds from Broetje Orchard to support programs and projects throughout the country and the world.

[21]The Center for Sharing is a faith community of Christians in which members are encouraged to deepen their relationship with Jesus Christ and explore their spiritual gifts. Established in 1986 as a nonprofit organization, it provides a safe community in which people can prayerfully search for their God-given missions (calls).

[22]Jubilee Youth Ranch is one of Washington's premier private residential youth service organizations, founded in 1996 for young people in need of a new beginning. This Christ-centered ranch is a boarding school designed to minister to young men from across the U.S. Most of the young men who come to Jubilee have experienced personal, family, or educational difficulties and are struggling with rebellion, low self-esteem and/or destructive or antisocial behaviors.

[23]A nonprofit organization dedicated to asset building for low-income and disadvantaged populations.

[24]Cheryl Broetje, "Servant-Leadership Blossoms."

Chapter 14—HOME

[1]Rick is a consultant on CLTs. His Web site is www.rjacobus.com.

[2]From Sol Kinnis, "Community Land Trusts and Housing Co-operatives," *Co-operative Housing Today* (September 2000), online at http://web.uvic.ca/bcics/research/housing/land-trusts.html. See also "The Community Land Trust Model-Eight Distinctive Features" at http://www.public.iastate.edu/%7Etastaub/clt-features.html and "The Community Land Trust Model," at http://www.iceclt.org/clt/cltmodel.html

[3]In addition to providing affordable housing, CLTs may make land available for community gardens, playgrounds, economic development activities, farming, and timber and firewood, and may hold conservation easements to protect ecologically fragile areas or open.

[4]See "Understanding Subsidy Retention" at www.rjacobus.com, p. 2 of "Creating Permanently Affordable Homeownership Through Community Land Trusts."

[5]From chapter 1 of Robert Swann, *Peace, Civil Rights, and the Search for Community: An Autobiography*, available at the Schumacher Society Web site, http://www.smallisbeautiful.org/about/biographies/swann_autobiography/swann_toc.html.

[6]Ibid., chapter 19.

[7]Ibid.

[8]Molly Ivins, "This cooperative really works," July 15, 2004, Sacbee Press Club

[9]HOME helps to market the crafts in the craft store as well as find other markets for the products: smoked and dried salmon and pickled asparagus (from native peoples in North America); organically grown collard greens, sweet potatoes, and molasses (African American markets in Southern United States).

[10]Today we also have a rural education program that combines basic liberal arts with training in nonprofit management.

[11]Ivins, "This cooperative really works."

[12]Ibid.

[13]Women, Infants, Children–a government-funded food and nutrition program

[14]The only problem with a full-time minimum wage job is that it usually disqualifies a person from additional financial help through various government programs.

[15]If our lumber were not green, we would qualify for additional financing from Rural Development. Once we obtain a kiln, we will dry our lumber to meet codes for governmental help in construction.

Chapter 15— The Nehemiah Strategy

[1]A "relational institution" builds its power on the relationships built and sustained through its members, rather than building power upon the exercise of government or the conduct of business.

[2]Lee Stuart and John Heinemeier, *The Nehemiah Strategy: South Bronx Churches*, 2.

[3]The full story of this organizing effort can be read in Robert C. Linthicum, *Transforming Power: Biblical Strategies for Making a Difference in Your Community* (Downers Grove, Ill.: InterVarsity Press, 2003), 174-79.

[4]IAF (Industrial Areas Foundation), PICO (Pacific Institute for Community Organizing), DART (Direct Action Research Training), and Gamaliel Foundation are some faith-based community organizing groups. Christians Supporting Community Organizing is great place to learn more: http://www.cscoweb.

[5]For more basic information about the organizing effort and its effects, readers can refer to my Fall 2002 article in *Trinity News* titled "The South Bronx Churches Nehemiah Strategy"; Michael Gecan, *Going Public* (Boston: Beacon Press, 2002); and Jim Rooney, *Organizing the South Bronx* (Albany: State University Press of New York, 1989).

[6]Rooney, *Organizing the South Bronx.*

[7]Margaret Hornblower, "Homes, Hope Rising from N.Y. Rubble," *The Washington Post*, 12 July 1985, A1 and A6.

[8]Alfredo Lopez, *The Puerto Rican Papers: Notes on the Emergence of a Nation* (Indianapolis: Bobbs-Merrill, 1973).

[9]Robert A. Caro, T*he Power Broker: Robert Moses and the Fall of New York* (New York: Vintage Books, 1975).

[10]Rooney, *Organizing the South Bronx,* 107.

[11]The prior success of East Brooklyn Congregations with the Nehemiah Strategy gave SBC an advantage in approaching these judicatories

[12]Although the Roman Catholics were the largest single denomination in SBC, the Archdiocese of New York was not able to offer the leadership and support that Bishop Mugavero had in Brooklyn, because of its previous financial commitments to other housing programs more directly under their control.

[13]Bernard F. Loomer, " Two forms of Power" *Criterion* (Spring 1978).

[14]This happened at the last legal meeting of the Board of Estimates, a New York City commission that made land use decisions but had been declared unconstitutional by the United States Supreme Court for violating the principle of one person, one vote.

[15]New York City takes the enlightened approach that it is more important to have stable, rebuilt neighborhoods with decent housing for the workforce of the city than it is to maximize tax revenues. In fact, officials' calculation and willingness to extend this kind of benefit recognizes that in the long run, any loss in tax revenues will be more than offset by the true revitalization of the city's neighborhoods and the economic well being of its families.

[16]*From Siempre*, 28 October 2002.

Chapter 16—Setting the Stage

[1]Salvation Army, the Union Station (a year-round homeless shelter started by Bill Doulos with All Saints Episcopal Church), the AIDS Service Center, and Pacific Clinics.

[2]The church also hosts the Elizabeth House, a home for pregnant women needing protection from abuse.

[3]John Kretzmann and John McKnight, *Building Communities from the Inside Out: A Path toward Finding and Mobilizing a Community's Assets* (Chicago, ACTA Publications, 1993), 293.

[4]Ibid. Kretzmann and McKnight provide an overview of the various creative loans and possible new financial structures in their section on Building the Community Economy. Other structures are: credit unions, banks, Individual Development Accounts, community development loan funds, and revolving loans.

[5]Now the Federal Deposit Insurance Corporation–Savings Association Insurance Fund.

[6]Georgia Beaverson, "Defying the Lending Equation," *Metier*1, no. 2 (Summer 1993): 2–3.

[7]Ibid.

[8]Russ Pulliam, "Putting God to Work in Pittsburgh," *Christianity Today* (April 1982): 18.

[9]Deborah Mendenhall, "Making His Word His Business," *Pittsburgh Post-Gazette,* 1 October 2000: C1.

[10]Russ Pulliam, "Putting God to Work in Pittsburgh," *Christianity Today* (April 1982): 18.

[11]IAF (Industrial Areas Foundation), founded by Saul Alinsky in Chicago in 1940, now a national network of multiethnic, interfaith affiliate organizations in primarily low- and moderate-income communities across the United States and beyond. IAF affiliates are coalitions of local faith-based organizations. Each is involved with renewing democracy by fostering the competence and confidence of ordinary citizens to take action on problems facing their communities. To that end, IAF provides leadership training for more than sixty affiliates, representing over 1,000 institutions and a million families, principally in New York, Texas, California, Arizona, New Mexico, Nebraska, Maryland, Tennessee, the United Kingdom,

and South Africa. By thus reshaping the power base in politics, IAF transforms the civic and physical infrastructure of communities.

[12]Jim Wallis, *Faith Works: Lessons from an Activist Preacher* (New York: Random House), 306.

[13]Most of this information is taken from Jane Addams, *Twenty Years at Hull House*, A Signet Classic (New York; Scarborough, Ontario: New American Library, 1910, 1960), foreword from 1960 reprint.

Chapter 17—Getting Started

[1]From Katy Dudley's keynote address at CCDA's opening night, November 28, 2001.

[2]Robert Linthicum, *Transforming Power: Biblical Strategies for Making a Difference in Your Community* (Downers Grove, Ill., InterVarsity Press, 2003), 94.

[3]Trustworthy businesses who do quality work are difficult to find. Jubilee, our community development organization in St. Louis, is now offering reliable construction companies for home remodeling and other services the community wants and needs.

[4]These include paycheck advances, rent-to-own practices, and expensive mortgage rates. See "Innovations in Personal Finance for the Unbanked," (Washington, D.C.: Fannie Mae Foundation, 2003), accessed in January 2006 at http://www.fanniemaefoundation.org/programs/fscs.shtml

[5]Charles Swindoll, *Hand Me Another Brick: How Effective Leaders Motivate Themselves and Others* rev. ed. (Nashville: Word, 1998), 161.

[6]Martin Buber, *Ten Rungs: Hasidic Sayings* (New York: Shocken, 1947) 74.

[7]From a presentation by Sandra M. Speed entitled "The Nehemiah Model." Speed is CEO of Perfection Development Corporation.

[8]Useful resources include Fannie Mae; L.I.S.C.; Enterprise Foundation; HUD; S.C.A.N.P.H.; Nonprofit Housing Development; and the Federal home Loan Bank Internet resources: www.enterprisefoundation.org, www.scanph.org, www.nlihc,org, www.fanniemae.org, www.hud.gov/cdc.html, www.ncced.org. Useful magazines include *Affordable Housing Finance Magazine, shelterForce Magazine,* and HUD publications.

[9]Garciano currently works with Beckett Development and the Christian Outreach Ministries Enterprise in Colorado. For more information, the Web site is: http://housingministries.org/organization.htm

[10]Jean Burch, "The Small Church with a Big Dream," *Fuller in Focus* (Spring 2002): 20.

[11]Selected among Winn Residential's 400 properties nationwide.

[12]John Perkins, *Restoring at Risk Communities: Doing It Together and Doing It Right* (Grand Rapids Mich., Baker Books, 1995), 70.

[13]Sarah Anderson and John Cavanagh of the Institute for Policy Studies and Scott Klinger and Liz Stanton of United for a Fair Economy, "Executive Excess 2005: Defense Contractors Get More Bucks for the Bang," 12th Annual CEO Compensation Survey, August 30, 2005, available through www. faireconomy.org/press/2005.

[14]It began as a Bible study for homeless under the I-35 Bridge across from Baylor University, where 100 to 300 Baylor students, professors, prostitutes, and homeless people worship together.

[15]In addition to the predevelopment and development costs, insurance protects against risks, lawsuits, etc.

[16]Told by Dr. John Perkins to volunteers at the John M. Perkins Foundation for Reconciliation and Development, Jackson, Mississippi.

[17]From an interview with Bob Lavelle, Summer 2004.

[18]Ibid.

[19]Ibid.

[20]Lynette Clemetson, "A Black Enclave in Pittsburgh Is Revived," *The New York Times*, 9 August 2002.

[21]Speed, "The Nehemiah Model."

[22]Charles R. Swindoll, *Hand Me Another Brick,* rev. and exp. ed. (Nashville: Word, 1998), 163.

[23]Quoted in John Perkins, ed., *Restoring At-Risk Communities: Doing It Right and Doing It Together* (Grand Rapids: Baker Book House, 1995), 18.

Index